2025

Hauptschulabschluss

Original-Prüfungsaufgaben und Training

Baden-Württemberg

Englisch

© 2024 STARK Verlag GmbH, St.-Martin-Straße 82, 81541 München
18. ergänzte Auflage
www.stark-verlag.de

Das Werk und alle seine Bestandteile sind urheberrechtlich geschützt. Jede vollständige oder teilweise Vervielfältigung, Verbreitung und Veröffentlichung bedarf der ausdrücklichen Genehmigung des Verlages. Dies gilt insbesondere für Vervielfältigungen, Mikroverfilmungen sowie die Speicherung und Verarbeitung in elektronischen Systemen.

Inhalt

Vorwort
Hinweise zu den digitalen Zusätzen
Hinweise und Tipps zum Hauptschulabschluss

Hinweise, Tipps und Übungsaufgaben zu den Kompetenzbereichen

1	**Kompetenzbereich: Listening**	1
1.1	Strategien zum Kompetenzbereich „Listening"	1
1.2	Übungsaufgaben zum Kompetenzbereich „Listening"	5
	Listening Test 1: Short conversations	5
	Listening Test 2: A flight to London	6
	Listening Test 3: Weather forecast	6
	Listening Test 4: St Patrick's Day	7
	Listening Test 5: The meteorite	7
	Listening Test 6: A trip to the USA	8
	Listening Test 7: Youth Radio 2FM	9
	Listening Test 8: Music	10
	Listening Test 9: What do they eat?	10
2	**Kompetenzbereich: Reading**	11
2.1	Strategien zum Kompetenzbereich „Reading"	11
2.2	Übungsaufgaben zum Kompetenzbereich „Reading"	14
	Reading Test 1: Signs	14
	Reading Test 2: More signs	15
	Reading Test 3: India	16
	Reading Test 4: Book report	18
	Reading Test 5: Ghost walks	20
	Reading Test 6: Technology has value	23
	Reading Test 7: Insects for dinner	26
3	**Kompetenzbereich: Use of Language**	29
3.1	Strategien zum Vokabellernen ▶	29
3.2	Übungsaufgaben zum Wortschatz	31
3.3	Strategien zum Grammatiklernen	38
3.4	Übungsaufgaben zur Grammatik	38
3.5	Use of Language: Tests	48
4	**Kompetenzbereich: Writing**	51
4.1	Strategien zum Kompetenzbereich „Writing"	51
4.2	Hilfreiche Wendungen zur Textproduktion	54
4.3	Übungsaufgaben zum Kompetenzbereich „Writing"	57

5 Kompetenzbereich: Speaking ... 65
5.1 Hinweise zum Kompetenzbereich „Speaking" ... 65
5.2 Hilfreiche Wendungen zum Kompetenzbereich „Speaking" ... 67
5.3 Übungsaufgaben zum Kompetenzbereich „Speaking" ... 70

Aufgabe im Stil der Prüfung
A Listening Comprehension ... 77
B Text-based Tasks ... 80
C Use of Language ... 84
D Writing ... 85

Original-Abschlussprüfungsaufgaben

Hauptschulabschlussprüfung 2018
Listening Comprehension ... 2018-1
    Answer Sheet ... 2018-5
Reading Comprehension ... 2018-6
    Answer Sheet ... 2018-12
Writing ... 2018-13

Hauptschulabschlussprüfung 2019
Listening Comprehension ... 2019-1
    Answer Sheet ... 2019-5
Reading Comprehension ... 2019-6
    Answer Sheet ... 2019-12
Writing ... 2019-13

Hauptschulabschlussprüfung 2020
A Listening Comprehension ... 2020-1
B Text-based Tasks ... 2020-4
C Use of Language ... 2020-8
D Writing ... 2020-9

Hauptschulabschlussprüfung 2021
A Listening Comprehension ... 2021-1
B Text-based Tasks ... 2021-4
C Use of Language ... 2021-8
D Writing ... 2021-9

Hauptschulabschlussprüfung 2022
A Listening Comprehension ... 2022-1
B Text-based Tasks ... 2022-4
C Use of Language ... 2022-8
D Writing ... 2022-9

Hauptschulabschlussprüfung 2023

A   Listening Comprehension 2023-1
B   Text-based Tasks 2023-4
C   Use of Language 2023-8
D   Writing 2023-10

Hauptschulabschlussprüfung 2024 .... www.stark-verlag.de/mystark

Sobald die Original-Prüfungsaufgaben 2024 freigegeben sind, können sie als **PDF** auf der Plattform **MySTARK** heruntergeladen werden (Zugangscode auf der Umschlaginnenseite vorne im Buch).

Hördateien

Listening Test 1: Short conversations

Listening Test 2: A flight to London

Listening Test 3: Weather forecast

Listening Test 4: St. Patrick's Day

Listening Test 5: The meteorite

Listening Test 6: A trip to the USA

Listening Test 7: Youth Radio 2FM

Listening Test 8: Music

Listening Test 9: What do they eat?

Aufgabe im Stil der Prüfung

Abschlussprüfung 2018

Abschlussprüfung 2019

Abschlussprüfung 2020

Abschlussprüfung 2021

Abschlussprüfung 2022

Abschlussprüfung 2023

Abschlussprüfung 2024

Hinweis: Die Audio-Dateien befinden sich auf der Plattform **MySTARK**, auf die du über den **Zugangscode** vorne im Buch gelangst.

Hörtexte gesprochen von: Eva Adelseck, Daniel Beaver, Em Filer, Blair Gaulton, Esther Gilvray, Clare Gnasmüller, Daniel Holzberg, Rees Jeannotte, Paul Jenkinson, Daria Kozlova, Barbara Krzoska, Jennifer Mikulla, Julian Powell, Veronica Stivala, Rachel Teear, Benjamin Tendler, Roger Voight
Die Soundeffekte stammen aus folgenden Quellen: pacdv, Partners in Rhyme und freesound

Aufgaben und Lösungen verfasst von:

Ariane Last (Übungsaufgaben *Listening*, *Reading* und *Writing*, Lösungen zu den vom Kultusministerium gestellten Prüfungsaufgaben)

Paul Jenkinson (Aufgabe im Stil der neuen Prüfung)

Redaktion

Vorwort

Liebe Schülerin, lieber Schüler,

mit dem vorliegenden Buch kannst du deine Englischkenntnisse dauerhaft verbessern und dich so selbstständig auf die Hauptschulabschlussprüfung im Fach Englisch vorbereiten.

- Jedes Kapitel widmet sich einem **Kompetenzbereich** der Prüfung. Am Anfang erfährst du jeweils, welche Anforderungen auf dich zukommen können und wie du dich am besten darauf vorbereitest. Du kannst also bestimmte Bereiche herausgreifen, die du besonders üben möchtest.
- Anhand der **Übungen und der Abschlussprüfungsaufgaben** kannst du trainieren, wie man mit verschiedenen Aufgabenstellungen in den einzelnen Fertigkeitsbereichen umgeht und wie man sie löst.
- Mit der Hauptschulabschlussprüfung 2020 gab es Änderungen, was die Aufgabenformate in der Prüfung angeht. Anhand der **Übungsaufgaben** im Trainingsteil, der **Aufgabe im Stil der Prüfung** und der **Original-Abschlussprüfungsaufgaben ab 2020** hast du die Möglichkeit, die aktuellen Aufgabenformate zu trainieren.
- Die **Original-Prüfungen** der Jahre **2018 und 2019** eignen sich aber ebenfalls noch gut zur Vorbereitung. Lies dir dazu auch die Hinweise und Tipps zum Hauptschulabschluss durch.
- Am Ende des Buches findest du ein **Lösungsheft** mit ausführlichen Lösungsvorschlägen und hilfreichen **Hinweisen** und **Tipps** zum Lösen der Aufgaben.

Sollten nach Erscheinen dieses Bandes noch wichtige Änderungen in der Abschlussprüfung vom Ministerium für Kultus, Jugend und Sport bekannt gegeben werden, findest du aktuelle Informationen dazu auf MySTARK.

Wir wünschen dir viel Spaß beim Üben und viel Erfolg in der Prüfung!

Dein Stark Verlag

Auf alle **digitalen Inhalte** zu deinem Band (Prüfung 2024, Hördateien, MindCards, Kurzgrammatik und interaktive Aufgaben) kannst du online über die Plattform **MySTARK** zugreifen. Verwende dazu deinen **persönlichen Zugangscode** auf der Umschlaginnenseite vorne im Buch.

Hinweise zu den digitalen Zusätzen

Auf die folgenden digitalen Inhalte zu deinem Band kannst du online über die Plattform **MySTARK** zugreifen. Verwende dazu deinen persönlichen **Zugangscode** auf der Umschlaginnenseite vorne im Buch.

Original-Prüfungsaufgaben 2024

Die Plattform MySTARK enthält auch die Original-Prüfungsaufgaben 2024. Du kannst sie dir herunterladen, sobald sie freigegeben sind.

Hördateien

MySTARK enthält auch die MP3-Dateien zu den Hörverstehenstexten der Übungsaufgaben und der Original-Prüfungsaufgaben.

Kurzgrammatik

In der Kurzgrammatik werden alle wichtigen grammatischen Themen knapp erläutert und an Beispielsätzen veranschaulicht. Hier kannst du nachschlagen, wenn du in der Grammatik einmal unsicher sein solltest.

Web-App „MindCards"

Die Web-App „MindCards" ermöglicht es dir, am Smartphone **hilfreiche Wendungen** zu den Kompetenzen „Writing" und „Speaking" zu wiederholen. Über nebenstehende QR-Codes oder die unten angegebenen Links gelangst du zu den MindCards.
https://www.stark-verlag.de/mindcards/writing-1
https://www.stark-verlag.de/mindcards/speaking-1

Interaktive Aufgaben

Zusätzlich zu den Aufgaben im Buch hast du die Möglichkeit, **Grundlagen** wie **Wortschatz und Grammatik** interaktiv zu üben. Diese Grundlagen brauchst du u. a. auch für die Kompetenzbereiche **Hör- und Leseverstehen**, die du hier ebenfalls trainieren kannst.

Die interaktiven Aufgaben zu den „Basic Language Skills" bieten dir:

▶ „Listening Comprehension" – unterschiedliche Hörtexte (*Announcements*, *Conversations* und Dialoge) mit Aufgaben zum Hörverstehen
▶ „Reading Comprehension" – zwei Sachtexte mit verschiedenen Aufgabenformaten zum Leseverstehen
▶ „Vocabulary Practice" – Aufgaben z. B. zu Wortfeldern, Definitionen, *Opposites* und *Words in context*
▶ „Grammar Practice" – Aufgaben zu einzelnen grammatischen Strukturen
▶ Alle Aufgaben sind interaktiv, d. h., du kannst sie direkt am PC/Tablet bearbeiten und erhältst sofort eine Rückmeldung zu deinen Antworten.

Hinweise und Tipps zum Hauptschulabschluss

1 Ablauf der Prüfung

Die Hauptschulabschlussprüfung besteht aus einem schriftlichen Prüfungsteil, der zentral gestellt wird, und aus einer Kommunikationsprüfung, die deine Schule erstellt:

Schriftliche Prüfung:

| A Listening Comprehension |
| Pause |
| B Text-based Tasks |
| C Use of Language |
| D Writing |

Kommunikationsprüfung:

| A Monologisches Sprechen |
| B Dialogisches Sprechen |
| C Sprachmittlung |

Die schriftliche Prüfung und die Kommunikationsprüfung werden dabei im Verhältnis **3:2** gewertet, d. h., die schriftliche Prüfung zählt mehr. Das Ergebnis deiner Jahresleistung und deiner Prüfungsleistung (schriftlich und Kommunikationsprüfung) machen zu **jeweils 50 %** dein gesamtes Prüfungsergebnis aus.

2 Inhalte und Themen

Die Prüfung hat kein alle Aufgaben übergreifendes Thema. Nur in den Prüfungsteilen B und C beziehen sich die Aufgaben jeweils auf einen Text. Es handelt sich dabei um authentische Texte, die oft aus der Lebenswelt junger Menschen stammen.

3 Leistungsanforderungen

Allgemeine Kenntnisse und Fertigkeiten

Von dir wird erwartet, dass du geschriebene oder gesprochene Texte zu bekannten Themen verstehst, auch wenn darin unbekannte Wörter enthalten sind. Das Schreiben von E-Mails oder einfachen Texten nach Vorgaben sollte dir auch keine Probleme bereiten. In der Kommunikationsprüfung kommt es u. a. darauf an, dass du in Alltagssituationen zwischen zwei Personen vermitteln kannst und dass du Fragen stellen und auf Fragen reagieren kannst.

Listening Comprehension

Dieser Prüfungsteil besteht aus vier Teilen. Nachdem du Zeit hattest, dir die Aufgaben anzusehen, hörst du die Texte jeweils immer zweimal. Bei den Aufgaben musst du z. B. die richtigen Bilder oder Aussagen ankreuzen, einzelne Wörter in einen Lückentext eintragen oder eine Zuordnung vornehmen. Selbst

Hinweise und Tipps zum Hauptschulabschluss

formulierte Sätze werden nicht gefordert. Dein Wortschatz muss aber groß genug sein, um auch schwierigere Aussagen zu verstehen, unbekannte Wörter aus dem Kontext zu erschließen und die Kernaussage längerer Texte zu erfassen. Im Gegensatz zu allen anderen Teilen der Prüfung darfst du hier kein Wörterbuch verwenden.

Text-based Tasks

Du sollst hier zeigen, dass du z. B. Texte auf Hinweis- oder Verbotsschildern und einen längeren Sachtext verstehst. Dabei musst du die richtigen Antworten (z. B. A, B, C oder *true/false/not in the text*) auswählen, aber auch Überschriften den richtigen Textstellen zuordnen. Auch musst du zu vorgegebenen Sätzen diejenigen im Text finden, die dasselbe bedeuten. Bei der Bearbeitung der Aufgaben darfst du ein Wörterbuch zu Hilfe nehmen.

Use of Language

Hier werden deine Wortschatz- und Grammatikkenntnisse geprüft. Es wird dir dabei ein kurzer Text vorgelegt, der mehrere Lücken enthält. Du musst nun entscheiden, welches der vorgegebenen Wörter jeweils in die Lücke gehört. Weiterhin musst du zu Vokabeln aus dem Text Synonyme finden sowie Wörter mit der gegenteiligen Bedeutung. Auch sollst du zu manchen Wörtern Definitionen angeben und zum Thema des Textes Fragen formulieren. Das Wörterbuch kann dir dabei behilflich sein.

Writing

Im letzten Teil der Prüfung musst du zeigen, dass du eigene Texte auf Englisch verfassen kannst. Du kannst dabei das Wörterbuch verwenden. Der Prüfungsteil „Writing" besteht aus zwei Teilen, die du beide bearbeiten musst. Im ersten Teil verfasst du eine E-Mail, z. B. an einen Brieffreund. Es werden dir dabei mehrere Punkte vorgegeben, auf die du eingehen sollst. Wichtig ist auch, dass du mindestens 60 Wörter schreibst. Der zweite Teil ist etwas umfangreicher, da du mindestens 80 Wörter schreiben musst. Hier sollst du einen Text zu einem bestimmten Thema, z. B. deinem Lieblingsstar, verfassen. Es werden dir dabei verschiedene Ideen auf Englisch vorgegeben, die du in deinem Text verwenden kannst.

Kommunikationsprüfung

Die Kommunikationsprüfung dauert insgesamt 15 Minuten und wird einzeln oder zu zweit abgelegt. Sie findet vor der schriftlichen Prüfung statt und besteht aus folgenden Teilen:

Teil A: Monologisches Sprechen: Dieser Teil ist eine Einzelprüfung. Hier präsentierst du dein Schwerpunktthema, d. h., du musst über ein bestimmtes Thema selbstständig sprechen. Versuche, so frei wie möglich vorzutragen.

Teil B: Dialogisches Sprechen: In diesem Prüfungsteil seid ihr zu zweit und bekommt jeweils eine „prompt card". Auf der einen Karte stehen Informationen, auf der anderen Karte Stichworte für Fragen. Sind alle Fragen gestellt und beantwortet, wechselt ihr die Rollen. Hierfür bekommt ihr neue Karten.

Teil C: Sprachmittlung: Hier sollst du in einer Situation, die dir auf Englisch erklärt wird, zwischen zwei Personen vermitteln. Person A spricht nur Deutsch, Person B nur Englisch. Du musst abwechselnd einmal ins Deutsche und einmal ins Englische übertragen. Es geht hier nicht darum, Wort für Wort zu übersetzen, sondern den Inhalt sinngemäß wiederzugeben.

4 Bewertung

In den Prüfungsteilen A–C musst du v. a. die richtigen Lösungen ankreuzen und nur kurze Definitionen und Fragen formulieren. Im Prüfungsteil „Writing" sollst du dagegen ganze Texte verfassen. Hier geht es vorrangig um Verständlichkeit: würde z. B. eine Engländerin verstehen, was du geschrieben hast? Auch in der mündlichen Prüfung gilt als Mindestanspruch: würde ein Muttersprachler das verstehen? Darüber hinaus achten die Prüfer*innen auch auf deine Aussprache und deine Flexibilität: Ist dein Wortschatz umfangreich oder benutzt du immer die gleichen Worte? Kannst du ein Gespräch in Gang halten?

5 Hinweise und Tipps zur schriftlichen Prüfung

- Lies die Aufgaben und Anweisungen **genau** durch. Achte darauf, was von dir verlangt wird.
- Versuche zunächst, unbekannte Wörter aus dem Zusammenhang zu erschließen. Vielleicht verstehst du einen Satz auch ohne dieses Wort. Das Nachschlagen im Wörterbuch (in den Teilen B–D) braucht **viel Zeit** und muss gut geübt sein.
- Verwende nicht zu viel Zeit für Aufgaben, die dir schwierig erscheinen. Besser ist es, zuerst alle Aufgaben zu bearbeiten und am Schluss noch einmal zu den Aufgaben zurückzukehren, die dir Probleme bereitet haben.
- Für die Prüfungsteile B bis D solltest du dir eine Uhr mit in die Prüfung nehmen. Es ist wichtig, dass du dir die Zeit sinnvoll einteilst.

Hinweise und Tipps zum Hauptschulabschluss

6 So kannst du dich mit diesem Buch auf die aktuelle Prüfung vorbereiten

Seit dem Prüfungsjahrgang 2020 sieht die Hauptschulabschlussprüfung etwas anders aus. So ist z. B. der Teil „Use of Language" neu hinzu gekommen und im „Writing"-Teil sind die Aufgaben „Letter" und „Dialogue" entfallen. Anhand der **Übungsaufgaben** in diesem Band und der **Aufgabe im Stil der Prüfung** sowie der **Originalprüfungen ab 2020** kannst du dich optimal auf die Prüfung 2024 vorbereiten.

Da jedoch viele Aufgabenformate gleich oder sehr ähnlich geblieben sind, kannst du auch die **Original-Prüfungsaufgaben der Jahre 2018 und 2019** gut zur Vorbereitung verwenden. Auch wenn eine Aufgabe nicht 1:1 mit einer Aufgabe im Stil der neuen Prüfung übereinstimmt, schadet es nicht, diese zu Übungszwecken ebenfalls zu bearbeiten. Im Folgenden findest du eine Übersicht, welche alten Prüfungsaufgaben zu welchen neuen Prüfungsteilen passen.

Prüfungsteile der neuen Prüfung:	Mit welchen alten Original-Prüfungsaufgaben kann ich üben?
A *Listening Comprehension*	*Listening Comprehension* 2018 und 2019: Part 1, 2, 3 und 5
B *Text-based Tasks* (früher: *Reading Comprehension*)	*Reading Comprehension* 2018 und 2019: Part 1, 2, 3 und 5
C *Use of Language*	*Reading Comprehension* 2018 und 2019: Part 4
D *Writing*	*Writing* 2018 und 2019: Part 3

▶ Übungsaufgaben zu den Kompetenzbereichen

Bildnachweis: © 123rf.com

1 Kompetenzbereich: Listening

Zu verstehen, was andere Menschen in der Fremdsprache sagen, ist eine wichtige sprachliche Fertigkeit im alltäglichen Leben. Es hilft dir sehr, dich in einem anderen Land zurechtzufinden, wenn du z. B. eine Wegbeschreibung verstehst. Deshalb ist es wichtig, das Hörverstehen intensiv zu üben. Die Texte der Höraufgaben in diesem Buch und in der Abschlussprüfung spiegeln daher auch Sprech- und Hörsituationen wider, die einem im Alltag begegnen können, z. B. ein Gespräch zwischen zwei Freunden.

1.1 Strategien zum Kompetenzbereich „Listening"

Ablauf des Hörverstehensteils in der Abschlussprüfung

Hier ist es wichtig, dass du selbst einmal die Höraufgaben der Original-Abschlussprüfungen ausprobierst. Der Hörverstehenstest läuft folgendermaßen ab:

- Die Anweisungen und Texte werden euch vorgespielt. Die Texte hört ihr dabei immer zweimal.
- Dir wird Zeit gegeben, dich mit den Arbeitsanweisungen und Aufgaben vertraut zu machen.
- Nun geht der Hörverstehenstest los. Wenn ein Hörtext das erste Mal vorgespielt wird, kannst du die Aufgaben bereits bearbeiten.
- Wenn der Hörtext wiederholt wird, kannst du deine Antworten überprüfen oder noch vervollständigen.
- Zum Schluss wird dir noch einmal Zeit gegeben, alles durchzusehen.
- Die Lösungen notierst du dabei direkt auf deinem Aufgabenblatt.

TIPP

Vor dem ersten Hören
- Lies dir die Aufgaben genau durch. Achte dabei auf Schlüsselwörter, die auf die richtige Antwort hinweisen können.
- Höre genau auf die Anweisungen.

Beim ersten Hören
- Höre genau zu. Worum geht es im Text? Achte dabei wieder auf Schlüsselwörter.
- Verwende beim ersten Hören evtl. einen Bleistift, damit du noch etwas ändern kannst.

Beim zweiten Hören
- Die Fragen folgen der Reihenfolge im Text. Wenn du eine Frage beim ersten Hören nicht beantworten konntest, dann versuche, beim zweiten Hören die Stelle im Text zu finden.
- Bearbeite möglichst alle Aufgaben. Auch wenn du die richtige Lösung nicht weißt, kreuze z. B. bei *Multiple Choice*-Aufgaben eine Antwort an. Vielleicht liegst du ja richtig.
- Überprüfe noch einmal deine Antworten.

Vorgehen beim Üben

Bevor du die Original-Abschlussprüfungen bearbeitest, die in diesem Buch enthalten sind, kannst du anhand der Übungsaufgaben und der Aufgabe im Stil der Prüfung schon einmal Schritt für Schritt für die Prüfung trainieren. Versuche, wie in der echten Prüfung, die Aufgaben nur durch Zuhören zu bearbeiten. Erst wenn du gar nicht auf die richtige Lösung kommst, solltest du die Hörverstehenstexte im Lösungsteil lesen. Bei der Bearbeitung der Übungsaufgaben kannst du wie folgt vorgehen:

- ▶ Lies dir erst einmal, wie in der Prüfung, die Aufgaben durch. Hast du sie verstanden? Frage dich, ob du die Hörsituation schon erkennst – handelt es sich z. B. um ein Interview? Wichtig ist, dass du auf Schlüsselwörter achtest, die dir einen Hinweis auf die Lösung geben.

- ▶ Höre dir den entsprechenden Text nun einmal an, sodass du weißt, worum es geht. Achte wiederum auf Schlüsselwörter (z. B. „o'clock" oder „am", wenn nach der Uhrzeit gefragt wird). Manchmal geben auch Hintergrundgeräusche einen Hinweis auf die Lösung.

- ▶ Höre dir den Text jetzt noch einmal an und versuche dabei, alle Aufgaben zu lösen. Wenn dir dies immer noch Probleme bereitet, kannst du den Text noch ein drittes oder viertes Mal anhören. Versuche dabei, nicht in die Lösungen zu schauen.

- ▶ Erst wenn du alles bearbeitet hast oder gar nicht weiterkommst, kannst du deine Antworten mit den Lösungen im Lösungsteil vergleichen.

- ▶ Während der Überprüfung solltest du dir einige Fragen stellen: Wie könnte ein Fehler zustande gekommen sein? Habe ich den Hörtext oder die Aufgaben nicht richtig verstanden?

- ▶ Höre dir gegebenenfalls den Hörtext mithilfe der Lösung noch einmal an. In diesem Fall solltest du diese Höraufgabe nach ein paar Tagen wiederholen.

- ▶ Versuche, mit der Bearbeitung jeder weiteren Aufgabe die Zahl der Hördurchgänge zu reduzieren, bis du bei der in der Prüfung üblichen Anzahl (zwei Mal) angelangt bist.

Kompetenzbereich: Listening 3

Mögliche Aufgabenformate in der Prüfung

Die folgenden Aufgabenformate können in der Abschlussprüfung vorkommen:

Auswahlaufgabe (Multiple choice)

Bei diesem Aufgabentyp hörst du mehrere kurze Dialoge oder ein längeres Gespräch. Bei den kurzen Hörtexten gibt es jeweils eine Frage mit drei Antwortmöglichkeiten, von denen du die richtige auswählen musst.

Text:

Tour guide: The tour starts at 9 am every Saturday and Sunday. The meeting point is in front of the train station.

Task and solution:

When does the tour start?

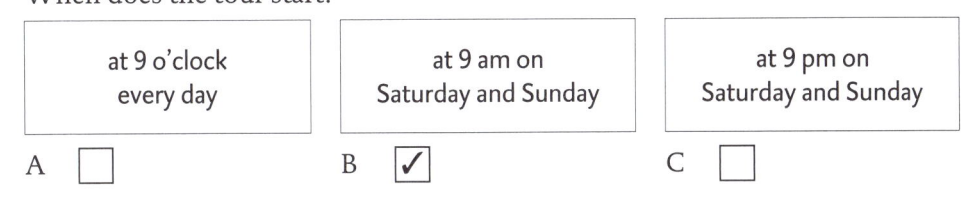

at 9 o'clock every day	at 9 am on Saturday and Sunday	at 9 pm on Saturday and Sunday
A ☐	B ☑	C ☐

Beim längeren Gespräch bekommst du einen Satzanfang vorgelegt und mehrere Möglichkeiten, den Satz zu vervollständigen. Beachte, dass die Formulierung in der Aufgabe oft anders lautet als im Hörtext.

Text:

Tour guide: The tour starts at 9 am every Saturday and Sunday. The meeting point is in front of the train station.

Task and solution:

The tour starts at …

☐ 9 o'clock in the evening every Saturday.

☑ 9 o'clock in the morning every Saturday.

☐ 9 am every day.

Einsetzaufgabe (Fill in the grid)

Bei diesem Aufgabentyp geht es darum, Lücken in einer Tabelle zu vervollständigen. Manchmal musst du nur ein Wort, manchmal mehrere Wörter, und manchmal auch Zahlen eintragen. Wichtig ist, dass du dir die Aufgabenstellung vor dem Abspielen des Hörtextes gut durchliest, damit du weißt, auf welche Informationen du beim Zuhören besonders achten musst.

Text:

Sam: On Monday, I went to a shop where I bought something to drink because I was thirsty. Then I went to the cinema and watched a movie.

Task and solution:

a)	Sam went to the cinema on _____Monday_____.

Kompetenzbereich: Listening

Zuordnungsaufgabe *(Matching)*

Bei diesem Aufgabenformat werden dir z. B. Begriffe vorgegeben, die du den richtigen Personen zuordnen musst. Es können auch mehr Wörter vorgegeben sein, als du brauchst. Achte beim Hören genau auf die Begriffe (Schlüsselwörter).

Beispiel

Text:

Lisa: Let's do a guided tour. I'd love to see Buckingham Palace!
Tom: Yes, great idea. I would like to visit the Houses of Parliament.
Sam: I'd like to see Westminster Abbey, of course.

Task and solution:

What do the tourists want to see?

a) Lisa $\boxed{B}$ A The London Eye
b) Tom $\boxed{C}$ B Buckingham Palace
c) Sam $\boxed{E}$ C The Houses of Parliament
                                 D Westminster Cathedral
                                 E Westminster Abbey

1.2 Übungsaufgaben zum Kompetenzbereich „Listening"

Listening Test 1: Short conversations

Listen to the following five conversations. Listen to them twice.
There is one question for each conversation.
Mark A, B or C.

Question 1
What are the friends going to give Sue as a birthday present?

sports shop voucher	cinema ticket	concert ticket
A ☐	B ☐	C ☐

Question 2
Which film are they going to watch?

James Bond	Meeting Mr Right	Squirrels Gone Nuts
A ☐	B ☐	C ☐

Question 3
What is the name of the app?

FOTIE2GETHER	FOOTOGETHER	FOOTIE2GETHER
A ☐	B ☐	C ☐

Question 4
For which date does Mr Smith finally book the room?

the weekend before Christmas	between Christmas and New Year	from 2 to 3 January
A ☐	B ☐	C ☐

Question 5
Which dress is the customer going to try on?

the blue one	the black one	the purple one
A ☐	B ☐	C ☐

Kompetenzbereich: Listening

Listening Test 2: A flight to London

Listen to a flight captain speaking.
Listen twice and fill in the grid.

© Monika Wisniewska.
Shutterstock

	flight number:	175
a)	flight delay:	_____ minutes
b)	duration of the flight:	_____ hour _____ minutes
c)	altitude:	_____ feet
d)	average speed:	_____ miles per hour
e)	at about ten past three:	_____ the Channel

Listening Test 3: Weather forecast

Listen to a weather forecast.
Listen twice and fill in the grid.

a)	time:	_____
b)	weather in the morning:	_____ with _____ periods
c)	rain:	in the _____
d)	temperature the next day:	_____ °C
e)	temperature expected at the weekend:	_____ °C

© Denijal photography. Shutterstock

Listening Test 4: St Patrick's Day

© AnatolyM. Shutterstock

Listen to a report about St Patrick's Day.
Listen twice and fill in the grid.

a)	Saint Patrick lived	_____ years ago.
b)	He died on	_____.
c)	During the public celebration there are	parades, music, _____ and _____.
d)	typical colour for the holiday:	_____
e)	in former times:	people went to _____ on that day

Listening Test 5: The meteorite

© Bjoern Wylezich. Shutterstock

Listen to a radio show about a meteorite.
Listen twice.
Mark A, B or C.

a) When the meteorite came down it was ...
- A ☐ 9 am.
- B ☐ 9 pm.
- C ☐ night-time.

b) The meteorite crashed through the roof of the McDonalds' ...
- A ☐ kitchen.
- B ☐ living room.
- C ☐ garage.

c) There was a loud noise and it got very ...
- A ☐ bright.
- B ☐ smelly.
- C ☐ dusty.

d) Lisa found the rock under ...
- A ☐ the sofa.
- B ☐ the PC.
- C ☐ the table.

e) The rock will be given to … 　A ☐ a school.
　B ☐ a scientist.
　C ☐ a museum.

Listening Test 6: A trip to the USA

Listen to a conversation between two friends.
Listen twice.
Mark A, B or C.

© Thomas Pajot.
Shutterstock

a) Jenny also went to …　A ☐ Miami.
　B ☐ Chicago.
　C ☐ New York.

b) Jenny took the ferry to …　A ☐ Central Park.
　B ☐ Ellis Island.
　C ☐ the Empire State Building.

c) On the Top of the Rock observation desk …　A ☐ people can buy toy cars.
　B ☐ Jenny was afraid of the height.
　C ☐ Jenny had a perfect view of New York.

d) Jenny bought …　A ☐ seven pairs of trousers.
　B ☐ several pairs of shoes.
　C ☐ seven T-shirts.

e) Jenny's friend hoped to get some …　A ☐ souvenirs.
　B ☐ money for the driving test.
　C ☐ good jeans.

Listening Test 7: Youth Radio 2FM

Listen to a radio show about young people.
Listen twice.
Mark A, B or C.

a) The radio show is about …
   - A ☐ graduating from school.
   - B ☐ young people's jobs.
   - C ☐ young people's hobbies.

b) Today's guest, Jason, works as …
   - A ☐ a carpenter.
   - B ☐ a carver.
   - C ☐ a model.

c) His training took …
   - A ☐ less than two years.
   - B ☐ more than two years.
   - C ☐ two years.

d) Sometimes Jason works …
   - A ☐ from Monday to Friday.
   - B ☐ from Monday to Saturday.
   - C ☐ from Monday to Sunday.

e) Jason loves his job because …
   - A ☐ it feels great when a piece of work is done.
   - B ☐ he has three weeks of vacation.
   - C ☐ he gets a lot of money.

Kompetenzbereich: Listening

Listening Test 8: Music

Listen to some people talking about music.
What headline matches which person? Listen twice.
Write a letter, A–H, next to each person.

© Pavel K. Shutterstock

a) Jacob ☐
b) Amber ☐
c) Thomas ☐
d) Grace ☐
e) Amelia ☐

A Making music yourself
B Great songs in a show
C Music from the radio
D Composing music
E Turning up the music
F Favourite band live on stage
G Winning a music show
H Mozart's life

Listening Test 9: What do they eat?

Listen to some people talking about food.
What kind of food do the people like? Listen twice.
Write a letter, A–H, next to each person.

a) Clare ☐
b) Finn ☐
c) Colin ☐
d) Hannah ☐
e) Tessa ☐

A All kinds of meat
B Only organic food
C Vegetarian food
D Vegetarian with exceptions
E Only Indian food
F Vegan food
G Meat – but only organic
H No meat and fewer carbohydrates

© pkruger.
123rf.com

Weitere Hörverstehensübungen findest du online bei den interaktiven Aufgaben auf der Plattform MyStark.

2 Kompetenzbereich: Reading

Es gibt viele verschiedene Arten von Lesetexten. Ebenso vielfältig können die Aufgabenstellungen dazu sein. Die Textsorten und Aufgabenstellungen, die am häufigsten im Unterricht, in Klassenarbeiten und in der Abschlussprüfung vorkommen, werden wir dir hier vorstellen. In der **Prüfung ab 2020** findest du die Aufgaben zum Leseverstehen im **Teil B „Text-based Tasks"**. Beachte, dass du in der Prüfung deine Lösungen zu diesem Teil auf einem extra Schülerbogen und nicht auf den Aufgabenblättern notieren musst.

2.1 Strategien zum Kompetenzbereich „Reading"

Ganz gleich, welche Art von Lesetext oder welche Art von Aufgabenstellung du bearbeiten musst, die Vorgehensweise ist dabei immer dieselbe.

Zunächst einmal ist es sinnvoll, den Text an sich ganz genau zu betrachten. Manchmal kannst du bereits am **Layout**, d. h. an der Gestaltung des Textes erkennen, um welche Textsorte es geht. Wenn du weißt, ob der dir vorliegende Text eine Werbeanzeige, ein Zeitungsartikel oder ein Interview ist, dann bist du schon einen Schritt weiter. *Arbeitsschritt 1*

Nun solltest du die **Aufgabenstellungen genau lesen**, damit du weißt, nach welchen Aspekten du den Text durchsuchen sollst. Wenn du dann den Lesetext liest, kannst du ganz gezielt wichtige **Schlüsselwörter bzw. Textpassagen markieren**, damit du sie bei der Bearbeitung der Aufgaben schnell wiederfindest. *Arbeitsschritt 2*

Jetzt solltest du den Text **genau lesen**. Suche dir gezielt die Informationen heraus, die du für das Bearbeiten der Aufgaben brauchst. Deswegen hast du bereits die Aufgabenstellungen gelesen und wichtige Stellen markiert. Unbekannte Wörter kannst du **im Wörterbuch nachschlagen**. Achte aber darauf, dass du nicht zu viele Vokabeln nachschaust, denn das kostet wertvolle Zeit. Manche Wörter kannst du außerdem ganz leicht aus dem **Sinnzusammenhang erschließen**. Entscheidend ist, dass du dir bei diesem Arbeitsschritt einen Überblick über den Inhalt deines Textes verschaffst. *Arbeitsschritt 3*

> **TIPP**
> - Versuche, beim ersten Lesen zu verstehen, worum es in dem Text geht.
> - Lies den Text dann noch einmal genau durch. Du musst nicht alle Wörter kennen – einige kannst du auch durch den Sinnzusammenhang erschließen.
> - Sieh dir die Aufgabenstellungen genau an. Markiere beim nochmaligen Lesen des Textes Textstellen im Hinblick darauf, nach was in der Aufgabe gefragt wird.

Mögliche Aufgabenformate in der Prüfung

Die folgenden Aufgabenformate können dir im Leseverstehensteil der Prüfung begegnen:

Auswahlaufgabe (Multiple choice)

Hier bekommst du eine Frage mit verschiedenen Antworten vorgelegt, oder einen Satzanfang und mehrere Möglichkeiten, den Satz zu vervollständigen.

Beispiel

Text:

The guided tour starts at 9 am every Saturday and Sunday. The meeting point is in front of the train station.

Tasks and solutions:

1. The tour starts at …
   a) ☐ 9 o'clock in the evening every Saturday.
   b) ✓ 9 o'clock in the morning every Saturday.
   c) ☐ 9 am every day.

2. Where does the tour start?
   a) ☐ next to the train station
   b) ☐ behind the train station
   c) ✓ in front of the train station

Lies die Aufgaben immer genau durch. Beachte, dass die Fragen bzw. Sätze oft anders formuliert sind als im Text, z. B. *9 o'clock in the morning* anstatt *9 am*. Versuche nun, die Antwort herauszufinden, die zum Text passt. Wenn du dir unsicher bist, dann probiere es andersherum: Schließe zuerst die Antworten aus, die falsch sind. Dann findest du vielleicht die richtige Antwort leichter. Die Reihenfolge der Fragen entspricht normalerweise dem Textaufbau, sodass du abschätzen kannst, wo im Text die Antwort stehen muss.

True/false/not in the text

Bei diesem Aufgabentyp erhältst du eine Aussage *(statement)*. Du musst entscheiden, ob diese Aussage im Vergleich mit der Information im Text richtig oder falsch ist *(true or false)* oder im Text nichts dazu zu finden ist *(not in the text)*.

Beispiel

Text:

Yesterday, Sam went to a shop where he bought something to drink because he was thirsty. Then he went to the cinema and watched a movie.

Task and solution:

Sam went to a shop and bought something to eat.

This statement is ☐ true ✓ false ☐ not in the text

Sehr hilfreich ist es, wenn du dir die Schlüsselwörter in der Aussage und den Satzbau gut anschaust und dann im Text suchst. Oft gelingt es schnell, die passende Textstelle zu finden.

Kompetenzbereich: Reading

Find the corresponding sentence parts or sentences

Dein Leseverstehen wird hier überprüft, indem du zu vorgegebenen Sätzen diejenigen Sätze im Text findest, die inhaltlich dasselbe aussagen.
Die Reihenfolge der Sätze entspricht der Reihenfolge der dazu passenden Sätze im Text. Gehe den Text also Schritt für Schritt durch. Beachte, dass in den vorgegebenen Sätzen der jeweilige Textinhalt anders formuliert oder auch knapp auf den Punkt gebracht wird. Es kann jedoch hilfreich sein, wenn du dir Schlüsselwörter in den Sätzen markierst und dann im Text suchst.

Text:

Yesterday, Sam went to a shop where he bought something to drink because he was thirsty. Then he went to the cinema and watched a movie.

Task and solution:

Find the corresponding sentence parts or sentences in the text that mean the same and write them down.

Sam watched a film in the cinema.
<u>Then he went to the cinema and watched a movie.</u>

Zuordnungsaufgabe (Matching)

Bei diesem Aufgabenformat werden dir z. B. Überschriften vorgegeben, die du den passenden Abschnitten im Text zuordnen musst. Lies die Überschriften genau durch und achte auch hier wieder auf Schlüsselwörter, die du in den passenden Textabschnitten finden kannst.

Text:

1 The guided tour starts at 9 am on Saturday.
You will meet the tour guide in front of Nelson's Column on Trafalgar Square.
The tour lasts about 2.5 hours.
You will see Trafalgar Square, Buckingham Palace, Westminster Abbey, and the
5 Houses of Parliament.

Task and solution:

Match the headings (a–d) with the correct letter of the parts of the text.
Write down the correct answer next to each heading.

a)	Sights on the tour	D	A	line 1
b)	Duration of the tour	C	B	line 2
c)	Meeting point	B	C	line 3
d)	Time when the tour starts	A	D	lines 4–5

2.2 Übungsaufgaben zum Kompetenzbereich „Reading"

Reading Test 1: Signs

Where can you find these signs?
Mark A, B or C.

a) **→ EMERGENCY** Patient Drop-Off & Pick-Up

- A ☐ in front of a school
- B ☐ at a drive-in
- C ☐ at a hospital

b) **ALL PETS MUST BE ON A LEASH**

- A ☐ in a park
- B ☐ at school
- C ☐ in a public swimming pool

c) **EXPECT DELAYS**

- A ☐ at a motorway
- B ☐ in a restaurant
- C ☐ in a plane

d) **All visitors must report to reception**

- A ☐ at the airport
- B ☐ in an office
- C ☐ on a train

Abbildungen: © Stephen Finn. Shutterstock, © fallesenphotography. 123rf.com, © Mr Doomits. Shutterstock

Reading Test 2: More signs

What information do these signs give you?
Mark A, B or C.

a) **[Sign: Fire assembly point]**
- A ☐ Fire can occur at this point.
- B ☐ Meet at this point in case of a fire.
- C ☐ Don't make a fire at this point.

b) **[Sign: ONE WAY →]**
- A ☐ Turn right and go along the street.
- B ☐ You can drive in this direction, for example.
- C ☐ You are only allowed to drive in one direction.

c) **[Sign: SCHOOL SPEED LIMIT 25 ON SCHOOL DAYS WHEN CHILDREN ARE PRESENT]**
- A ☐ Don't drive faster than 25 at the weekends.
- B ☐ Don't drive faster than 25 on school days.
- C ☐ Drive more slowly than the speed limit.

d) **[Sign: CAUTION HIGH NOISE AREA HEARING PROTECTION REQUIRED]**
- A ☐ You need to wear ear protectors.
- B ☐ Don't use headphones.
- C ☐ A headset is required to listen to music.

e) **[Sign: NO PARKING THIS SIDE OF STREET 8 A.M.–NOON 1ST & 3RD TUESDAY STREET SWEEPING]**
- A ☐ There is no parking in this street on Tuesdays.
- B ☐ You can't ever park on this side of the street.
- C ☐ There is no parking on one side of the street on certain days.

Abbildungen: © Alvaro Cabrera Jimenez. Shutterstock, © Stakes. Shutterstock, © Chad Zuber. Shutterstock

Reading Test 3: India

India

© Aliaksandr Mazurkevich. 123rf.com

1 With a population of about 1.43 billion the Republic of India is the most populous country on earth. More than sixteen million people live in or around the
5 capital city, New Delhi.
India is also one of the world's oldest civilisations. Throughout the centuries, the subcontinent has been settled and ruled by various dynasties and cultures.
10 The last to arrive were the British, who began to colonise India in the 17th century and only left in 1947, when India declared its independence.
Today, the two main official languages
15 are English and Hindi. However, there are many more languages spoken in India (122 major languages and 1599 other languages or dialects, according to 2001 Census of India).
People in India belong to a variety of faiths: more than 80 per cent of the
20 Indian population are Hindus, around 13 per cent are Muslims and over two per cent are Christians. The rest of the population are Sikhs or Buddhists, or practise one of the many minor faiths.
In Europe and the USA, people have always been interested in the spiritual[1] side of India. A lot of Westerners travel to India to practise yoga, enjoy Ayur-
25 vedan medical treatments, or visit India's many cultural sites. Other business sectors are booming as well. The textile industry, the car industry and the IT sector, for example, have all been growing fast over the last few decades. However, most people continue to work in traditional fields, for instance as farmers.
30 Not all people have been able to benefit from India's growing wealth. Millions of people still live in poverty and do not have enough to eat. Children often have to work as well and cannot go to school. Moreover, women and members of the lower castes do not have a high status in society and are often looked down upon and treated badly. *(302 words)*

Vocabulary
1 spriritual – *spirituell, geistig, nicht körperlich*

1. Match the headings with the correct letter for the parts of the text.

   a) Religions ☐ A lines 1–5
   b) Problems ☐ B lines 6–13
   c) Variety of languages ☐ C lines 14–18
   d) Number of inhabitants ☐ D lines 19–22
   e) Different influences ☐ E lines 23–29
   f) Culture and economy ☐ F lines 30–34

2. Decide whether the statements are 'true', 'false' or 'not in the text'. Mark the correct answers.

	true	false	not in the text
a) Most Indians live in the capital.	☐	☐	☐
b) The British came to India in the 17th century.	☐	☐	☐
c) Children learn English and Hindi at school.	☐	☐	☐
d) Yoga was brought to India by Westerners.	☐	☐	☐
e) The textile industry is booming.	☐	☐	☐
f) In India many people are poor.	☐	☐	☐

Reading Test 4: Book report

"I am Malala"

© Russell Watkins/UK Department for International Development, Wikimedia Commons, lizenziert unter cc-by-2.0

1 Many of us here in the UK might not know her name, but Malala Yousafzai is actually one of the most famous people in the world and one of the most important
5 children's rights activists. On her sixteenth birthday, Malala gave a speech in front of the United Nations. At the age of seventeen, she received the Nobel Peace Prize. "I am Malala" is the bestselling memoir of
10 this extraordinary young woman and her brave fight for children's right to education.

Malala was born in 1997 in the northwest of Pakistan. The Swat Valley, where
15 she grew up, used to be a popular destination for tourists. This changed when the Taliban began taking control of the area, terrorising the population and destroying schools for girls.

Malala's father, Ziauddin Yousafzai, is a teacher and has always believed that
20 girls should have the same right to education as boys. He founded his own school and his daughter Malala attended classes there. Both father and daughter also spoke out publicly for girls' right to education.

In 2008, the BBC was looking for a schoolgirl who would be willing to report anonymously[1] about life under the terror regime of the Taliban. Ziaud-
25 din Yousafzai suggested his own daughter, and Malala (then eleven years old) began writing a blog about her experiences under the name "Gul Makai".

Malala's activism soon attracted the hatred of the Taliban. When she was going home from school one day in 2012, a Taliban gunman stopped the school bus and shot Malala right in the head. Malala survived and was
30 brought to England to recover from the attack. Although she was nearly killed and still receives threats from the Taliban, Malala continues to fight for the right to education for every child.

Reading her book, I felt shocked by what Malala had to go through and was impressed by how brave she is. It made me realise how lucky we are here to
35 live in peace and that everyone can go to school. Malala is a true role model for all young people and an inspiration to fight for what's right. "I am Malala": a real must-read!

(356 words)

Vocabulary
1 anonymously – *anonym, ohne den echten Namen zu nennen*

Kompetenzbereich: Reading | 19

1. Match the headings with the correct letters for the parts of the text.
   a) The attack ☐   A lines 1–8
   b) Malala's blog ☐   B lines 9–12
   c) Opinion of the book ☐   C lines 13–22
   d) A famous book ☐   D lines 23–26
   e) Malala's achievements ☐   E lines 27–32
   f) Her childhood ☐   F lines 33–37

2. Complete the sentences by choosing the correct ending according to the text. Mark the correct answers.
   a) Malala is famous for her …
      ☐ childhood.
      ☐ children's rights movement.
      ☐ special name.

   b) Malala's aim is for …
      ☐ both girls and boys to get an education.
      ☐ boys to be able to go to school too.
      ☐ school to be easier for everyone.

   c) Malala's father …
      ☐ was a reporter for the BBC.
      ☐ supported his daughter.
      ☐ tried to stop his daughter.

   d) When Malala was 11 years old she …
      ☐ wrote for a magazine.
      ☐ published a book.
      ☐ wrote a blog.

   e) Malala was shot by the Taliban …
      ☐ in 2008.
      ☐ in 2012.
      ☐ on her sixteenth birthday.

   f) Malala was very brave because she …
      ☐ travelled around the world.
      ☐ lived on her own after the attack.
      ☐ went on fighting for children's rights.

Reading Test 5: Ghost walks

Ghost walks

1 Edinburgh has always been the perfect setting for ghost stories: Scotland's capital looks back on a long history full of tragedy, cruelty and crime. Besides, Edinburgh's grey buildings, its dark vaults[1] and the thick fog that sometimes covers the town for days make it a creepy[2] place. These might be the reasons
5 why so many people claim to have seen ghosts or other paranormal[3] phenomena in and around the town. For those who come to Edinburgh in the hope of catching a glimpse of a Scottish ghost, a guided ghost walk around town is a must.

The guides not only know a lot about history, they also know how to create a
10 creepy atmosphere and make visitors shudder. They are often studying history or working as historians, and thanks to their special training, they know every detail of Edinburgh's history. The walks start in the Old Town, which is the scene of most real historical events. The events usually have to do with executions, murder and other terrible crimes. They are often as gruesome as
15 the paranormal ghost stories, though sometimes a bit exaggerated[4]. Besides getting the creeps, visitors can also learn a lot about Scottish history and everyday life in medieval[5] Edinburgh.

The paranormal stories are mostly based on legends of ghosts, witches and unsolved mysteries. Some of them also rest on tourists' reports of ghost
20 sightings. Visitors are usually taken to graveyards or old vaults and basements. Some of the ghost walks are like theatre performances, with tour guides in monster costumes and actors dressed up as ghosts, suddenly jumping out of nowhere. In the dark, this can be very frightening, so loud and fearful shrieks are not unusual in Edinburgh at night.

25 Ghost walks are a great experience for those who enjoy the thrill, but they are not for the faint-hearted. Visitors who want to get to know Edinburgh without shivering with fear should do a normal guided tour and just enjoy the beautiful historical buildings and monuments.

(335 words)

Vocabulary
1 vault – *Gewölbe* 2 creepy – *gruselig* 3 paranormal – *übernatürlich, übersinnlich*
4 exaggerated – *übertrieben* 5 medieval – *mittelalterlich*

1. Decide whether the statements are 'true', 'false' or 'not in the text'.
   Mark the correct answers.

	true	false	not in the text
a) Edinburgh is an ideal place for ghost stories.	☐	☐	☐
b) Some people have seen ghosts on guided ghost walks.	☐	☐	☐
c) Specially trained guides perform creepy tours.	☐	☐	☐
d) Historical stories about the city are based on ghosts, witches and monsters.	☐	☐	☐
e) Some ghost walks are like a theatre play.	☐	☐	☐
f) Visitors can also book normal tours through the city for less money.	☐	☐	☐

2. Complete the sentences by choosing the correct ending according to the text. Mark the correct answers.

   a) Grey buildings and the thick fog make Edinburgh …
      - [ ] unattractive.
      - [ ] creepy.
      - [ ] ugly.

   b) Tour guides in Edinburgh are often …
      - [ ] historians.
      - [ ] actors.
      - [ ] ghost fans.

   c) Besides old legends, you can learn about …
      - [ ] the city's most famous buildings.
      - [ ] monsters.
      - [ ] Scottish history.

   d) Some guides are dressed up as monsters and …
      - [ ] try to chase away ghosts.
      - [ ] frighten the visitors.
      - [ ] join a costume parade.

   e) Ghost walks are perfect for people who …
      - [ ] want to bring their dog.
      - [ ] are not interested in history.
      - [ ] like to be frightened.

3. Find the corresponding sentences or parts of sentences in the text that mean the same and write them down.

   a) There can be a lot of fog in town.
      _____
      _____

   b) Visitors who want to spot a ghost should join a ghost tour.
      _____
      _____

   c) The guides are well-informed about Edinburgh and its history.
      _____
      _____

   d) On the tour you also learn about how people lived in the Middle Ages.
      _____
      _____

e) It can be really scary in the darkness.

f) It is not unusual to hear people scream at night.

Dunkle Gasse © Can Stock Photo/rabbit75can, Silhouetten © Alan49. Shutterstock

Reading Test 6: Technology has value

Technology has value

1 Technology is widely available[1] to students in classrooms across the United States, a study shows. It found that nearly
5 nine in 10 U.S. public school students say they use digital learning tools at least a few days a week. And more than half of those questioned said they use
10 digital technology to learn every day.

In the survey, digital learning tools include websites, application software programs, and online classes, games, videos and programs.

The survey found that classroom technology gets high marks from educa-
15 tors[2]. At least eight in 10 teachers and school administrators said they see great value in using classroom technology tools now and in the future. 65 percent of U.S. teachers use digital tools to teach every day and more than three-fourths of teachers said technology makes their teaching more successful. Educators think it especially helps with activities like research, information
20 searches, reports and presentations.

Derek Kelley agrees. He coordinates technology for Fairfax County Public Schools. He says: "the important thing is to help prepare the students for real world experience" and knowledge about technology is something students need. Kelley said technology is just one of many tools available to teachers.
25 As students learn differently, technology can help teachers support their students by offering different methods for providing information.

Critics of technology in classrooms say that students are spending too much time looking at screens on their computers or electronic devices. Concerns about technology overuse is something Derek Kelley's office hears about
30 from the community. "So we are making sure that there is a balance with student use of technology," he says.

Nearly all elementary students say digital learning tools are fun. Most say the technology helps them learn things on their own and at their own speed. Almost three-fourths of secondary students say the technology tools help
35 them learn things on their own. Over half said they make school more interesting. Forty-two percent would like to use it more often at school, and only eight percent said they would like to use them less.

One thing everyone agrees on: technology is here to stay in American classrooms.

(357 words)

Abridged and adapted from: Ann Ball and George Grow (editor): 'Study Finds Educators, Students Agree: Technology has value', in: Voice of America Learning English

Vocabulary
1 available – *verfügbar*
2 educators – *Lehrer*innen, Erzieher*innen*

Kompetenzbereich: Reading

1. Decide whether the statements are 'true', 'false' or 'not in the text'. Mark the correct answers.

	true	false	not in the text
a) Less than half of U.S. public school students use digital learning tools.	☐	☐	☐
b) Some students use the tools every day in the evening.	☐	☐	☐
c) Digital learning tools are websites, games and videos, for example.	☐	☐	☐
d) 65 per cent of U.S. teachers use digital tools in their classrooms once a week.	☐	☐	☐
e) Mr Kelley tries to make sure that students don't use digital technology too much.	☐	☐	☐
f) Most elementary students confirm that digital tools are fun to learn with.	☐	☐	☐
g) All students who were questioned want to use digital tools at school more often.	☐	☐	☐

2. Complete the sentences by choosing the correct ending according to the text. Mark the correct answers.

   a) A study says that almost all students use digital learning tools …
      - ☐ once a week.
      - ☐ at least several days a week.
      - ☐ at home only.

   b) Digital tools can help teachers make their lessons …
      - ☐ shorter.
      - ☐ less boring.
      - ☐ more successful.

   c) Thanks to the tools, it is easier for students to …
      - ☐ chat with friends.
      - ☐ search for information.
      - ☐ get in touch with other people.

   d) Digital tools can also help students to …
      - ☐ prepare them for real world experience.
      - ☐ learn quicker.
      - ☐ get prepared for their final exams.

   e) Critics say that …
      - ☐ electronic devices can be dangerous.
      - ☐ students use electronic devices too often.
      - ☐ students should use books for learning.

3. Find the corresponding sentences or parts of sentences in the text that mean the same and write them down.

   a) Many students across the United States use technology at school.

   b) Educators think classroom technology is a good thing.

   c) It is important for students to know about technology.

   d) Teachers should not only use technology in their classrooms.

   e) We ensure that technology is not overused.

Reading Test 7: Insects for dinner

Insects for dinner

1 It may sound sickening, but many people can and do eat insects. Edible[1] insects are a great source of protein and minerals known to be important for good health, like calcium
5 and iron. Insect larvae, for example, offer all that, as well as high quality fat, which is good for brain development. Insects are food in many parts of the world, but not in the United States. Concerns about and even fear of the
10 creatures mean serving insects as meals is extremely rare.
But that is starting to change. Wendy Lu McGill is opening a shipping container near Denver, Colorado. She steps into a little room that is lined with small white boxes. Machines keep the room's temperature around 26 degrees Celsius. The relative humidity, or level of wetness in the air, is 80 per-
15 cent. This is just right for the extremely small creatures McGill is raising: mealworms[2]. *Rocky Mountain Micro Ranch* is Colorado's first and only edible insect farm. We raise crickets and mealworms to sell to restaurants and food manufacturers."
The United Nations Food and Agricultural Organization has said that the
20 world's demand for protein from beef and even chicken is unsustainable[3]. Protein from bugs is one possible solution.
McGill grows nearly 275 kilograms of insects every month. She feeds them crushed, wet grain. A carrot supplies their water needs. Each mealworm is about half the size of the smallest finger on a human hand. Ms. McGill says:
25 "I want to be part of trying to figure out how to feed ourselves better as we have less land and water and a hotter planet and more people to feed."
Amy Franklin, a visitor to the insect farm, already likes the idea of using bugs as food: "I'm founder of Farms for Orphans. And what we do is farm bugs for food because in other countries where we work, they're a really, really
30 popular food." Franklin works in the Democratic Republic of Congo. In its markets, people sell live wild-caught crickets[4] and African Palm weevil larvae to eat.
Bugs also taste yummy at Linger, a Denver restaurant. Jeremy Kittleson is Linger's food director. He says the restaurant is working to change American
35 food interests. "As much as we love beef, there's no scientist, there's no environmentalist that's gonna tell you cattle farming is a sustainable[5] practice. We should eat more insects." Amy Franklin gives a toast with a forkful of noodles and crickets: "Bug Appetit."

(412 words)

© Napat. Shutterstock

Abridged and adapted from: Shelley Schlender (VOA News) and Caty Weaver (adaptation for Learning English), George Grow (editor): 'Would Americans Let Edible Insects Come to Dinner?', in: Voice of America Learning English

Vocabulary
1 edible – *essbar* 2 mealworm – *Mehlwurm* 3 unsustainable – *nicht nachhaltig, umweltschädigend*
4 cricket – *Grille* 5 sustainable – *nachhaltig*

Kompetenzbereich: Reading | 27

1. Match the headings with the correct letters for the parts of the text.
   a) An alternative to beef ☐   A lines 1–7
   b) A protein alternative ☐   B lines 11–18
   c) An insect farm ☐   C lines 19–21
   d) Healthy insects ☐   D lines 22–26
   e) Food for the insects ☐   E lines 33–38

2. Decide whether the statements are 'true', 'false' or 'not in the text'. Mark the correct answers.

	true	false	not in the text
a) Insects contain many important substances for human beings.	☐	☐	☐
b) Mealworms can die at temperatures less than 26 degrees Celsius.	☐	☐	☐
c) The United Nations Food and Agricultural Organization says that getting protein from beef and chicken is the best solution.	☐	☐	☐
d) Mealworms eat carrots to be supplied with water.	☐	☐	☐
e) In a Denver restaurant you can eat live crickets and weevil larvae.	☐	☐	☐

3. Complete the sentences by choosing the correct ending according to the text. Mark the correct answers.

   a) Eating insects is not yet popular in …
      ☐ India.
      ☐ the U.S.A.
      ☐ the Democratic Republic of Congo.

   b) Wendy Lu McGill sells her insects to …
      ☐ private customers.
      ☐ zoos.
      ☐ restaurants.

   c) Her insects eat …
      ☐ grass.
      ☐ earth.
      ☐ grain.

   d) Ms McGill says we need to feed ourselves better because …
      ☐ we will have less land but more people.
      ☐ cattle shouldn't be killed.
      ☐ it is healthier.

e) Amy Franklin … ☐ grows almost 275 kilograms of insects every month.

☐ has a bug farm in the Democratic Republic of Congo.

☐ works with Ms McGill in Colorado.

4. Find the corresponding line/lines in the text that mean the same.
Write down the correct letter.

a) In many parts of the world people eat insects.

b) Ms. McGill enters a small room.

c) … trying to find an answer to how we can produce and eat better food …

d) People really like to eat this food.

e) Insects can also be delicious.

| lines 1–2 A | lines 4–5 B | lines 8–9 C | line 10 D | line 12 E |

| lines 20–21 F | line 25 G | lines 29–30 H | line 33 I | line 37 J |

Weitere Übungen zum Leseverstehen findest du bei den interaktiven Aufgaben auf der Plattform MyStark.

3 Kompetenzbereich: Use of Language

Die Aufgaben, die dir im Unterricht, in Klassenarbeiten und in Prüfungen zum Bereich „Sprache" begegnen, sind sehr vielfältig. Ziel dieser Aufgaben ist es, deinen Wortschatz bzw. deine Grammatikkenntnisse zu testen. In der Abschlussprüfung wird dieser Bereich im Teil **„Use of Language"** geprüft, aber ein umfangreicher Wortschatz und gute Grammatikkenntnisse sind auch die Grundlage für das Hör- und Leseverstehen sowie das Schreiben und Sprechen. In diesem Kapitel hast du die Gelegenheit, anhand einer Vielzahl von Aufgaben deinen **Wortschatz** und deine **Grammatik** zu erweitern bzw. zu verbessern. Am Ende des Kapitels kannst du dann zwei **Tests im Stil der Prüfung** bearbeiten.

Weitere Übungen zu Wortschatz und Grammatik findest du übrigens online auf der Plattform **MyStark**.

3.1 Strategien zum Vokabellernen

Um einen umfangreichen Wortschatz aufzubauen, ist es wichtig, dass du intensiv übst. Je mehr Wörter du kennst und in Gesprächen oder beim Schreiben anwenden kannst, desto treffender und abwechslungsreicher kannst du dich in der Fremdsprache ausdrücken. Es gibt verschiedene Methoden, um den Wortschatz zu erweitern.

Eine Übersicht zu verschiedenen Methoden des Vokabellernens gibt dir auch ein **Video**, zu dem du über nebenstehenden QR-Code gelangst.

Natürlich ist zunächst einmal das **Vokabelheft** zu erwähnen. Richte dir auf einer Doppelseite drei Spalten ein: eine für den englischen Begriff, eine für die deutsche Bedeutung und eine für einen englischen Satz, in dem die Vokabel vorkommt. Zum Lernen deckst du dann jeweils eine Spalte ab.

Methode 1

Wesentlich effektiver ist es jedoch, die **Vokabeln auf Karteikarten** zu notieren. Natürlich kannst du auch ein spezielles Programm auf dem Computer **oder eine App** auf deinem Smartphone verwenden. Oft kannst du dir ein Wort oder eine Wendung aber besonders gut einprägen, wenn du sie dir auch handschriftlich notierst. Schreibe dabei den englischen Begriff auf die Vorderseite einer Karte. Notiere dazu auch einen englischen Satz, in dem die Vokabel vorkommt. So lernst du gleich die Verwendung des Wortes mit. Notiere auch sonst alles, was zu der Vokabel gehört (z. B. bei Verben nicht nur den Infinitiv, sondern z. B. auch die Präpositionen, die nach den jeweiligen Verben stehen). Auf die Rückseite der Karteikarte schreibst du die deutsche Bedeutung der Vokabel. Die Karteikartenmethode hat im Vergleich zum herkömmlichen Vokabelheft **Vorteile**:

Methode 2

▶ Du kannst die Karteikarten drei Stapeln zuordnen.
   Stapel 1: **Wörter, die neu für dich sind.** Diese Wörter solltest du mindestens jeden zweiten Tag durchgehen. Lies dabei auch immer den englischen

Satz durch, den du auf der Karteikarte notiert hast. Manchmal ist es leichter, sich ein Wort im Satzzusammenhang zu merken, als als einzelne Vokabel. Sobald du die neue Vokabel kennst, legst du sie auf Stapel 2 ab.

Stapel 2: **Wörter, die du noch nicht so sicher im Kopf hast.** Diesen Stapel solltest du regelmäßig durchgehen und dabei die Vokabeln üben. Wenn du eine Vokabel sicher weißt, legst du sie auf Stapel 3 ab.

Stapel 3: **Wörter, die du schon sicher im Kopf hast.** Diesen Stapel solltest du hin und wieder einmal durchblättern, um zu sehen, ob du alle Vokabeln noch weißt.

Eine App nimmt dir die oben genannten Schritte ab und ist sehr praktisch, da sie in der Regel selbst erkennt, welche Wörter du schon weißt und welche du dir noch einmal anschauen solltest. Die handschriftliche Methode hat jedoch auch Vorteile: So kannst du die Karteikarten beispielsweise ganz flexibel nach **Wortfeldern** (z. B. *weather: wind, snow, sun*) oder nach **Wortfamilien** (z. B. *business, businessman, businesswoman, busy*) ordnen. Dabei kannst du die Wortfelder bzw. Wortfamilien jederzeit erweitern bzw. umbauen.

Methode 3

Du kannst natürlich auch kreativ sein und dir deine eigene Methode zum Vokabellernen ausdenken. Das macht am meisten Spaß und bringt langfristig gesehen sicherlich den besten Lernerfolg.

▶ Zeichne dir z. B. **Mindmaps** zu gelernten Vokabeln. Du kannst sie nach Wortfeldern oder Wortfamilien ordnen. Diese Mindmaps kannst du an gut sichtbaren Stellen in deinem Zimmer aufhängen. Jedes Mal, wenn du daran vorbeikommst, gehst du die entsprechenden Vokabeln im Kopf durch.

Beispiel

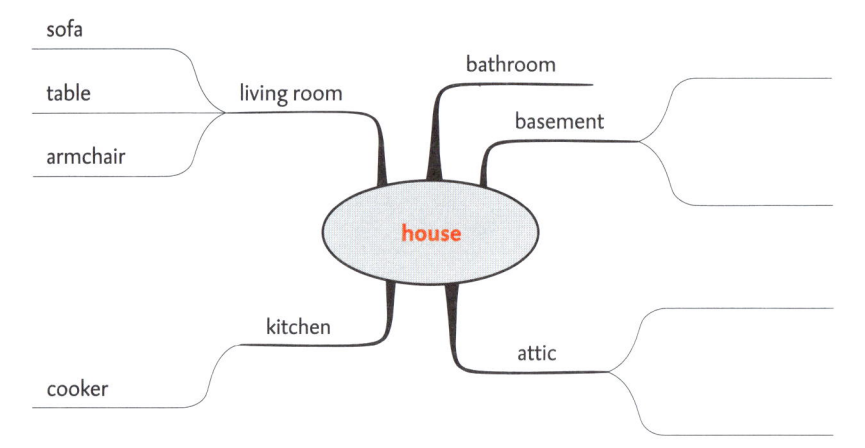

Mindmap mit zentralem Begriff "house" und Ästen zu: living room (sofa, table, armchair), bathroom, basement, attic, kitchen (cooker).

▶ Immer wenn du eine neue Vokabel gelernt hast, schreibst du den Begriff z. B. auf ein Post-It und befestigst es am entsprechenden Gegenstand bei dir zu Hause. So klebst du beispielsweise einen **Zettel** mit dem Begriff „cupboard" an euren Küchenschrank. Das funktioniert zum Teil auch mit abstrakten Begriffen: Die Vokabel „proud" könntest du z. B. an das Regalfach heften, in dem sich deine Schulsachen befinden. Denn sicherlich bist du stolz darauf, dass du in der Schule schon so weit gekommen bist.

▶ Versuche, die **neuen Vokabeln** immer wieder in einem vollständigen englischen Satz **anzuwenden**. Beteilige dich auch so oft wie möglich am Unterricht und unterhalte dich mit Klassenkameraden auf Englisch – vielleicht könnt ihr daraus ein Spiel machen. Ihr könntet auch kurze Smartphone-Videos mit Dialogen zu bestimmten Wortfeldern (z. B. *friendship*) drehen.

Welche Methode du auch anwendest oder mit anderen Strategien kombinierst, lerne nie zu viele Vokabeln auf einmal! Am besten ist es, wenn du neue Vokabeln immer in **kleinen Einheiten von sechs bis sieben Wörtern** lernst. Lies sie zunächst ein paar Mal durch, wiederhole sie laut – in einer modernen Fremdsprache kommt es auch auf die korrekte Aussprache an! – und lege sie dann für etwa 20 Minuten zur Seite. Dann fängst du von vorne an. Diese Pausen sind wichtig, damit sich das gerade Gelernte setzen kann. So wird es dir ein Leichtes sein, deinen englischen Wortschatz zu erweitern.

> - **Lerne langfristig.** In der Fremdsprache einen umfangreichen aktiven Wortschatz zu haben, ist sehr wichtig und hilft dir beim Hör- und Leseverstehen sowie beim Schreiben.
> - Lerne deine Vokabeln immer in **Einheiten von sechs oder sieben Wörtern**. Mache beim Lernen regelmäßig kurze Pausen, damit du das Gelernte besser behältst.
> - Trainiere beim Lernen auch die **Aussprache**.

TIPP

In diesem Buch kannst du mithilfe verschiedener Aufgaben deinen Wortschatz trainieren und erweitern, z. B. indem du Wörter zu bestimmten Wortfeldern, oder den passenden englischen Ausdruck finden musst *(collocation)*. Manchmal musst du zu einem Wort auch ein Synonym oder die entgegengesetzte Bedeutung finden. Auch gibt es Lückentexte oder einzelne lückenhafte Sätze, bei denen du erkennen sollst, welches Wort in den Satzzusammenhang passt. Meist sind die Wörter vorgegeben, für die du dann die jeweils richtige Lücke finden musst. Eine anspruchsvollere Aufgabe besteht darin, die Lücken ohne vorgegebene Wörter zu füllen und selbst ein passendes *(suitable)* Wort zu finden.

3.2 Übungsaufgaben zum Wortschatz

Word fields

1. Find the words from the box that fit each noun (a–c).

   suntan • bird • chalk • monkey • teacher • pupil • guinea pig • desk • tent
   swimming • horse • beach • bear • sunshade • blackboard • hiking • chair

   a) school: _____

   b) holidays: _____

   c) animals: _____

2. Find at least three words that fit the collective nouns *(Sammelbegriffe)*.

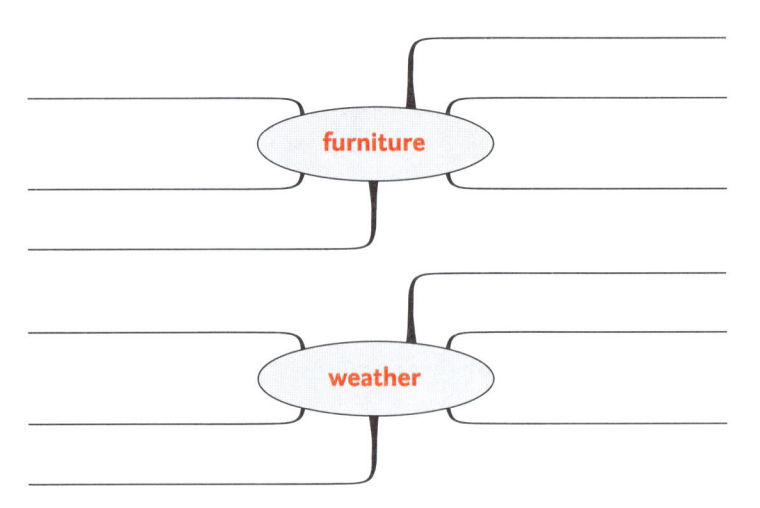

furniture

weather

3. Find collective nouns for the following words/pictures.

   Example: banana, cherry, apple: ____fruit(s)____

   a) green, yellow, blue: _____

   b) _____

   v.l.n.r.: © Rob Wilson. Shutterstock, © wacpan. Shutterstock, © vladimiroquai. 123rf.com

   c) English, Dutch, French: _____

4. Odd-one-out: Find the word that does not go together with the others in the list.

   Example: fruits: banana, cherry, ~~potato~~, apple

   a) vegetables: carrot, salad, beans, pineapple

   b) jobs: cleaner, CV, waiter, car mechanic

   c) drinks: water, vinegar, juice, tea

   d) meals: fork, breakfast, dinner, lunch

   e) sweets: chips, chocolate, jelly beans, lollipop

   © Africa Studio. Shutterstock

5. Cross out the word that is wrong and find the collective noun.

   Example: banana, cherry, ~~potato~~, apple → ____fruit(s)____

   a) shirt, jeans, skirt, bag, pullover → _____

   b) violin, piano, singer, flute, guitar → _____

   c) arms, legs, food, eyes, hands → _____

d) potatoes, peas, carrots, beans, knife → _____

e) ice-cream, cake, pudding, meat, sweets → _____

6. Where can you find these people and things?

   Example: teacher, pupil, blackboard, chalk → _school_

   a) menu, waiter, drinks → _____

   b) actors, seats, curtain → _____

   c) doctor, nurse, patient → _____

   d) priest, candles, prayer books → _____

   e) trees, playground, bench → _____

7. **Countries, languages and nationalities:** Complete the grid.

the people	the country	the language
	England	
(the) French		
(the) Spanish		
		Italian
(the) Americans		
	Germany	
		Dutch
		Turkish
	Canada	

© CanStockPhoto@Boarding1Now105

Words with the same sounds

8. In the following box there are seven words that sound the same as seven other words. Find the pairs that sound the same.

   Example: would – wood

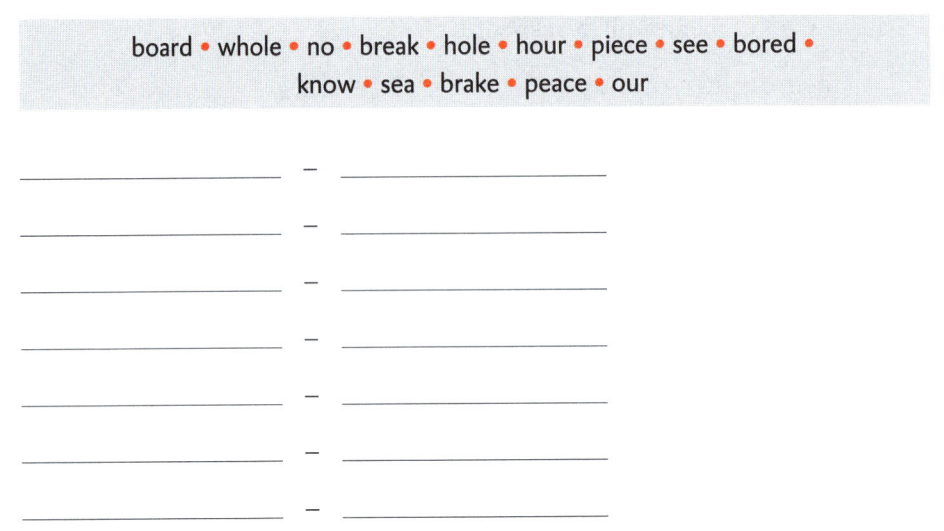

   > board • whole • no • break • hole • hour • piece • see • bored •
   > know • sea • brake • peace • our

   _____ – _____

   _____ – _____

   _____ – _____

   _____ – _____

   _____ – _____

   _____ – _____

   _____ – _____

Opposites and synonyms

9. Find the opposites of the following words.

   Example: come – **go**

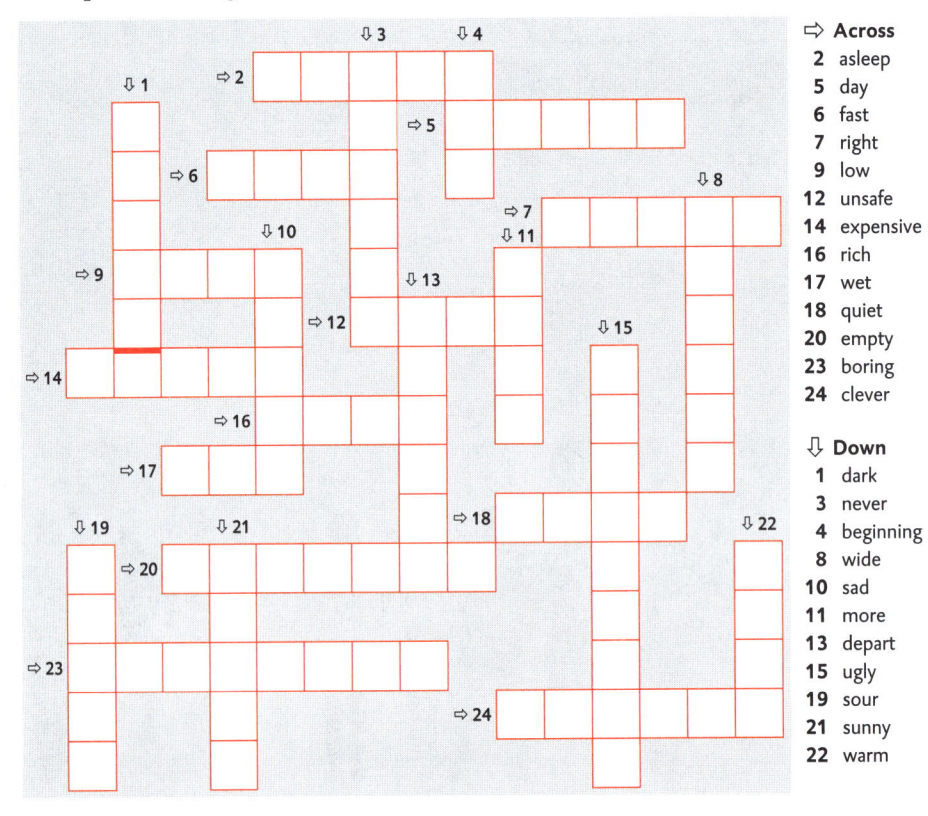

   ⇨ **Across**
   2 asleep
   5 day
   6 fast
   7 right
   9 low
   12 unsafe
   14 expensive
   16 rich
   17 wet
   18 quiet
   20 empty
   23 boring
   24 clever

   ⇩ **Down**
   1 dark
   3 never
   4 beginning
   8 wide
   10 sad
   11 more
   13 depart
   15 ugly
   19 sour
   21 sunny
   22 warm

10. Find the opposite of the words underlined.

    Example: It was dark in the <u>morning</u>. – It was dark in the <u>evening</u>.

    a) I <u>arrived</u> early this morning.
    _____

    b) The plane was <u>late</u>.
    _____

    c) I have just <u>missed</u> the train!
    _____

    d) Sarah has <u>lost</u> her watch.
    _____

    e) James <u>bought</u> a car yesterday.
    _____

    f) My water bottle is <u>full</u>.
    _____

11. Find words with the same meaning (synonyms).

    a) maybe   – _____
    b) small   – _____
    c) <u>Close</u> the door, please. – _____
    d) quick   – _____
    e) (to) phone   – _____

12. Jobs: Write down the forms which are used for women.

    a) policeman   – _____
    b) prince   – _____
    c) actor   – _____
    d) waiter   – _____

Collocations

13. Choose the correct word to complete the sentence.

    a) When do you _____ in the morning?
       stand up ☐
       go up   ☐
       get up   ☐

© Carlos Caetano. Shutterstock

b) I don't want to _____ a lot of money at the weekend.
- give out ☐
- spend ☐
- pay ☐

c) The shop assistant asks you: "What are you _____ for?"
- seeing ☐
- watching ☐
- looking ☐

d) I am _____ my homework at the moment.
- doing ☐
- making ☐
- having ☐

e) _____, the film was very interesting.
- In my opinion ☐
- In my decision ☐
- Personally ☐

f) Sarah, please _____ me the truth!
- speak ☐
- say ☐
- tell ☐

g) Wait, it's not your _____!
- turn ☐
- row ☐
- line ☐

h) Look, Sarah is _____ a photo!
- making ☐
- taking ☐
- doing ☐

© HONGQI ZHANG. Shutterstock

Complete the text

14. Jack is on a journey through Europe. Complete the following text with words from the box. There is one more word than you need.

> too • language • born • example • capital • country • different

a) As Jack doesn't speak any Spanish yet, he started a _____ course in Malaga.

b) The other students are from many _____ countries.

c) Sarah, for _____, is from England.

d) Massimo is from Rome, the _____ of Italy.

e) Louise from France speaks German and English, _____.

f) Alicia was _____ in Quebec in Canada. Her native language is French.

15. Lukas from Cologne has just spent a year in Australia. Complete the following text by choosing the correct word.

   a) Lukas had always wanted to go **for/to/after** Australia for a year.

   b) However, a holiday at the other end of the world is **many/much/very** expensive and Lukas didn't have enough money.

   c) One of Lukas' friends had a great idea: Lukas **could/was/wanted to** go on a "work and travel" holiday.

   d) Lukas was happy! Now he would be able to afford the stay in his **favourable/favourite/favour** country.

   e) When Lukas finally got to Australia, he **worked/had worked/will work** on a sheep farm.

   f) **Before/After/While** working for six weeks, Lukas travelled around the country with some friends he had met at the farm.

Rahmen © Vector Dude. Shutterstock, Bild © Leah-Anne Thompson. Shutterstock

3.3 Strategien zum Grammatiklernen

Auf den folgenden Seiten kannst du anhand einer Vielzahl von Aufgaben dein grammatikalisches Wissen üben und vertiefen. Solltest du dir einmal unsicher sein, kannst du in der **digitalen Kurzgrammatik** auf der Plattform **MyStark** nachschlagen, zu der du über den Code auf der Umschlaginnenseite vorne im Buch kommst.

In der Kurzgrammatik haben wir für dich die wichtigsten Bereiche der Grammatik übersichtlich zusammengestellt. In der linken Spalte findest du die Regeln, in der rechten Spalte die entsprechenden Beispiele dazu. Lies dir die Regeln genau durch und überlege dir zu jeder von ihnen auch ein eigenes Beispiel. Präge dir die Regel immer zusammen mit einem Beispiel ein, so merkst du sie dir besser. Anhand der folgenden Aufgaben kannst du schließlich überprüfen, ob du die Regeln anwenden kannst.

3.4 Übungsaufgaben zur Grammatik

Adverbs

16. Write down the adverbs.

    Example: easy → _easily_

    a) nice → _____

    b) careful → _____

    c) bad → _____

    d) good → _____

17. Complete the sentences. Use the adverb and the correct verb form in the present tense.

    Example: Lisa __never gets up__ (get up/never) early in the morning.

    a) Sarah _____ (have/always) some cornflakes for breakfast.

    b) Joe _____ (play/often) football with his friends.

    c) Tom and Jessica _____ (have/sometimes) dinner in a restaurant.

    d) Lisa's parents _____ (go/mostly) to Greece on holiday.

    e) Tom _____ (do/never) his homework properly.

Comparisons

18. Describe the pupils in Jenny's class and make comparisons.
    Use the words from the box. Sometimes you have to use them twice.

    than • old • tall • good • long • small

    Example: Jenny is ___smaller___ than Tina.

    a) At 1.75 m Evan is _____ than Jack, who is 1.69 m in height.

    b) Sarah is _____ girl in the class – she is 1.80 m.

    c) Sarah, who turns 16 in April, is _____ than Jack, who was born in June.

    d) Jessica's hair is _____ than Tina's.

    e) Emma is _____ at maths _____ Evan.

    f) But Jessica is _____ pupil in the class!

19. Danny and Luisa are talking about their holidays.
    Fill in the missing words.

    The weather in France was much _____ (bad) than last year. It was raining almost all the time. Our flat, however, was _____ (comfortable) last year. I also like the French food. It's much _____ (good) than the food in England. In my opinion, France is _____ _____ (beautiful) country in Europe.

    I went to Spain with a youth group. The weather in San Sebastian was almost as _____ (bad) in France, but it was _____ (exciting) to spend the holidays there than with my parents in Scotland. In my opinion, Spanish food is the _____ (good) in Europe. My holiday in Spain was great, and I met _____ (many) people _____ in all my holidays before!

Conjunctions

20. Complete the following sentences. Use the conjunctions from the box.

> before • because • although • since • and • while

a) Danny wants to become a kindergarten teacher _____ he did an internship in a kindergarten last year. He likes the job _____ working with children is never boring.

b) Luisa wants to be a flight attendant. She has always wanted to be up in the air and see the world, _____ she knows that she will often be away _____ miss her friends and family.

c) Elise would like to become a doctor. _____ still at school, she is doing some voluntary work at a hospital near her home. _____ she starts to study medicine, however, she is going on a trip through South America.

If-clauses

21. Tom's mum. Complete the if-clauses type I. Sometimes you can also use modal auxiliaries in the main clause.

Example: "If the weather __is__ (be) nice on Saturday, we __will go__ (go) to the beach."

a) "If you _____ (help) me in the kitchen, I _____ (give) you some extra money for your new bike."

b) "If you take the train, you _____ (be) in time."

c) "You _____ (get) wet if you _____ (not take) an umbrella with you!"

d) "If you _____ (not study) hard, you _____ (fail) your test."

e) "If it _____ (get) cold, you _____ (put on) a jacket."

22. Holidays. Complete the if-clauses type II. Sometimes you can also use modal auxiliaries in the main clause.

    Example: "If the weather __was__ (be) better, we __would go__ (go) to the beach."

    a) If we _____ (save) enough money, we could fly to Australia.

    b) I _____ (go) to the USA if I could choose where to go on holiday.

    c) If I _____ (go) to the USA, I would visit Las Vegas.

    d) If I _____ (have) a lot of money, I _____ (travel) around the world!

    e) My parents _____ (pay) for my trip to Spain if I _____ (learn) some Spanish.

Modal auxiliaries

23. School trip. Fill in the correct modal auxiliaries from the box. Use them only once. Decide whether the sentence is positive or negative and use the correct tense.

    > can/be able to • may/be allowed to • must/have to • mustn't • need

    Mr Parker:

    a) Before we go on our trip to Washington, your parents _____ fill in the form I have given you.

    b) If you _____ take part, just give the form back to me.

    c) You _____ give me the money for the trip now. I'll collect it next week.

    d) Perhaps we _____ visit the National Air and Space Museum.

    e) You _____ forget to take something to eat and drink with you!

Pronouns

24. Fill in the correct pronouns.

Mrs Brown comes into the classroom, looks out of the window and asks her class in surprise, "Whose jacket is that lying outside?" John answers, "_____ is Lisa's." "Lisa, is that _____ jacket?" Mrs Brown asks. "Go and get _____, please." Then Mrs Brown notices that Lisa is not in the classroom. "Where is _____ today?" "_____ think _____ is ill," says Maggie, who sounds as if she has been crying, "_____ didn't wait for _____ this morning like _____ usually does. _____ borrowed _____ jacket yesterday and _____ told me to look after _____. But this morning, Jack and Tim took the jacket and threw _____ around. _____ couldn't catch _____, and then _____ threw _____ out of the window." "Is that true, _____ two?" asks Mrs Brown, "Did _____ do that? Go and get the jacket immediately, give _____ back to Maggie and say sorry to _____. _____ will stay behind after school and clean up the classroom." Jack is very angry and says, "_____ wasn't _____!" _____ points at Tim: "_____ did it – _____ was all _____ fault!" Mrs Brown turns to the whole class and says, "All of _____ saw _____ take the jacket and throw _____ out of the window, and did any of _____ help Maggie? No, _____ didn't. _____ have decided that _____ will all stay behind after school and clean up the classroom. Maggie, _____ go to Lisa's house straight after school, return the jacket to _____ and explain what _____ did at school today.
And now, everyone, please show _____ _____ homework!"

Passive voice

25. Put the parts of the sentences into the correct order.

Example: was read / by Jack / the book.   <u>The book was read by Jack.</u>

a) by Laura / the message is written

   _____

b) by Sarah / was bought / the last ticket

   _____

c) the window / by Paul / has been closed

   _____

d) was eaten / the hamburger / by Lisa.

e) is given / to Jack by Tony / the pen

Prepositions

26. Fill in the correct prepositions from the box. There are more prepositions than you need.

   a) The teacher is sitting _____ the table.
   b) Jessica has never been _____ Australia.
   c) What do you think _____ my new dress?
   d) The new boy in our class is _____ Singapore.
   e) I am waiting _____ you at the bus stop.

   Box: to, in, at, of, for, from, on, after

Question words

27. Write down the questions to the following answers. Use question words for the words underlined.

   Example: _What has Ethan bought?_
              Ethan has bought a new pair of jeans.

   a) _____
      Jack enjoyed the film.

   b) _____
      It's 10 o'clock now.

   c) _____
      Lisa has (got) a new bike.

   d) _____
      Sarah buys the red dress, not the green one.

   e) _____
      The Smiths are going on holiday to Spain.

   f) _____
      The train arrives at 3:30.

Tenses

28. Find the correct endings to each sentence.

1	At the moment	A	the Smiths bought their new car.
2	Two months ago,	B	Sarah washes her hair.
3	Tomorrow	C	Jason is doing his homework.
4	Every day	D	the weather will be fine.

1	2	3	4

29. Jackie shows her friends pictures from her holidays. What is happening in the photos?

    Example: Lisa ___is riding___ her bike. (ride)

    a) What is your sister _____ in this photo? (do)

    b) My brother _____ in the sea. (swim)

    c) Here I _____ my new dress! (wear)

    d) The sun _____ in every picture. (shine)

    e) In this picture we _____ some delicious ice-cream. (eat)

30. Put the verbs in brackets into the simple past.

    On Saturday morning Kelly and Sara _____ (meet) in town to do some shopping. They _____ (be) invited to a birthday party in the evening and _____ (want) to buy a present. At first they _____ (cannot) really decide what to buy, but then they _____ (see) a cool smartphone case and _____ (be) sure that that would be the right present for Tim. Now they _____ (can) take a look around for some trendy clothes for the party. Kelly _____ (buy) a T-shirt, but Sara _____ (do not) find anything. Afterwards they _____ (go) home to get changed for the party.

31. Emily is talking about next week. Complete the sentences with the will-future or the going-to-future. Use the notes on the right.

   a) I _____ for dinner on Saturday.

   b) On Monday, I _____ at 3 p.m.

   c) After that I _____ for my brother.

   d) He _____ next Sunday.

   e) I hope the weather _____ on Sunday.

   meet Jessie
   go to hairdresser's
   buy birthday present
   turn 12
   weather good

   © Picsfive. Shutterstock

32. Fill in the correct tense.

   a) I _____ (feel) very sick yesterday, so I went to bed early. Now I _____ (feel) much better.

   b) "I _____ (be) to the cinema for ages. Thank you so much for the ticket!"

   c) My little brother _____ (be) born in 2010.

   d) My parents _____ (marry) for 20 years.

   e) I _____ (travel) to Australia for three weeks in January. I can't stand the winter here any longer.

   f) "Jenny, _____ (eat) my cake?! There's nothing left!"

   g) My parents _____ (give) me these headphones for my birthday last week.

33. Emma is in the ticket shop. Put the verbs in brackets into the correct tense.

   Emma: _____ (you/have) tickets for the Rihanna concert?

   Shop assistant: No, I'm sorry. We _____ (sell) the last one yesterday.

   Emma: What a pity! But what about the open air festival which _____ (take place) in August?

   Shop assistant: Yes, we _____ (still have) tickets for the festival.

Relative clauses

34. Connect the parts of the sentences with the correct relative pronoun. Write the correct pronoun and letter (A–E) in the grid.

   1 Mia is the girl
   2 The boy
   3 Have you already read the book
   4 The train
   5 The little girl

   who   which

   A is playing in the garden is Tony's sister.
   B goes to Brighton departs from platform 16 today.
   C is new in my class is from York.
   D I'm in love with.
   E I gave you for your birthday?

	1	2	3	4	5
pronoun					
letter					

Reported speech

35. Read the following messages. Then put the sentences into reported speech. Mind the tenses.

   a) **Sam**: I am going to Spain this summer.

   Sam writes _____

   b) **Jason**: My bus arrives at 8 p.m.

   Jason wrote _____

   c) **Emily and Jessica**: We had a test last week.

   Emily and Jessica told me _____

   d) **Daniel**: I am going to buy a new smartphone tomorrow.

   David wrote _____

   e) **Lisa**: My sister is not at home.

   Lisa wrote me _____

f) **Mum:** I have left for Dublin to go shopping.

   Mum told me _____

g) **Jackie:** My brother works in New York.

   Jackie mentioned _____

Word order

36. Put the parts of the sentences into the correct word order.

    Example: summer / a / holidays / start / few / weeks / the / in
    　　　　　The summer holidays start in a few weeks.

    a) visit / California / aunt and uncle / is going to / his / in
       Paul _____

    b) summer / the / with / invited / to spend / him / them
       They _____

    c) that / jealous / her / take / brother / is / a trip / is going to
       Zoe _____

    d) promises / can / that / she / them / aunt / visit / soon / too
       Zoe's _____

3.5 Use of Language: Tests

Test 1: London

Part 1

Read the text and mark the correct words.

London

1 London is Britain's capital, and it is a very big city – almost nine million **(a)** live in the Greater London area. In London, there is something for **(b)**: famous sights and a great nightlife, **(c)** example. There are lots of clubs, restaurants, theatres, and,
5 of course, pubs. There is always a lot to do and see. Visit Buckingham Palace, **(d)** the Queen lives, or have a look at 10 Downing Street, the prime minister's home. If you want to have a fantastic view of London from above, then go on the London Eye, a big ferris wheel **(e)** to the River
10 Thames. However, a ride on the London Eye is very expensive! Anyway, the best way to **(f)** London is on foot or by using the red double-decker buses. Come to London – it's definitely worth a visit!

© PeterSVETphoto. Shutterstock

a) ☐ peoples ☐ people ☐ men
b) ☐ someone ☐ everyone ☐ everything
c) ☐ for ☐ with ☐ by
d) ☐ who ☐ which ☐ where
e) ☐ at ☐ next ☐ not far
f) ☐ discover ☐ go to ☐ leave

Part 2

Find the opposites in the text. Write down the correct answer.

a) small _____
b) never _____

Part 3

Find the synonyms in the text. Write down the correct answer.

a) great _____
b) many _____

Part 4

Choose two of the following words from the text and give a definition.

a) famous (line 3): _____

b) sights (line 3): _____

c) expensive (line 11): _____

Part 5

You would like to go on a trip to London and you want to know more about the city. Ask three different questions about London.

_____

_____

_____

Test 2: The Grand Canyon

Part 1

Read the text and mark the correct words.

The Grand Canyon

1 The Grand Canyon is one of the seven natural wonders of the world, and one of the **(a)** canyons on earth. It stretches for
5 450 kilometers. Parts of the canyon are more **(b)** 30 kilometers wide and one kilometer deep. The canyons of America's Southwest are
10 deep, ancient openings in the earth. They look as if they formed as the earth split apart. In reality, rivers formed these canyons.
(c) its size, the weather at the top of the Grand Canyon is often much **(d)** from the bottom. On some winter days, for example, you may find cold winds and snow at the top. But at the bottom of the canyon, you may find
15 warm winds and flowers.
Five million people visit the Grand Canyon National Park every year. Most of them walk along paths down the canyon. It **(e)** several hours to walk to the bottom, and even longer to climb back up. Some visitors ride on mules to the bottom of the canyon. Hundreds of thousands of people also pay a helicopter
20 or an airplane pilot to fly them above and around the canyon, and thousands of people every year explore the Grand Canyon by boat from the Colorado River. Visitors can also see the canyon from a huge glass walkway called the Skywalk. The Skywalk is on the Hualapai Indian Reservation in the western part of the Grand Canyon. The Hualapai Indians built it to increase tourism

© Christophe Testi. Shutterstock

Kompetenzbereich: Use of Language

25 at the reservation. For visitors hoping to get a view of the entire Grand Canyon, they will have to travel well beyond the state of Arizona. The only **(f)** to see the entire canyon at once is from outer space.

Abridged and adapted from: Ashley Thompson and Hai Do (editor), with materials from VOA Learning English archive and the National Parks Service: 'The Grand Canyon: Beyond Words', in: Voice of America Learning English

a) ☐ more large ☐ most large ☐ largest
b) ☐ as ☐ than ☐ then
c) ☐ Because of ☐ Because ☐ As
d) ☐ differing ☐ diffident ☐ different
e) ☐ need ☐ takes ☐ makes
f) ☐ state ☐ part ☐ place

Part 2

Find the opposites in the text. Write down the correct answer.

a) rarely _____
b) below _____

Part 3

Find the synonyms in the text. Write down the correct answer.

a) might _____
b) to look at _____

Part 4

Choose two of the following words from the text and give a definition.

a) ancient (line 10): _____
b) to pay (line 20): _____
c) huge (line 23): _____

Part 5

For a school project you need to know more about the Grand Canyon.
Ask three different questions about the Grand Canyon.

_____
_____
_____

4 Kompetenzbereich: Writing

Viele Schüler*innen sind der Meinung, dass sie sich auf den Bereich „Schreiben" nicht vorbereiten können, da die Note – wie im Deutschunterricht – vermeintlich von der individuellen Einschätzung der Lehrkraft abhängt. Erschwerend kommen im Fach Englisch noch die Fremdsprache und die damit verbundenen Fehler hinzu. Aus diesen Gründen üben viele im Vorfeld einer Prüfung die Textproduktion gar nicht erst, was von Nachteil ist, wenn man bedenkt, dass man im Teil „Schreiben" viele Punkte erreichen kann.

Mache nicht den gleichen Fehler, sondern arbeite die folgenden Seiten gut durch. Du wirst sehen: Eine sinnvolle Vorbereitung auf das Schreiben kurzer englischer Texte ist möglich und bringt in der Prüfung viel.

4.1 Strategien zum Kompetenzbereich „Writing"

Langfristige Vorbereitung

Genau wie auf die anderen Prüfungsteile auch, kannst du dich auf die Textproduktion in Tests, Klassenarbeiten und Prüfungen nur langfristig gut vorbereiten. Wenn du dir erst wenige Tage vor der Prüfung überlegst, dass du in diesem Bereich noch Schwächen hast, dann ist das für eine sinnvolle Beschäftigung mit diesem Thema zu spät. Beginne also rechtzeitig mit der Vorbereitung.

Schaue bzw. höre dir englischsprachige Interviews mit deinen Lieblingsstars z. B. im Internet an, schaue Filme oder Serien im Original und lies viel auf Englisch. Bücher und Zeitschriften sowie DVDs kannst du dir in der Bücherei ausleihen. Bei Filmen und Serien kannst du zu Beginn die Sprache auswählen und dir dann den Film einfach auf Englisch anschauen, evtl. auch mit deutschen oder englischen Untertiteln. Du wirst sehen: Mit der Zeit verstehst du immer mehr und Redewendungen werden dir immer vertrauter. Eine gute Übung ist es auch, sich mit Freunden oder Familie Textnachrichten in der Fremdsprache zu schicken. So wird dir das eigenständige Formulieren zunehmend leichter fallen.

Das Schreiben des Textes

Ganz gleich, welche Art von Texten du schreiben musst, die Vorgehensweise ist dabei immer dieselbe.

▶ Lies die **Aufgabenstellung** gut durch und überlege genau, was darin von dir verlangt wird. Erhältst du mit der Aufgabenstellung irgendwelche **Vorgaben** (z. B. Punkte, auf die du eingehen sollst), die du in deinen Text einbringen musst? Oder musst du einen Text ohne Vorgaben schreiben? Wenn du einen Brief oder eine E-Mail schreiben sollst, überlege dir, wer sie empfängt und wie du mit dem Adressaten/der Adressatin sprechen würdest. In einem persönlichen Brief verwendest du eine andere Anrede als z. B. in einem Bewerbungsschreiben.

Arbeitsschritt 1

Arbeitsschritt 2 ▸ Es kann hilfreich sein, wenn du dir vor dem Ausarbeiten deines Textes **Stichpunkte** notierst, die du dann ausformulierst. Beachte dabei genau die Vorgaben in der Aufgabenstellung (z. B. in Form von Stichworten) und überlege dann, was du eventuell noch hinzufügen musst. Wenn es dir hilft, halte deine Gedanken in einer Mindmap fest. So kannst du sie strukturieren.

Arbeitsschritt 3 ▸ Nun musst du den **Text ausarbeiten**. Achte dabei darauf, dass du Zusammenhänge im Satz durch entsprechende **Bindewörter** (Konjunktionen wie *and*, *but*, *because* etc.) deutlich machst. Greife auch auf **Redewendungen** zurück, die du gelernt hast. Schreibe kurze, überschaubare Sätze – so kannst du Grammatikfehler leichter vermeiden. Achte auch darauf, Wiederholungen zu umgehen. Auf den Seiten 72–74 haben wir viele Redewendungen zusammengestellt, die dir beim Verfassen deines Textes helfen werden. Lerne sie auswendig – du wirst sie immer wieder verwenden können. Zusätzlich hast du die Möglichkeit, viele Redewendungen mithilfe unserer „**MindCards**" interaktiv zu wiederholen. Auf Seite 72 findest du den QR-Code, über den du auf die MindCards zugreifen kannst.

Arbeitsschritt 4 ▸ Nimm dir auf jeden Fall Zeit, am Ende alles noch einmal in Ruhe durchzulesen. Ist dein Text logisch aufgebaut? Gibt es auch keine Gedankensprünge? Wichtig ist aber auch, dass du deinen Text noch einmal gezielt auf Rechtschreibung und Grammatik durchsiehst und Fehler verbesserst.

Tipp
- Lies die Aufgabenstellung genau durch. Was wird von dir verlangt?
- Erstelle eine Stoffsammlung.
- Arbeite deinen Text sorgfältig aus.
- Variiere deine Sätze. Dauernde Wiederholungen wirken beim Lesen ermüdend.
- Verknüpfe die einzelnen Sätze mit entsprechenden Bindewörtern (Konjunktionen).
- Lies deinen Text abschließend noch einmal genau durch und überprüfe dabei, ob alles logisch aufgebaut und verständlich geschrieben ist. Verbessere Rechtschreib- und Grammatikfehler.

Mögliche Aufgabenformate in der Prüfung

In der Prüfung können dir im Teil „Schreiben" u. a. folgende Aufgaben begegnen:

Eine E-Mail oder einen Brief verfassen

In der Prüfung kann von dir verlangt werden, z. B. eine E-Mail zu schreiben. Das kann sowohl eine formelle als auch eine persönliche E-Mail sein. Allgemein wird hier überprüft, wie gut du dich in Alltagssituationen schriftlich auf Englisch ausdrücken kannst.

▸ **Formelle E-Mails oder Briefe:** Hier kann es sich z. B. um eine Beschwerde, eine Nachfrage oder eine Bitte um Information handeln. Achte darauf, dass du keine umgangssprachlichen Formulierungen verwendest. Bleibe in deiner Ausdrucksweise sachlich und verwende keine Kurzformen (z. B. *I'm* statt *I am*). Gehe auf alle Aspekte ein, die in der Aufgabenstellung genannt werden. Bekommst du z. B. eine Stellenanzeige vorgelegt, ist es auch wichtig, genau zu lesen, was von den Bewerbern/Bewerberinnen erwartet wird, sodass du darauf Bezug nehmen kannst.

▶ **Persönliche Briefe und E-Mails:** Du musst dich in eine vorgegebene Situation hineinversetzen, und z. B. einem Brieffreund/einer Brieffreundin schreiben. Dabei sollst du auf die Stichpunkte eingehen, die in der Aufgabenstellung aufgeführt werden. Sprache und Stil können bis zu einem gewissen Grad umgangssprachlich sein und du kannst z. B. Kurzformen wie *I'm* verwenden.

Creative Writing

Hier schreibst du über eigene Erfahrungen bzw. Erlebnisse oder du äußerst deine Meinung zu einem bestimmten Thema, z. B. „My favourite star". Dir werden dabei schon verschiedene Ideen, z. B. in einer „idea box", vorgegeben, die dir beim Verfassen deines Textes helfen können. Da du bei dieser Art von Aufgabe beim Schreiben viel Freiheit hast, kannst aber auch eigene Ideen einbringen.

4.2 Hilfreiche Wendungen zur Textproduktion

Anrede und Schlussformeln

Persönlicher Brief/persönliche E-Mail

Liebe Jenny,	Dear Jenny,
Hi/Hallo Jenny,	Hi/Hello Jenny,
Viele Grüße	Best wishes/Kind regards
Liebe Grüße	Love *(nur bei guten Freunden, häufiger von Frauen verwendet als von Männern)*
Mach's gut/Tschüss, Ciao	Take care/Cheers

Formelles Schreiben

wenn du den Namen des Ansprechpartners nicht kennst

Sehr geehrte Damen und Herren,	Dear Sir/Madam,
Mit freundlichen Grüßen	Yours faithfully

wenn du den Namen des Ansprechpartners kennst

Sehr geehrte Frau Roberts,	Dear Mrs Roberts,
Sehr geehrter Herr James,	Dear Mr James,
bei einer unverheirateten Frau	Dear Miss Berry,
wenn du nicht weißt, ob die Frau verheiratet ist	Dear Ms Bell,
Mit freundlichen Grüßen	Yours sincerely

Einleitung und Schluss eines Briefes/einer E-Mail

Danke für …	Thank you for …
Ich hoffe, dass …	I hope that …
Wie geht es dir/Ihnen?	How are you?
In deiner letzten E-Mail hast du mir über … erzählt.	In your last e-mail you told me about …
In deiner letzten E-Mail hast du mir erzählt, dass …	In your last e-mail you told me that …
Entschuldige, dass ich … vergessen habe, aber …	Sorry that I forgot to …, but …
Sage bitte … / Richte … bitte aus	Please tell …
Es wäre schön, wenn wir uns treffen.	It would be nice if we could meet.
Bitte richte … Grüße aus.	Best wishes to … (Please) say hi/hello to …
Bitte schreibe mir bald zurück.	Write soon.
Ich freue mich darauf, bald von dir zu hören.	I'm looking forward to hearing from you soon.

Ich freue mich auf deine E-Mail.	I'm looking forward to your e-mail.
Ich werde dich anrufen.	I'll call/phone/ring you.

Häufig vorkommende Redewendungen/Ausdrücke

sich entschuldigen	I'm sorry
etwas bedauern	It's a pity/shame that … / I'm disappointed that …
an etwas erinnern	Please remember to …
Überraschung äußern	I was surprised that …
eine Bitte äußern	Could you/Would you …, please?
einen Wunsch äußern	I'd like to …
einen Entschluss mitteilen	I've decided to … I've made up my mind to … I'm going to …
eine Absicht mitteilen	I intend to/I'm planning to … I want to/I will …
eine Meinung äußern	I think that … I believe that … I'm of the opinion that …
Interesse ausdrücken	I'm interested in …
Freude ausdrücken	I'm happy/glad about …
Überzeugung ausdrücken	I'm convinced that … I'm sure that …
nach dem Preis fragen	How much is it?/ How much does it cost?
Ich hoffe, dir hat … gefallen.	I hope you liked/enjoyed …
Ich muss jetzt …	I have (got) to …
Ich denke, es ist besser …	I think it's better to …

Auskunft über sich selbst geben

Ich wohne in …	I live in …
Ich wurde am … in … geboren.	I was born in … on …
Ich interessiere mich für …	I'm interested in …
Ich war schon in …	I've (already) been to …
Ich möchte gerne … werden.	I'd like to be a/an …
Mir geht es gut.	I'm fine.
Mir geht es nicht gut.	I'm not well.
Ich mag …	I like … / I enjoy …
Ich mag … lieber (als …).	I prefer to … / I like … better (than …)
Ich weiß … noch nicht genau.	I still don't know exactly.

Ich plane, … zu tun.	I plan to …
Ich freue mich (sehr) auf …	I'm looking forward to …
	I'm excited about …
Ich konnte … nicht …	I wasn't able to … / I couldn't …
In meiner Freizeit	In my free time/spare time
Ich nehme (regelmäßig) an … teil.	I take part in …

Layout eines formellen englischen Briefs

```
                                              24 Castle Street      ⎫
                                              Blackburn             ⎬  Absender*in
                                              Lancashire            ⎪  (ohne Namen)[1]
                                              LK6 5TQ               ⎭

                                              6 March 20…              Datum[2]

   Mrs J. Fox                                                        ⎫
   Dane Cleaners                                                     ⎪  Empfänger*in
   3 Arthur Road                                                     ⎬  (nur in förmlichen
   Doddington                                                        ⎪  Briefen)
   NE3 6LD                                                           ⎭


   Dear Mrs Fox,                                                        Anrede

   Thank you for your letter …                                          Brief


   Yours sincerely,                                                     Schlussformel
   Adam Smith                                                           Unterschrift
   Adam Smith                                                           Name
```

[1] Die Adresse des Absenders kann auch auf der linken Seite stehen
[2] Auch möglich: 6th March 20… oder March 6, 20…; das Datum kann auch links stehen

Häufig vorkommende Redewendungen/Ausdrücke in einem Bewerbungsschreiben (Brief/E-Mail)

Zur Zeit besuche ich die …-Schule und werde (im Juni) meinen Abschluss machen.	At the moment/Currently I go to … school and will take my final exams (in June).
Ich suche nach einer Stelle, weil …	I am looking for a … job because …
Ich interessiere mich sehr dafür, als … zu arbeiten, weil …	I am very interested in working as a … because …
Ich habe Erfahrung in/im …	I am experienced in …
Ich kann …	I am able to …
Ich bin jederzeit für ein Interview verfügbar.	I am available for an interview at any time.
Anbei finden Sie meinen Lebenslauf.	I enclose my CV.
Ich freue mich, von Ihnen zu hören.	I look forward to hearing from you.

4.3 Übungsaufgaben zum Kompetenzbereich „Writing"

Sprachliche Ausdrucksfähigkeit

1. Find suitable *(passende)* words in the box to describe the words underlined. Sometimes more than one word is possible.

   small • light • beautiful • loud • old • dirty • summer

   a) The _____ house at the end of the street is ours.

   b) Mum told me to give away my _____ T-shirts.

   c) Jack loves sitting in his room and listening to _____ music.

   d) Take off your _____ shoes!

   e) I live in a/an _____ village.

   f) Sarah wore a _____ blue dress at her birthday party.

   g) We travelled a lot during our _____ holidays.

2. Fill in the correct conjunctions.

   when • while • although • because • but

   a) I took an umbrella with me this morning _____ it was raining.

   b) _____ I'm 18 years old I will move out.

   c) I'd love to visit New York, _____ I don't have enough money.

   d) _____ Jack had studied a lot, he did not pass the exam.

   e) Claire washes the dishes _____ she is talking to her best friend on the phone.

E-Mails und Briefe

3. What is the correct start and ending for a letter or an e-mail?
   You are writing to:

   a) your aunt Mary: _____

   b) Mrs Smith at the bank: _____

   c) your friend Luke: _____

   d) Mr O'Brien, your English teacher: _____

   e) a postcard to your grandparents: _____

   f) the addressees of your job application: _____

4. You read a post in a music blog. It says that musicals are boring. Below, you find your response to the post. Answer the questions to complete the text.

   Dear Jack,

   I read your post about musicals.
   (Do you agree or disagree with the post?)

   _____
   _____
   _____

   (Have you ever been to a musical? Write something about it: where it was, how you liked it.)

   _____
   _____
   _____
   _____
   _____
   _____

   (What is your general opinion on musicals? Do you recommend that people go and see one?)

   _____
   _____
   _____

   Kind regards,
   (your name)

5. You are going to visit your exchange partner Danny from your school's partner school in Dublin in March.

   Write an e-mail to Danny.
   In your e-mail, write about …
   - yourself and your family.
   - your school.
   - the town or village you live in.

   And ask about …
   - Danny himself.
   - what you could do in Dublin during your visit.

   Write at least **60** words.

   © Thorsten Pohl

Kompetenzbereich: Writing

6. Write an e-mail to a volunteer agency.

   You want to do some volunteer work in England. So you ask an English volunteer agency for some information.

   Include the following points:
   - what kind of volunteer work?
   - your age and qualifications
   - how long?
   - accommodation?

   Write at least **60** words.

7. Write an e-mail to your pen friend.

   Last summer you went to Italy with your family. Tell your pen friend about your holiday.

   Include the following points:
   - where?
   - how long?
   - accommodation?
   - weather?

   Write at least **60** words.

Creative Writing

8. Write about your perfect place to live. The following ideas can help you. Write at least **80** words.

- where?
- why?
- with whom?
- What do you do there?

idea box:

countryside • city • to live • weather • temperature • to swim • landscape • food • people • house • apartment • …

9. Write about your dream job.
   The following ideas can help you.
   Write at least **80** words.

- what?
- why?
- You know someone who does the job?

idea box:

kind of job • work experience • advantages/disadvantages • working hours • salary/pay • …

5 Kompetenzbereich: Speaking

Die **Kommunikationsprüfung** im Fach Englisch wird von der Schule gestellt, an der du deine Hauptschulabschlussprüfung ablegst. Aus diesem Grund kann die Prüfung von Schule zu Schule verschieden sein. Erkundige dich rechtzeitig bei der zuständigen Lehrkraft nach den Prüfungsanforderungen.

5.1 Hinweise zum Kompetenzbereich „Speaking"

Ablauf der Prüfung

- Es werden in der Regel zwei Schüler*innen gleichzeitig geprüft. Du musst dich also auch auf Englisch unterhalten können. Dabei brauchst du aber keine Angst zu haben, wenn der Mitschüler/die Mitschülerin vielleicht nicht so gut in Englisch ist – du kannst trotzdem die volle Punktzahl bekommen.
- Es sind in der Regel zwei Lehrkräfte dabei. Eine Lehrkraft führt das Prüfungsgespräch, die andere Lehrkraft sitzt dabei und hört genau zu.

Prüfungsteile

Die Kommunikationsprüfung besteht aus drei Teilen: **monologisches** und **dialogisches Sprechen** sowie **Sprachmittlung**. Im ersten Teil (monologisches Sprechen) sprichst du alleine, im zweiten Teil (dialogisches Sprechen) musst du zeigen, wie gut du dich in einem Gespräch auf Englisch ausdrücken kannst.

Du erzählst hier etwas zu einem Schwerpunktthema, das du vorher einüben kannst. Es soll aber kein Gespräch zwischen dir und dem Prüfer/der Prüferin zustande kommen. Insgesamt dauert dieser Prüfungsteil ca. 5 Minuten. Mögliche Themen könnten sein: Familie, Freunde, Haustier, Urlaub, Hobby, Film.

Monologisches Sprechen

TIPP

- Nenne in der **Einleitung** das **Thema** deines Vortrags.
- Der **Hauptteil** soll alle wichtigen Informationen enthalten.
- Im **Schluss** fasst du den Inhalt noch einmal kurz zusammen, äußerst deine Meinung oder ziehst ein Fazit.
- Formuliere deinen Vortrag **mit eigenen Worten**.
- **Übe** vor der Prüfung **das freie Sprechen**. Sprich gut hörbar und nicht zu hastig und achte auf eine deutliche Aussprache. Am besten übst du vor Freunden oder deinen Eltern.
- Beantworte Fragen der Prüfer*innen ausführlich und in englischer Sprache.
- Folgende Gesichtspunkte fließen in die Bewertung deines Vortrags ein:
  - Hatte dein Referat den vereinbarten Umfang? War der Vortrag inhaltlich vollständig, gut strukturiert und verständlich? Konntest du den Inhalt sicher vortragen? Konntest du die Fragen der Prüfer*innen verstehen und beantworten? Waren Wortschatz, Grammatik und Aussprache insgesamt angemessen?

Kompetenzbereich: Speaking

Dialogisches Sprechen

Im Prüfungsteil zum dialogischen Sprechen sollst du mit einem Mitschüler/einer Mitschülerin ein kurzes Gespräch nach Vorgaben („prompts") führen.

▶ Dazu erhaltet ihr zu einem bestimmten **Thema** Kärtchen mit Vorgaben in Form von Stichpunkten, die euch als roter Faden für das Gespräch dienen sollen.

▶ Auf diesen Karten werden euch Rollen vorgegeben, die ihr im Dialog einnehmen sollt. Eine Person von euch wird Fragen stellen, die andere wird diese beantworten. Die Details der Situation und der Rollen, die ihr einnehmen sollt, könnt ihr den Karten entnehmen. Mit einem neuen Paar *prompt cards* werden dann die Rollen getauscht. Dieser Prüfungsteil dauert wieder 5 Minuten.

Sprachmittlung

Der letzte Teil in der mündlichen Prüfung überprüft deine Fähigkeit der „Sprachmittlung", also wie gut du zwischen den Sprachen Deutsch und Englisch vermitteln kannst.

▶ Die Lehrkraft beschreibt dir die Situation. Im Rollenspiel wird dein Mitschüler/deine Mitschülerin nur Deutsch sprechen und die Lehrkraft nur Englisch. Damit sie sich verständigen können, musst du zwischen ihnen dolmetschen.

▶ Falls du die Möglichkeit hast, solltet ihr euch zu dritt auf die Sprachmittlung vorbereiten. Zwei Mitschüler*innen können dann den Dialog vortragen, während der Dritte dolmetscht. Falls du alleine übst, kannst du das Gespräch aufnehmen (denke an Pausen, die du zum Übersetzen brauchst) und anschließend dolmetschen. Vergleiche deine Lösung in einem zweiten Durchlauf Satz für Satz mit der Musterlösung. Beachte aber, dass es häufig mehrere richtige Lösungen gibt, die hier vielleicht nicht angegeben sind.

▶ Es ist in jedem Fall **hilfreich**, sich vorher **Situationen zu überlegen**, in denen man dolmetschen müsste, wie z. B. beim Einkaufen oder im Hotel. So kann man sich schon einmal Vokabeln und Wendungen dazu überlegen.

TIPP

- Mithilfe der digitalen Kurzgrammatik auf MyStark kannst du deine Kenntnis der englischen Grammatik noch einmal vertiefen und verbessern.
- Sieh so oft wie möglich Filme oder Serien in englischer Sprache. Dies stellt eine Hilfe zum Hörverstehen dar, aber auch für die Sprachmittlung, da du Aussprache, Satzmelodie und Wendungen verinnerlichst.
- Bei der Bewertung in der Prüfung ist wichtig, ob du schnell reagierst, ob du dem Gespräch folgen kannst, und ob deine Übersetzungen richtig und verständlich sind. Es wird auch bewertet, wie sicher und gewandt du dich ausdrückst und wie du Verständigungsprobleme meisterst, etwa wie du den Faden wieder aufgreifst, wenn du nicht weiterweißt oder dir ein Wort nicht einfällt.

5.2 Hilfreiche Wendungen zum Kompetenzbereich „Speaking"

Hilfreiche Wendungen für den Prüfungsteil „Monologisches Sprechen":

Mein Thema ist …	My topic/subject is …
Ich möchte über das folgende Thema sprechen: …	I'd like to talk about the following topic/subject: …
Ich möchte/werde über … sprechen.	I'd like to/I'm going to talk about …
Ich habe folgende Punkte ausgewählt: …	I chose these aspects: …
Ich werde mich auf folgende Punkte konzentrieren: …	I'm going to concentrate on the following aspects: …
Zuerst …, dann …, später …	First …, then …, afterwards …
Mein erster/zweiter/dritter/letzter Punkt ist …	My first/second/third/last point is …
Am Ende/Abschließend möchte ich über … sprechen.	Finally, I'd like to talk about … / To finish, I'm going to talk about …

Hilfreiche Wendungen für den Prüfungsteil „Dialogisches Sprechen":

Seine Meinung äußern/seine Einschätzung zum Ausdruck bringen:

Meiner Meinung nach …	In my opinion … / I think/believe that …
Ich kann/könnte mir vorstellen, dass…	I can/could imagine that …
Ich würde (nicht) gerne …	I would/wouldn't like to …
Ich bevorzuge …	I prefer …
Ich mag… lieber als …	I like … better than …
Ich stimme zu, dass … / Ich stimme nicht zu, dass …	I agree that … / I disagree that …
Ich kann/könnte mir vorstellen, dass …	I can/could imagine that …

Andere nach ihrer Meinung/nach einer Auskunft fragen (Asking other people for their opinion/some information):

Was ist deine/Ihre Meinung zu …?	What's your opinion/view (of) …?
Was denkst du/denken Sie über …?	What do you think about …?
Könntest du/könnten Sie mir das erklären?	Could you explain that to me?
Was hältst du/halten Sie von …?	What about …?

Zustimmen und widersprechen (Agreeing and disagreeing):

I agree (with you). Ich bin deiner/Ihrer Meinung.	→ (I'm sorry but) I disagree (with you). Ich bin nicht deiner/Ihrer Meinung.

That's a good idea. *Das ist ein guter Vorschlag.*	→ (Excuse me, but) I don't think that's such a good idea. *Das ist keine so gute Idee.*
You're right. *Du hast/Sie haben Recht.*	→ (I'm sorry, but) you're wrong. *Es tut mir leid, aber du hast/Sie haben nicht Recht.*

Wenn du dir mit deiner Meinung nicht sicher bist, verwende Ausdrücke wie:

Ich bin nicht sicher.	I'm not sure/certain.

Jemanden unterbrechen (Interrupting someone)

Kann ich dich/Sie etwas fragen?	Can I ask you something?
Kann ich bitte etwas sagen?	Can/May I (just) say something, please?
Entschuldigung, aber …	Excuse me, but …
Ich möchte dich/Sie nicht unterbrechen, aber … / Ich unterbreche dich/Sie ungern, aber …	I don't wish/I'm sorry to interrupt/stop you but …
Entschuldigung, könntest du/könnten Sie das wiederholen?	I'm sorry, could you repeat that, please?
Es tut mir leid, aber …	I'm sorry, but (I'd just like to say) …

TIPP

> Well, actually, I think …, I guess …, etc. eignen sich gut als Pausenfüller. Verwende sie, wenn du einen Augenblick Zeit brauchst, um zu überlegen, was du als Nächstes sagen möchtest.

Hilfreiche Wendungen für den Prüfungsteil „Sprachmittlung":

Entschuldigung, ich habe dich/Sie nicht verstanden.	Sorry, I didn't understand you.
Könntest du/Könnten Sie das bitte wiederholen?	Could you please repeat that?
Könntest du/Könnten Sie mir bitte erklären, was … ist?	Could you please explain what a … is?
Könntest du/Könnten Sie mir bitte erklären, was Sie mit … meinen?	Could you please explain what you mean by …?
Was meinst du/meinen Sie, wenn Sie … sagen?	What do you mean when you say …?

Hier sind ein paar Beispiele für typische Alltagssituationen für den Prüfungsteil **„Sprachmittlung"**:

At the hotel	*Im Hotel*
At the souvenir shop	*Im Souvenirgeschäft*
On the telephone	*Am Telefon*
In a restaurant	*In einem Restaurant*

At the station Am Bahnhof
Asking the way Nach dem Weg fragen
At the tourist information centre Im Fremdenverkehrsamt /
 In der Touristeninformation
At the travel agent's Im Reisebüro

Viele hilfreiche Wendungen mehr kannst du mithilfe unserer App „**Mind-Cards**" interaktiv wiederholen. Verwende dazu den nebenstehenden QR-Code.

5.3 Übungsaufgaben zum Kompetenzbereich „Speaking"

Monologisches Sprechen

TIPP

Vortrag zu einem bestimmten Thema
Für deinen Vortrag musst du ein **Schwerpunktthema** wählen, das du mit deiner Lehrkraft absprichst. Als Hilfestellung in der Prüfung darfst du meist einen Stichwortzettel verwenden, auf dem du kurze Notizen zu deinem Referat vermerken kannst. Solltest du einmal den Faden verlieren, kannst du auf deine Aufzeichnungen zurückgreifen.
Gliedere dein Referat in Einleitung, Hauptteil und Schluss: in der **Einleitung** nennst du das Thema deines Referats und evtl. auch, warum du es gewählt hast. Im **Hauptteil** gehst du auf einzelne Aspekte des Themas ein, über die du gerne etwas erzählen möchtest. Runde dein Referat mit einem **Schluss** ab. Du kannst dabei z. B. alles noch einmal in einem Satz zusammenfassen oder eine Bewertung abgeben. Beachte jedoch immer, dass du für deinen Vortrag nur bis zu **5 Minuten** Zeit hast!

1. Thema „Holidays": Vervollständige als Vorbereitung auf deinen Vortrag folgende Mindmap.

2. Vortrag: „Holidays". Bereite mithilfe der Mindmap ein Referat über einen deiner letzten Urlaube vor. Verwende nicht mehr als 500 Wörter.

Kompetenzbereich: Speaking

3. Thema „Harry Potter": Vervollständige als Vorbereitung auf deinen Vortrag folgende Mindmap.

Illustrationen © Vik CG. Shutterstock

4. Vortrag: „Harry Potter": Bereite mithilfe der Mindmap ein Referat über die Harry Potter-Bücher vor. Verwende nicht mehr als 500 Wörter.

Kompetenzbereich: Speaking

Dialogisches Sprechen

TIPP

Reacting to prompts (Gesprächsführung nach Vorgaben)
Diese Prüfung legt ihr zu zweit ab. Ihr erhaltet Kärtchen mit Gesprächsvorgaben. Auf der einen Karte stehen die Informationen zu einer bestimmten **Situation**, auf der anderen Karte Punkte, zu denen im Gespräch Fragen gestellt werden sollen. Eure Aufgabe ist nun, anhand der jeweiligen Vorgaben ein kurzes Gespräch zu führen, in das ihr die Vorgaben einbaut. Ihr habt dafür ca. **5 Minuten** Zeit. Achte auf folgende Punkte:
- Verwende alle Vorgaben in dem Gespräch.
- Formuliere ganze, verständliche Sätze. Sprich deutlich.
- Verwende Redewendungen und achte auf Aussprache und Grammatik.

5. Renting a bike

   Prompt A

   BRISTOL BIKES – Rent a Bike
   You are calling **Bristol Bikes – Rent a Bike**.
   Find out some details. Ask at least 5 questions.
   ➢ what?
   ➢ how long?
   ➢ prices?
   ➢ special offers?
   ➢ insurance?
   ➢ some more information?

   Prompt B

   BRISTOL BIKES – Rent a Bike
   You work for Bristol Bikes – Rent a Bike.
   Please give some information about it.
   ➢ huge choice of bikes
   ➢ several hours to one week
   ➢ £9 a day per person
   ➢ special rates for families: £60 for four people for one week
   ➢ insurance in case of damage or theft
   ➢ addresses of small hotels that have storage places for bikes

Fahrrad © kurtcan. Shutterstock

6. At the cinema

Prompt A

STARDUST CINEMA

You are interested in the cinema programme.
Find out some details. Ask at least 5 questions.

- new films?
- when?
- prices for students?
- snacks and drinks?
- posters on sale?
- special offer?

Prompt B

STARDUST CINEMA

You work for the cinema.
Please give some information about it.

- new films: "Squirrels Gone Nuts 2" and "All About You"
- at 4 pm and 8 pm
- special prices for students: £4 per ticket
- soft drinks, popcorn, several snacks
- film posters on sale
- special offer: Tuesday's ticket plus snack and soft drink for £7.50

Illustrationen © Viktorija Reuta. Shutterstock

Sprachmittlung

TIPP

Hier musst du in einer bestimmten Situation zwischen zwei Personen dolmetschen. Die Rolle der Person, die nur Englisch spricht, wird von der Lehrkraft übernommen, die Rolle der Person, die nur Deutsch kann, von deinem Mitprüfling. Es ist nun deine Aufgabe, die Fragen und Aussagen ins Englische bzw. Deutsche zu übertragen. Du erhältst keine Vorlage des Gesprächs, sondern musst die Inhalte dem entnehmen, was die anderen beiden Personen sagen.

- Beachte, dass du beim Übersetzen Aussagen häufig in die 3. Person übertragen musst.
  Beispiel: Sagt der deutsche Tourist „Ich brauche ein Taxi zum Flughafen", übersetzt du "He/She needs a taxi to the airport".
- Versuche das Gesagte sinngemäß zu übertragen.
  Beispiel: "Here you are." → „Bitte schön."

- Umschreibe Wörter, die du nicht kennst, oder verwende ein ähnliches Wort.
  Beispiel: „Mein Pass ist weg."
  → "He can't find his passport." / "He thinks he has lost his passport."
- Keinesfalls solltest du nichts sagen, wenn du nicht weißt, wie du etwas dolmetschen sollst. Du solltest stattdessen versuchen, das Gespräch trotzdem fortzusetzen. Ist die Vorgabe zum Verständnis nicht unbedingt nötig, kannst du sie notfalls überspringen.
  Beispiel: Beim Einkaufen: „Nein, danke. Das ist mir zu teuer. Auf Wiedersehen."
  "No thanks. (…). Goodbye."
- Manchmal ist es auch möglich, die Körpersprache einzusetzen, um einen Gegenstand/Sachverhalt zu beschreiben.
  Beispiel: In der Apotheke: "Could you please give me something for …?"
  → auf Kopf, Nase etc. zeigen

7. You are at a bike rental in Dublin. A German tourist also wants to rent a bike but he doesn't understand what the bike rental assistant tells him. Try to help the German tourist.

German tourist (other student)	Mediation (you)	Assistant (teacher)
Entschuldigen Sie, ich würde hier gerne ein Fahrrad mieten. Können Sie mir helfen?		
	Ja, gerne. The lady/gentleman …	
		Yes, of course. How long would he/she like to rent the bike for?
	…	
Ich möchte gerne eines für zwei Tage mieten. Wie viel kostet das?		
	…	
		That would be € 30.
	…	
Das passt. Kann ich mir gleich eines aussuchen?		
	…	
		Yes, sure. We have a lot of different bikes on offer. Where would he/she like to ride the bike – in the city or in the countryside?
	…	
Ich würde nur in der Stadt fahren. Welches Rad kann er/sie mir empfehlen?		
	…	
		This nice red city bike, for example.

© Jethita. Shutterstock

	…	
Ja, das sieht schön aus. Kann ich es ausprobieren?		
	…	
		Yes, of course. Go ahead.
	…	
Dankeschön.		

8. You are at a hotel in New York. A German tourist has just arrived and needs help because her English is not very good and she cannot understand what the receptionist says. You offer to help her.

German tourist (other student)	Mediation (you)	Receptionist (teacher)
Hallo, mein Name ist Elisabeth Schmidt. Ich habe für meinen Mann und mich ein Zimmer reserviert.		
	Mrs Schmidt …	
		Yes, Mrs Schmidt … Your reservation is from August 15th to 18th. Could I have your passports and your credit card, please?
	…	
Hier sind unsere Pässe und die Kreditkarte.		
	…	
		Thank you very much.
	…	
Können Sie uns morgen um 7 Uhr aufwecken?		
	…	
		Sure, we can do that. Here's your key. Your room number is 223.
	…	
Dankeschön. Wo und wann können wir denn das Frühstück zu uns nehmen?		
	…	
		Breakfast is served from 7 to 10 am. The breakfast room is on the first floor (= "Erdgeschoss" in the US).
	…	

© VectorsMarket. Shutterstock

Kompetenzbereich: Speaking

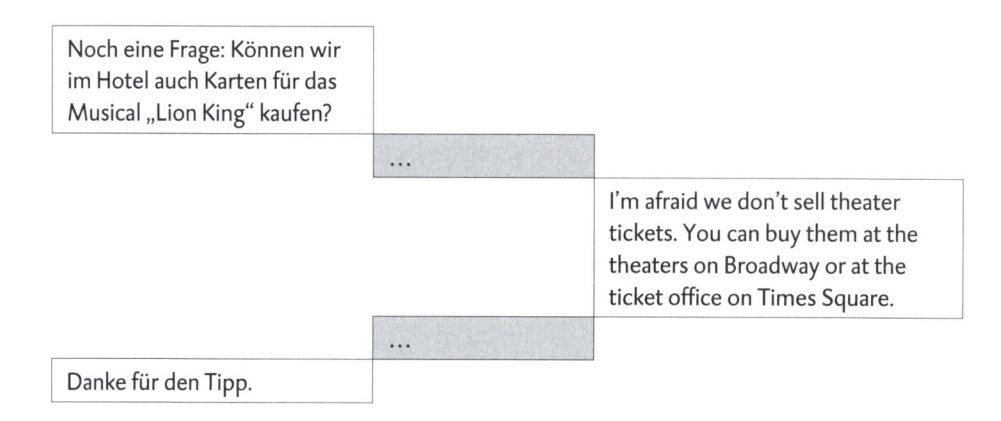

Noch eine Frage: Können wir im Hotel auch Karten für das Musical „Lion King" kaufen?	
	...
	I'm afraid we don't sell theater tickets. You can buy them at the theaters on Broadway or at the ticket office on Times Square.
	...
Danke für den Tipp.	

9. You are at a souvenir shop. An English tourist needs some help, but the shop assistant doesn't understand what he/she is saying. You help the tourist.

English tourist (teacher)	Mediation (you)	Shop assistant (other student)
Hello, could you help me, please? I would like to have this T-shirt in blue.		
	Die Dame/Der Herr ...	
		Ja, klar, hier bitte.
	...	
Thank you. Where can I put it on?		
	...	
		Da drüben sind die Umkleidekabinen.
	...	
Thank you. *(A while later)* This T-shirt is too big. Can I have it in a size smaller?		
	...	
		Sicher, hier ist Größe S.
	...	
Thanks. That should fit now.		
	...	
		Möchten Sie noch etwas?
	...	
I'll take these two postcards as well. Do you sell stamps?		
	...	
		Ja, verkaufen wir auch.
	...	
Great. Thank you!		

Einkaufstasche © Thomas Soellner. Shutterstock

▶ **Prüfungsaufgaben**

Bildnachweis: © wavebreakmedia. Shutterstock

Hauptschulabschlussprüfung in Baden-Württemberg
Aufgabe im Stil der Prüfung

♪ 77

A Listening Comprehension

20 pts

Part 1

5 pts

You will hear five short conversations. There is one task for each conversation. You will hear each conversation twice. For tasks a)–e) tick (✓) A, B or C.

a) Where does Tom want to go on holiday?

Japan	Australia	South Africa
A ☐	B ☐	C ☐

b) What does the man need?

a credit card	some change	a £ 5 note
A ☐	B ☐	C ☐

c) How many minutes late is the train today?

3	13	30
A ☐	B ☐	C ☐

d) What did the bird take?

ice cream	fish	chips
A ☐	B ☐	C ☐

e) Which question is difficult?

14	15	16
A ☐	B ☐	C ☐

Digitalziffern © DVARG. Shutterstock

Aufgabe im Stil der Prüfung

5 pts

Part 2

You will hear a report about Route 66 in the USA.
You will hear the information twice.
For tasks a)–e) fill in the grid.

	The highway is	_____3,900_____ km long.
a)	The highway wasn't the first, the longest or the	_____.
b)	The dust storms happened during the	_____.
c)	The people who left wanted	_____ life in California.
d)	The 1940s and 50s saw the rise of the	_____ culture.
e)	The new highways were faster and didn't have many	_____.

5 pts

Part 3

You will hear a conversation between Greg and Sina about Yellowstone National Park. You will hear the conversation twice.
For tasks a)–e) (✓) A, B or C.

Vocabulary:
stagecoach: *Postkutsche*

a) In the summer, the hotels …
   A ☐ are usually very full.
   B ☐ have parties every night.
   C ☐ do something very unusual.

b) In Yellowstone there is always …
   A ☐ a lot to do and see.
   B ☐ a risk of snow.
   C ☐ somewhere nice to walk.

c) Greg finds …
   A ☐ Sina silly.
   B ☐ Yellowstone's attractions great.
   C ☐ the stories more interesting than the sights.

d) The robbery happened in ...
   A ☐ 1904.
   B ☐ 1914.
   C ☐ 1940.

d) The robber was ...
   A ☐ eventually caught.
   B ☐ never found.
   C ☐ made up for visitors.

Part 4

5 pts

You will hear five people talking about holidays.
What kind of holiday do the people like?
You will hear the texts twice.
For tasks a)–e) write a letter, A–H, next to each person.

a) John   ☐   A Staying in a small hostel
b) Olivia ☐   B Camping in the wilderness
                 C Staying in a comfortable mobile home
c) Hailey ☐   D Staying in a luxury hotel
d) Carter ☐   E Doing a road trip by car
e) Josh   ☐   F Couchsurfing with locals
                 G Going on a city trip by train
                 H Staying at home

You now have 2 minutes to check your answers.

25 pts **B Text-based Tasks**

5 pts **Part 1**

Where can you find these signs? Tick (✓) the correct answer.
Example: B – Part 1: f) A

a)

**Keep off the ice!
Drowning hazard.
Ice may break.**

A ☐ on an icy road
B ☐ at a swimming pool
C ☐ at a frozen lake

b)

P PAY & DISPLAY

A ☐ at a supermarket
B ☐ at a self-service restaurant
C ☐ at a car park

c)

**No swimming
unless lifeguard
on duty!**

A ☐ in a gym
B ☐ at a beach
C ☐ in a bath tub

What information do these signs give you? Tick (✓) the correct answer.

d)

**Smoke Free Inside & Out
SMOKING IS NOT PERMITTED
• ALL BUILDINGS ON CAMPUS
• ALL OUTDOOR AREAS
• ALL PARKING LOTS**

A ☐ Smoking is not allowed inside the buildings and outside.
B ☐ Smoking is only allowed in the car park.
C ☐ Smoking is only allowed in some buildings.

e)

NO TEXTING WHILE DRIVING!

A ☐ You cannot receive text messages while you drive.
B ☐ You should not write text messages while steering a car.
C ☐ It is not possible to write text messages in a car.

Pay & Display © Wansfordphoto. Shutterstock, Smoking is not permitted © Robert J. Beyers II. Shutterstock, No texting while driving © StacieStauffSmith Photos. Shutterstock

Part 2 – Part 5: text

Green roofs benefit people

Water is a necessity of life. Rain, especially, helps plants grow and stay green. But too much rain – especially in cities – can lead to flooding. That can cause waste water systems, like sewers, to overflow and send pollutants into rivers and other waterways. To fight the problem, several cities in the United States are starting programs like rooftop gardens.

A team at the University of the District of Columbia in the nation's capital has created a garden on the top of one school building. The garden holds many kinds of plants to help absorb rainwater … and grow food at the same time. Rainwater is collected in large containers and sent through a system that waters the rooftop garden. The roof is filled with green life that appeals to insects.

In cities, "you don't have that many spaces to choose from and so rooftops are just (unused) space," says Caitlin Arlotta. She is a student in the school's Urban Agriculture program.

The project is part of a research program to see which plants do well on rooftops. The researchers are looking at plants including strawberries, tomatoes and sweet potatoes. "We have the same experiment running with tomatoes as we do with strawberries, so we're doing variety trials and we're trying just to see which variety grows the best in a green roof setting."

© Alisonh29/Dreamstime.com

One goal of the program is food justice; or in Arlotta's words, "bringing fresh food into cities where you wouldn't necessarily have that access." And that includes produce that might be more used by immigrants. "In the U.S., it may not seem very common to use hibiscus leaves and sweet potato leaves as food, but in many places around the world it is."

Sandy Farber Bandier helps run UDC's Master Gardener program. It seeks to improve cities and make them beautiful by training people to become Master Gardeners. She says she's been surprised by the garden's output. "My biggest surprise was that we produced 4,250 pounds of produce the first year and were able to give that to people in need."

She likes being able to show people who live in D.C. and others beyond the nation's capital what – and how – food can be grown on a rooftop. "This is the future for food."

(375 words)

Abridged and adapted from: Julie Taboh, Susan Shand and Caty Weaver: Green roofs benefit people, in: Voice of America Learning English

Part 2

5 pts

Match each part of the text with the correct heading.
Write down the correct letter.

a) lines 1–5   A A university team's solution

b) lines 6–11   B What the program tries to achieve

c) lines 18–25   C The consequences of too much rain

d) lines 26–30   D The result of the project

e) lines 31–35   E What the researchers want to find out

Solution:

a) _____   b) _____   c) _____   d) _____   e) _____

Part 3

5 pts

Decide whether the statements are 'true', 'false' or 'not in the text'. Tick (✓) the correct answer.

		true	false	not in the text
a)	Rainwater cannot be used to grow food in the garden because it is polluted.	☐	☐	☐
b)	Animals are attracted by the plants in the rooftop garden.	☐	☐	☐
c)	The researchers try to find out what plants grow best on the rooftop.	☐	☐	☐
d)	Most of the food they grow is commonly eaten in South America.	☐	☐	☐
e)	Ms Farber Bandier was happy with the amount of food produced in the garden.	☐	☐	☐

Part 4

5 pts

Find the corresponding line/lines in the text that mean the same.
Write down the correct letter.

Letter:

a) Water is needed for plants to grow.   _____

b) After being collected, the rainwater is distributed to the rooftop garden.   _____

c) Rooftops are areas in the city that can be made use of.   _____

d) The aim of the Master Gardener program is for cities to look nicer as well as to train people to become gardeners.   _____

e) This is how food will be grown in the future.   _____

line 27–28 A	lines 37–38 B	line 1 C	line 20–23 D	lines 9–10 E
line 14–15 F	lines 24–25 G	lines 31–33 H	lines 26–27 I	lines 12–13 K

Part 5

Tick (✓) the correct endings to complete the sentences according to the text.

5 pts

a) In the cities,
- A ☐ rain is not a problem at all.
- B ☐ too little rain can cause problems.
- C ☐ too much rain can cause problems.

b) The plants in the rooftop garden
- A ☐ soak up the rainwater.
- B ☐ do not absorb the rainwater.
- C ☐ do not need the rainwater.

c) A rooftop garden is perfect for cities because
- A ☐ food grows better on a rooftop than in a field.
- B ☐ there is not much space in cities.
- C ☐ you do not have to pay for a rooftop garden.

d) On the rooftop, the researchers
- A ☐ only grow vegetables.
- B ☐ only grow food from North America.
- C ☐ grow several different kinds of plants.

e) Sandy Farber Bandier
- A ☐ wants people in need to become gardeners.
- B ☐ thinks that not everyone can be a Master Gardener.
- C ☐ thinks that rooftop gardens will be a success.

15 pts | **C Use of Language**

6 pts | **Part 1**

Read the text and choose the correct word for each gap.
Tick (✓) the correct word.

The polar bear problem

1 Canada has got _____ (a) polar bears. They like to hunt seals on the ice of Hudson Bay. Thirty years _____ (b), ice was on the sea
5 from October to June but today it is often only there _____ (c) December to May.
Polar bears can only hunt the seals from the ice. They also have to eat a lot of them to gain fat because in the summer they live on the land where there is
10 not _____ (d) food for them. The polar bears used to hunt for more than eight months every year, now they are lucky if they can hunt for six months on the ice. A hungry bear is not a happy bear – and for the people in a town called Churchill, hungry bears are a big problem.
The bears _____ (e) came to Churchill in late October to wait for
15 the ice to start and they weren't a problem. Now they come early in July! And, _____ (f) they are hungry they are now coming close to people's homes where they look for things to eat in bins or they attack dogs. But a polar bear will attack a person, too. No one locks their car here; if a bear chases you, you can get into anyone's car, lock the door and you're safe.
20 Churchill has a special polar bear prison and polar bear police. If a bear is a problem, the polar bear police catch it and take it to the 'prison'. When there is some ice, the polar bear is taken by helicopter and put onto the ice so it can hunt and be happy once again.

© FloridaStock. Shutterstock

a)	☐	a lot	☐	a lot of	☐	lots
b)	☐	again	☐	after	☐	ago
c)	☐	of	☐	from	☐	for
d)	☐	no	☐	enough	☐	many
e)	☐	always	☐	also	☐	had
f)	☐	but	☐	although	☐	because

Aufgabe im Stil der Prüfung | 85

Part 2 — 2 pts
Find opposites for two of the three words in the text and write them down.

a) lose _____
b) less _____
c) early _____

Part 3 — 2 pts
Find synonyms for two of the three words in the text and write them down.

a) many of _____
b) near _____
c) search for _____

Part 4 — 2 pts
Choose two of the following words from the text and give a definition.

a) bin (line 17)
_____

b) to chase (line 18)
_____

c) to lock (line 18)
_____

Part 5 — 3 pts
For a presentation about the Arctic you need to know more about polar bears. Ask three different questions about polar bears.

a) _____
b) _____
c) _____

D Writing

Die Lösungen für den Teil D sind auf separaten Papierbögen zu notieren.

Part 1

Write an e-mail to your pen friend.
Your English friend Jason asked you about your holiday plans.
Include the following points:

- where?
- when?
- who is going with you?
- plans?

Write at least **60** words. Count your words.

© abdurahman.
123rf.com

Part 2

Write about your favourite star. The following ideas can help you.

| job? | age? | looks? | why? |

idea box
musician / singer / YouTuber / actor or actress / writer / a special person / …
famous / great / lyrics / professional / good cause / …

Write at least **80** words. Count your words.

Hauptschulabschlussprüfung in Baden-Württemberg
Englisch 2018

2018-1

I. Listening Comprehension

Part 1

You will hear five short conversations. You will hear each conversation twice. There is one question for each conversation. For questions 1–5 mark A, B or C.

1. What does the woman order at the bar?

   A ☐   B ☐   C ☐

2. What was Sally doing this morning?

   A ☐   B ☐   C ☐

3. Who is the new frontman?

   | Billy | Tommy | James |

   A ☐   B ☐   C ☐

4. Where will Danny spend his summer holidays?

   | Slovenia | Spain | Germany |

   A ☐   B ☐   C ☐

5. What time will the customer travel?

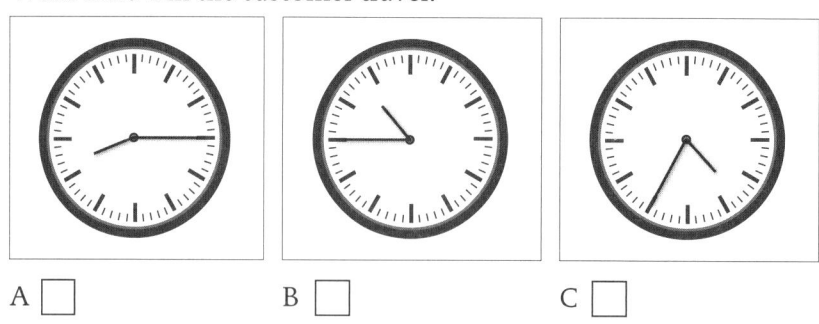

A ☐   B ☐   C ☐

Part 2

You will hear some information about a high school in Britain.
You will hear the information twice.
Listen and complete questions 6 to 10.

Hastings Castle High School

Name of the school		Hastings Castle High School
Press '3' to speak to	6	the _____
School times on Friday	7	8:45 a.m. – _____
Headmaster's phone number	8	01424 - _____
School uniform	9	tie, white _____ & _____ trousers
Not allowed in the classrooms	10	_____

Burg © iimages. 123rf.com

Part 3

You will hear a telephone conversation between a hotel clerk and a tourist.
You will hear the conversation twice.
For questions 11 to 15 mark A, B or C.

11. On 18th June Paula wants to
    A ☐ check out.
    B ☐ check in.
    C ☐ cancel the reservation.

12. Paula is going to stay for
    - A ☐ 4 nights.
    - B ☐ 5 nights.
    - C ☐ 18 nights.

13. The studio is
    - A ☐ for a single person only.
    - B ☐ not free for the time requested.
    - C ☐ still available.

14. The price for a night in the single suite is
    - A ☐ £124.90.
    - B ☐ £124.90 plus tax.
    - C ☐ £49 plus tax.

15. Paula's credit card number is
    - A ☐ 5497 5385 3000 9539.
    - B ☐ 5497 5853 0557 9539.
    - C ☐ 5497 5358 0577 9539.

Part 4
You will hear a climate expert talking about recycling. You will hear the report twice. For questions 16 to 20 mark 'true' or 'false'.

	true	false
16. Global warming has the power to destroy our environment.	☐	☐
17. With recycling you have to empty your trash bin as often as before.	☐	☐
18. With recycling natural resources will last longer.	☐	☐
19. Recycling shows others that the environment is important to you.	☐	☐
20. If we want to change the climate we need to close our windows.	☐	☐

Recyclingsymbol:
© Can Stock Photo/nickylarson974

Part 5

You will hear a radio report on the top five sights in New York.
Which feature belongs to each sight?
You will hear this report twice.
For questions 21 to 25 write a letter, A–H, next to each sight.

21. Empire State Building ☐
22. Times Square ☐
23. Statue of Liberty ☐
24. Central Park ☐
25. Museum of Modern Art ☐

A located on an island
B huge collection of pictures
C at times almost half a million people per day
D tallest skyscraper in the world
E made of steel
F sport opportunities
G constructed in 410 days
H symbol of injustice

Hauptschulabschlussprüfung Baden-Württemberg Englisch 2018

Listening – Answer Sheet

Part 1: Mark A, B or C.
Part 2: Fill in the correct answer.
Part 3: Mark A, B or C.
Part 4: Mark the correct answer.
Part 5: Fill in the correct letter.

Part 1

Number	A	B	C
1			
2			
3			
4			
5			

/5

Part 2

Number	
6	
7	
8	01424 –
9	/
10	

/5

Part 3

Number	A	B	C
11			
12			
13			
14			
15			

/5

Part 4

Number	true	false
16		
17		
18		
19		
20		

/5

Part 5

Number	Letter
21	
22	
23	
24	
25	

/5

_____ /25

II. Reading Comprehension

Part 1 – Signs

Where can you see these notices? Mark A, B or C on the answer sheet.

Example

Return books here

- A ☐ in a post office
- B ☐ in a bank
- C ☒ in a library

1. **Ducks crossing the road** Please drive **slowly**
   - A ☐ near a farm
   - B ☐ near a school
   - C ☐ near a crossroad

2. **CAUTION!** Bungee jumping overhead
   - A ☐ on a skyscraper
   - B ☐ on an airplane
   - C ☐ under a bridge

3. **DANGER!** Do not lean over the railings
   - A ☐ on a train
   - B ☐ in a classroom
   - C ☐ on a bridge

4. **This restroom is here for your convenience** Please help to keep it clean
   - A ☐ at a train station
   - B ☐ in a flat
   - C ☐ in a caravan

5. **Priority seat for** disabled passengers and expectant mothers
   - A ☐ in a church
   - B ☐ in a taxi
   - C ☐ on the underground

6. **express check-out** 10 items or less, cash only
   - A ☐ at an airport gate
   - B ☐ at a drug store
   - C ☐ in a bank

Schild „Duck crossing" © Can Stock Photo/Andrew45120

Part 2 – Signs

What information do these signs give you?
Mark A, B, C or D on the answer sheet.

7. *Where you look you will go*
   - A ☐ Walk, don't ride a motorbike!
   - B ☐ Always keep your eyes on the road!
   - C ☐ Look left, go right!
   - D ☐ Give your better look a go!

8. **This Skate Park is not supervised**
   All individuals understand and fully accept that they are using the facility at their own risk
   - A ☐ Only full skaters are accepted.
   - B ☐ This skate park is not very good.
   - C ☐ You have to understand all individuals.
   - D ☐ You skate here on your own responsibility.

9. *Gift Shop* **Open daily from 8 am – 8 pm except Sundays**
   - A ☐ You can buy souvenirs here on Sundays.
   - B ☐ You can buy food and drinks here every day.
   - C ☐ You can buy postcards and T-shirts in this shop.
   - D ☐ You can buy poisonous animals in this shop.

10. **Dog Walk** — Owners must clean-up and leash their dogs
    - A ☐ Dog holders are responsible for what their dogs leave behind.
    - B ☐ Dogs can run freely in this park and play with other dogs.
    - C ☐ Owners must keep their dogs close to them.
    - D ☐ Owners have to let go off the dog leash.

Part 3 – Text

Are the statements 'true' or 'false' or 'not in the text'?
Mark the correct answer on your answer sheet.

Healing Hooves

1. He might be quite small, but when he is doing his job he is larger than life. Petie is a Shetland pony that makes room-to-room visits at Akron Children's Hospital in Ohio.
5. For children, hospitals can be scary, so Petie brings fun and comfort to sick kids. "Some kids haven't smiled for a long time but they light up when they see Petie", trainer Susan Miller says. "He lays his head on the children's beds and his eyes get big and soft."
10. The pony has been a therapeutic horse since 1997. He gets three baths and is sprayed with safe-for-horses disinfectant before making his hospital rounds. That is to make sure of eliminating any bacteria for the patients.
And yes, if you were wondering, Petie is even house-trained: Although a person walks behind him with a bucket, just in case, Petie has learned to signal to
15. his handler when he needs a break.
After every visit Miller rewards Petie with his favorite treats: peppermint candy and popcorn. Then he goes back to his farm, where he likes to chase other horses. Miller says: "Petie is an angel at the hospital, but at home he's a little devil!"

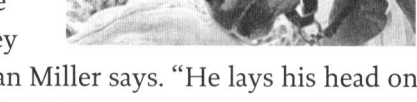

Adapted from/photo source: http://kids.nationalgeographic.com/explore/adventure_pass/amazing-animals/healing-hooves/; Stand: 01. 04. 2017

Statements – 'true' or 'false' or 'not in the text'

11. In hospitals in the USA you can often find therapeutic animals.
12. Whenever children in hospital see Petie they are happy.
13. In 1997 Petie started his career.
14. Ponies like being bathed.
15. At home on the farm Petie behaves as well as when he is with sick kids.

Part 4 – Text

Read the text and fill in the gaps. Mark A, B, C or D on the answer sheet.

A Cardboard Boat

1 Can you build a boat entirely _____ (16) cardboard? You might say "no", but some clever recyclers said "of course you can!"

5 Over ten days, Harry Dwyer and Charlie Waller turned their dream of a cardboard houseboat into reality, using about 300 old boxes they found in bins near their workshop.

10 They put a normal engine on the back of the boat. It was just a small one and _____ (17) it wouldn't rip the boat apart. In addition, they put up a flag made from a plastic bag – it's all from waste packaging.

It certainly looked good on land but what happened when it hit the water? You might think it turned into a soft and _____ (18) mess but you 15 would be wrong again. Instead of hitting the water and going straight down it worked – the boat _____ (19) sink.

Actually, boats _____ (20) made of the most unlikely materials. Steel, for example, rusts in water and then sinks. So, cardboard is probably not the obvious choice but it is definitely the cheapest houseboat you'll ever find.

Adapted from: www.ondemandnews.com 01. 04. 2017
Photo source: © Bircan Tulga/Media 10 Images

	A	B	C	D
16	off	from	by	through
17	hoping	hope	hoped	hopefully
18	wet	dry	hot	icy
19	shouldn't	didn't	don't	hadn't
20	can	could	are	is

Part 5 – Article

Complete the sentences by choosing the correct ending to each sentence.
Mark A, B or C on the answer sheet.

First People in Europe

1 Everyone knows that the oldest traces of human life were found in Africa. Now archaeologists put their focus on a place in Britain. But why? Hikers discovered the oldest human footprints
5 outside of Africa in Britain, dating back around a million years. This was one of the most important discoveries in the last years.

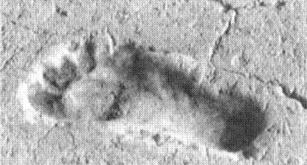

These footprints were found on a beach on the Norfolk coast in the east of England, and they are direct evidence of the earliest known humans in North-
10 ern Europe.

People first discovered the prints in May 2013 during low tide after the sand had eroded. Holes were revealed in the ground that looked like human footprints. Scientists recorded the surface using photogrammetry, which is a technique that can put together digital photographs to create a permanent record
15 and a 3D image of an imprint.

Technicians then presented the images and a model at a news conference at the British Museum in London. This presentation showed incredible pictures and was an archaeological sensation.

Scientists now say that the amazing discovery will rewrite our understanding
20 of human occupation of Britain and Europe. Now scientists can reconstruct the way of living of the first humans in Northern Europe much better and gain a more detailed insight.

Adapted from/picture source: http://www.nature.com/news/europe-s-first-humans-what-scientists-do-and-don-t-know-1.17815/; Stand: 10. 07. 2017

21. The first humans lived in

   A ☐ Africa.
   B ☐ Britain.
   C ☐ Northern Europe.

22. People found

   A ☐ hikers.
   B ☐ footprints.
   C ☐ bodies.

23. The holes looked like
    A ☐ feet.
    B ☐ sand.
    C ☐ hands.

24. The British Museum was the place of a
    A ☐ model show.
    B ☐ technicians' meeting.
    C ☐ presentation.

25. Scientists now have a better understanding of
    A ☐ Northern Europe.
    B ☐ the first humans.
    C ☐ the presentations.

Reading – Answer Sheet

Part 1: Mark A, B or C.
Part 2: Mark A, B, C or D.
Part 3: Mark the correct answer.
Part 4: Mark A, B, C or D.
Part 5: Mark A, B or C.

Part 1

Number	A	B	C
1			
2			
3			
4			
5			
6			/6

Part 2

Number	A	B	C	D
7				
8				
9				
10				/4

Part 3

Number	true	false	not in the text
11			
12			
13			
14			
15			/5

Part 4

Number	A	B	C	D
16				
17				
18				
19				
20				/5

Part 5

Number	A	B	C
21			
22			
23			
24			
25			/5

_____/25

III. Writing

Part 1 – Letter

5 pts

Karen is writing a letter to her grandma while taking part in a school exchange programme in Germany. Fill in the missing words.

Hello Granny,

I'm having a great _____ here in Berlin and have already _____ a lot of new friends.

School is different from England. _____ are no school uniforms and the lessons _____ very early in the morning: at 7.45 a.m.!

German is one of my favourite _____, as well as Maths and Science. After school we often _____ the bus to the city centre, go shopping or spend some time at the local youth _____.
My host family is awesome. They have a little _____, Marie, who is five years old and really sweet. When she talks to me it's always very fast and I can hardly _____ a word.

I hope you're _____.

I'll keep in touch and write again soon.

Lots of love,

Karen xxx

Part 2 – Dialogue

7 pts

You are on holiday in Wales and you want to spend a day in Cardiff.
Ask for information at the tourist office.
Complete the dialogue. Fill in the missing sentences.

Woman: Hello, what can I do for you?

You: _____

(Sage, dass du aus Deutschland kommst und einen Tag in Cardiff verbringen möchtest.)

Woman: Oh, there's plenty to do. You could go on a *Hop on – Hop off* Bus Tour, for example.

You: _____

(Frage, wie oft die Busse fahren.)

Woman: They run every half hour. From 10.00 a.m. to 3.30 p.m.

You: _____

(Frage, welche Sehenswürdigkeiten sie empfehlen kann.)

Woman: Well, I highly recommend Cardiff Castle and the National Museum of Wales.

You: _____

(Erzähle ihr, dass ein Freund von dir vor zwei Jahren in der 'Dr Who Experience' war.)

Woman: Unfortunately, the 'Dr Who Experience' closed last summer, it was only a seasonal exhibition.

You: _____

(Du findest das schade und hoffst, dass es andere interessante Dinge auf der Rundfahrt gibt.)

Woman: I'm sure you won't regret it. Do you want to buy the ticket now?

You: _____

_____

(Sage höflich ja und erkundige dich, was die Fahrkarte kostet.)

Woman: Well, it's £12.50 for adults and £9.50 for students.

You: _____

_____

(Du willst wissen, wie lange die Fahrkarte gültig ist.)

Woman: It's actually valid for 24 hours.

8 pts

Part 3 – E-mail

You want to spend your next summer holidays together with your friends at a youth camp abroad. Write an e-mail to the organization (info@ct-summer-camps.co.uk) that arranges special holiday packages for teenagers.

Include the following points:
- country you want to go to and time/duration of your stay
- activities you're interested in
- ask for accommodation and price

Write at least 60 words.

From:	To:
Subject:	

Now please count your words: _____

Hauptschulabschlussprüfung in Baden-Württemberg
Englisch 2019

I. Listening Comprehension

Part 1

You will hear five short conversations. You will hear each conversation twice. There is one question for each conversation. For questions 1–5 mark A, B or C.

1. Where did Clara put her mp3 player?

in her pocket	in her schoolbag	on her desk
A ☐	B ☐	C ☐

2. Which exercise should Henrietta do next?

exercise 4	exercise 7a	exercise 7b
A ☐	B ☐	C ☐

3. What ticket does the woman buy?

1.55 pm return ticket	12.30 pm single ticket	12.30 return ticket
A ☐	B ☐	C ☐

4. What is the man complaining about?

wrong colour	damaged	too expensive
A ☐	B ☐	C ☐

5. When will the football match be over?

in 6 minutes	in 1 minute	in 10 minutes
A ☐	B ☐	C ☐

Part 2

You will hear some information about poetry slams.
You will hear the information twice.
Listen and complete questions 6 to 10.

Poetry Slams

Poetry Slam		competition where poets perform their work
invented by Marc Smith in 1990 in San Francisco	6	_____
	7	first _____ poetry slam
careers of many slam poets	8	writers, _____, hip-hop artists
performance time	9	_____
poets mustn't use	10	costumes or _____

Part 3

You will hear a conversation between Karen and her mum in the kitchen.
You will hear the conversation twice.
For questions 11 to 15 mark A, B or C.

11. Karen could have been
    - A ☐ at the bus station.
    - B ☐ home earlier.
    - C ☐ on time.

12. For Karen the test at school
    - A ☐ went very well.
    - B ☐ was okay.
    - C ☐ was relaxed.

13. Wayne will
    - A ☐ celebrate his birthday at home.
    - B ☐ take some muffins to school.
    - C ☐ not touch the muffins.

14. Baking a cake is
    - A ☐ not difficult with enough practice.
    - B ☐ better than having dinner in an hour.
    - C ☐ something Karen is good at.

15. In the end Karen
    - A ☐ bakes a chocolate cake.
    - B ☐ eats a chocolate muffin.
    - C ☐ fixes a time with her mum.

Part 4

Mike is a fitness coach at a gym. He is presenting the sports centre to a group of people. You will hear the report twice. For questions 16 to 20 mark A, B or C.

16. In the main gym, you can do
    - A ☐ running, cycling, rowing.
    - B ☐ running, cycling, weights.
    - C ☐ rowing, cycling, weights.

17. In the main gym, you must
    - A ☐ wear trainers.
    - B ☐ use a towel.
    - C ☐ take a bottle of water.

18. The pool is always
    - A ☐ supervised by a lifeguard.
    - B ☐ closed for courses.
    - C ☐ open in the mornings.

19. The prices are higher because of
    - A ☐ the professional stuff.
    - B ☐ the exclusive changing rooms.
    - C ☐ the choice of activities.

20. The timetables for the classes are available
    - A ☐ online & on the noticeboard.
    - B ☐ in a brochure & online.
    - C ☐ on the noticeboard & in a brochure.

Part 5

You will hear some young people discussing what they plan on doing after leaving school. Which person has which plan?
You will hear this report twice.
For questions 21 to 25 write a letter, A–H, next to each person.

© CandyBox Images. Shutterstock

21. Nala ☐
22. Patrick ☐
23. Owen ☐
24. Christine ☐
25. Lennox ☐

A working with wood
B studying
C working as an au-pair
D working as a radio presenter
E travelling around
F doing a voluntary social year
G doing casual jobs
H doing work & travel

Listening – Answer Sheet

Part 1: Mark A, B or C.
Part 2: Fill in the correct answer.
Part 3: Mark A, B or C.
Part 4: Mark A, B or C.
Part 5: Fill in the correct letter.

Part 1

Number	A	B	C
1			
2			
3			
4			
5			/5

Part 2

Number	
6	
7	
8	
9	
10	/5

Part 3

Number	A	B	C
11			
12			
13			
14			
15			/5

Part 4

Number	A	B	C
16			
17			
18			
19			
20			/5

Part 5

Number	Letter
21	
22	
23	
24	
25	/5

_____/25

II. Reading Comprehension

Part 1 – Signs

Where can you see these notices?
Mark A, B or C on the answer sheet.

1. **Life vest under your seat.**
   - A ☐ in a train
   - B ☐ on a ferry
   - C ☐ in a bus

2. **☞ STAGE DOOR ☞**
   - A ☐ in a theatre
   - B ☐ at the zoo
   - C ☐ in a gym

3. **APPROACH SLOWLY GATE WILL OPEN**
   - A ☐ on a race track
   - B ☐ on a playground
   - C ☐ at a private property

4. **NO DRINKS TO BE TAKEN BEYOND THIS POINT THANK YOU**
   - A ☐ in a kitchen
   - B ☐ at a library
   - C ☐ at a train station

5. **PRIORITY SEATS** Please offer these seats to passengers with reduced mobility
   - A ☐ on a bus
   - B ☐ on a rollercoaster
   - C ☐ at the swimming pool

6. **BODY SHOP** High quality work – repairs, petrol, damages
   - A ☐ in a fitness studio
   - B ☐ at a doctor's surgery
   - C ☐ in a garage

Part 2 – Signs

What information do these signs give you?
Mark A, B, C or D on the answer sheet.

7.

SPRING BREAK
Coach break
to Scotland
£ 256

- A ☐ A coach broke down on the way to Scotland.
- B ☐ It costs £ 256 to meet a coach in spring in Scotland.
- C ☐ You'll have to spend £ 256 for your trip to Scotland.
- D ☐ There's a £ 256 penalty for coach drivers who avoid regular breaks.

8.

The library is open to resident members of the College only
Visitors by appointment

- A ☐ You have to make an appointment if you are a visitor.
- B ☐ Only resident members can use the library.
- C ☐ Visitors aren't allowed to use the library.
- D ☐ You can visit the college only if you are a resident member.

9.

BICYCLES MUST NOT BE PLACED AGAINST BOLLARDS OR CHAINS. ALL BICYCLES WILL BE REMOVED

- A ☐ Your bike isn't safe here.
- B ☐ You must remove the chains to place your bike here.
- C ☐ You are not allowed to leave your bike here.
- D ☐ The chains cannot be replaced.

10.

TERRACE IS FOR DINING ONLY
90-MINUTE LIMIT
Restrooms are located downstairs at the end of the bar

- A ☐ You have to finish your meal within 1.5 hours.
- B ☐ You must sit here for 90 minutes.
- C ☐ You can find the toilets on the upper floor.
- D ☐ You aren't allowed to sit outside the restaurant.

Part 3 – Text

Are the statements 'true' or 'false' or 'not in the text'?
Mark the correct answer on your answer sheet.

New Uses for Telephone Boxes

1. Red telephone boxes are as British as Buckingham Palace, bobbies and Big Ben. Tourists love them and they are a favourite photo motive. The problem is that since the arrival of mobile phones, nobody really needs public telephones any more.
   From almost 100,000 telephone boxes years ago there are less than 40,000 boxes left – and the number is decreasing. However, more and more red phone boxes are taking on a new life thanks to the *'Adopt a Kiosk'* scheme by British Telecom, a telecommunications company. For just £1, communities and charities can buy a phone box and use it for something completely different:
   Some phone boxes now house life-saving defibrillators. The *'Community HeartBeat Trust'* has installed them in the phone boxes across the country. If a person has a serious heart problem, help has to come quickly and that can be a problem in the countryside. Two people from Brighton run a business called 'Red Box Coffee'. They sell hot drinks and ice cream from the two boxes they've adopted in the seaside town. In Cheltenham, 10 of the boxes are being used as mini art galleries where local artists can show their works. So, the good old red phone boxes are being turned into something different and very useful.

adapted from: Moya Irvine: New Uses for Telephone Boxes. Read On, July 2017, Bremen: Ed. Schünemann

Statements – 'true' or 'false' or 'not in the text'

11. Phone boxes aren't used anymore because of the increasing number of tourists.

12. The number of re-used telephone boxes is growing.

13. In rural areas it is often hard to get medical help when a heart attack happens.

14. 'Red Box Coffee' sells hot drinks and ice cream for just £1.

15. All former telephone boxes in Cheltenham are used as mini galleries.

Hauptschulabschlussprüfung Baden-Württemberg Englisch 2019

Part 4 – Text

Read the text and fill in the gaps. Mark A, B, C or D on the answer sheet.

The Royal Ravens of the Tower of London

1 It is not known when the ravens first came to the Tower of London, but they are surrounded _____ (16) myth and legend.

5 Legend has it that in the 17th century the astronomical observer, John Flamsteed, complained to King Charles II that the ravens living in the tower were disturbing his work. So the king _____ (17) the killing of the
10 ravens.

© Vicky Jirayu. Shutterstock

But he was told that if the ravens _____ (18) the Tower, the Tower would fall and a great disaster would happen to his kingdom. Sensibly the King changed his mind and commanded that at least six ravens should be kept at the Tower at all times.

15 To prevent the birds from flying away one wing is clipped. This does not hurt nor does it harm them in _____ (19) way.

However, despite the wing clipping, there have been several escapes. The raven Grog was last seen outside an East End pub in 1981. He obviously felt he needed a change of _____ (20). Sometimes ravens even get lost
20 – and one of them, Mabel, is suggested to have been kidnapped!

adapted from https://www.historic-uk.com/HistoryMagazine/DestinationsUK/Tower-Ravens/, author: Ben Johnson

	A	B	C	D
16	buy	bye	by	be
17	ordered	blocked	stopped	prevented
18	leaves	left	will leave	are leaving
19	any	some	many	same
20	lane	platform	tracks	scene

Part 5 – Article

Complete the sentences by choosing the correct ending to each sentence. Mark A, B or C on the answer sheet.

Plans for 'Doghouse' Flats considered 'immoral'

1 Plans for very tiny flats in an area of London have come in for criticism. An architect wants to rebuild a very high office building into 254 flats, most of
5 them smaller than a standard hotel room. There are minimum standards for homes in Great Britain, but they do not apply if offices are converted into apartments.
10 Some of the new flats are just 16 square metres. They have a separate bathroom, a little kitchenette, a space for a bed, a wardrobe, a table with two chairs and one armchair. Once the furniture is in the room, there is only little space to
15 walk around. Other flats are a little bigger, but around 95 percent are smaller than the national minimum standard of 37 square metres for a single person. But these flats will be cheaper, won't they? This is definitely not the case, because this is London! They will be £800 a month to rent or £180,000 to buy. This is certainly a lot for a flat as big as a doghouse!
20 The average size of a European flat is about 90 square metres. In Britain it is 76 square metres. So you find comments on the council's website like: "This shouldn't be legal – it's inhuman!"

© Philafrenzy/wikipedia, CC BY-SA 4.0

Moya Irvine: Plans for "Doghouse" Flats considered "immoral". Read On, May 2017

21. The office building will be used as
    - A ☐ hotel rooms.
    - B ☐ doghouses.
    - C ☐ flats.

22. For the 'doghouse' flats UK standards are not
    - A ☐ recognized.
    - B ☐ converted.
    - C ☐ minimized.

23. Once furnished, the 16-m²-flats have
    - A ☐ almost no space to move.
    - B ☐ the national standard size.
    - C ☐ a bedroom with a walk-in cupboard.

24. The flats can be
    A ☐ rented cheaply.
    B ☐ bought.
    C ☐ sponsored.

25. Some online comments are
    A ☐ inhuman.
    B ☐ illegal.
    C ☐ critical.

Reading – Answer Sheet

Part 1: Mark A, B or C.
Part 2: Mark A, B, C or D.
Part 3: Mark the correct answer.
Part 4: Mark A, B, C or D.
Part 5: Mark A, B or C.

Part 1

Number	A	B	C
1			
2			
3			
4			
5			
6			/6

Part 2

Number	A	B	C	D
7				
8				
9				
10				/4

Part 3

Number	true	false	not in the text
11			
12			
13			
14			
15			/5

Part 4

Number	A	B	C	D
16				
17				
18				
19				
20				/5

Part 5

Number	A	B	C
21			
22			
23			
24			
25			/5

_____/25

III. Writing

Part 1 – Letter

Daniel writes a letter to his friend Jack from Maidstone Hospital.
Fill in the missing words.

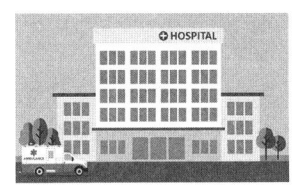

5 pts

Dear Jack,

I feel really _____ about not coming to your birthday party last Saturday. As my sister has already told you, I had this nasty fall with my skateboard and _____ taken to Maidstone Hospital with badly injured shoulders and knees.

The doctor told me I'd have to _____ here for at least another week! The staff, especially the nurses, are very _____ to me, caring and friendly. The food here is better _____ I expected. But we get our evening _____ at 5.30 pm. That's too early for me. I'm so glad that I'm _____ to use the DVD player because life in hospital can be very boring sometimes. There is no internet access and all the other _____ in my room are much older than me. It would be _____ if you could come and see me. Can I borrow a couple of your DVDs? I'm in room 3 _____ the second floor. Believe it or not, I really miss school!

See you soon,

Daniel

Part 2 – Dialogue

7 pts

You are waiting in Munich airport for your flight. A woman needs help.
Complete the dialogue.
Fill in the missing sentences.

Woman: Excuse me, I can't find the right gate and was wondering if you could help me.

You: _____

(Frage, wohin sie fliegen möchte.)

Woman: I'm on my way to Dubai to visit some friends there.

You: _____

(Frage, wann ihr Flug geht.)

Woman: I'm booked on the 11.30 a.m. flight.

You: _____

(Sage, dass man das Gate auf den Anzeigetafeln sehen kann.)

Woman: Oh right, thanks. But I can't find any of these boards.

You: _____

(Sage, dass sich eines rechts neben dem Kiosk befindet.)

Woman: Ah, ok. I think I know where you mean.

You: _____

(Schlage vor, ihr die Anzeigetafel zu zeigen.)

Woman: That's very kind of you. But I'll be fine now. Where are you flying to?

You: _____

(Sage, dass du nach Los Angeles fliegst und dort Verwandte besuchst.)

Woman: Lovely. I hope you'll have a great time there.

You: _____

(Bedanke dich und wünsche ihr einen guten Flug.)

Hauptschulabschlussprüfung Baden-Württemberg Englisch 2019   2019-15

Part 3 – E-mail

8 pts

Write an e-mail to Mrs Potter.
On your way to London you have just noticed that you left your coat in a bed & breakfast in Dover where you had stayed last night.
Write an e-mail to the landlady, Mrs Potter (potterbnb@dover.co.uk).

Include the following points:
- when and where you left the coat (1 pt)
- describe the coat (e. g. colour, size, fabric, label, buttons etc.) (1,5 pts)
- content of coat pockets (1,5 pts)
- how you could get the coat back (2 pts)

Write at least 60 words.

From:	To:
Subject:	

Now please count your words: _____

Schild© Can Stock Photo/lauraluchi, Mantel © Can Stock Photo/vectorchef

Hauptschulabschlussprüfung in Baden-Württemberg
Englisch 2020

2020-1

A Listening Comprehension

20 pts

Part 1

5 pts

You will hear five short conversations. There is one task for each conversation. You will hear each conversation twice. For tasks a)–e) mark A, B or C.

a) When will Ernest visit his grandma?

today	tomorrow	the day after tomorrow
A ☐	B ☐	C ☐

b) What time does the shop close today?

6.30 p.m.	8 p.m.	6 p.m.
A ☐	B ☐	C ☐

c) What's new in the house?

carpet / table	sofa / lamp	lamp / armchair
A ☐	B ☐	C ☐

d) Where did Peter sleep last night?

at Steven's house	at Harry's house	at William's house
A ☐	B ☐	C ☐

e) Which piece of clothing is in the washing?

grey T-shirt	black pullover	white T-shirt
A ☐	B ☐	C ☐

5 pts

Part 2

You will hear some information about Drake, a Canadian rapper.
You will hear the information twice.
For tasks a)–e) fill in the grid.

DRAKE

	Drake	_a Canadian rapper_
a)	born (year)	_____ in Toronto
b)	jobs (name two)	rapper, _____, _____
c)	name of song (2018)	_____
d)	things he gave away in the video clip (name two)	_____, _____
e)	number of sold records	more than _____

5 pts

Part 3

Listen to five people talking about their jobs. Which person has which job?
You will hear the information twice. For tasks a)–e) write a letter, A–H, next to each person.

a) Fiona ☐
b) Michael ☐
c) Susan ☐
d) Jeremy ☐
e) Vincent ☐

A tour guide
B nursery school teacher
C pilot
D travel agent
E shop assistant
F dentist
G doctor
H nurse

Part 4

You will hear a radio interview about summer camps.
You will hear the interview twice.
For tasks a)–e) mark A, B or C.

5 pts

a) Matthew went to a summer camp ...
   A every year. ☐
   B every two years. ☐
   C once every three years. ☐

b) With bow and arrow Matthew was good at ...
   A target shooting. ☐
   B figure shooting. ☐
   C distance shooting. ☐

c) In the summer camps Matthew also ...
   A went hiking. ☐
   B went stand-up paddling. ☐
   C played matches. ☐

d) Before roasting marshmallows at the campfire Matthew ...
   A listened to some songs. ☐
   B hoped for ghost stories. ☐
   C searched for sticks. ☐

e) At the summer camp Matthew felt more independent because ...
   A his parents picked him up. ☐
   B there were fewer regulations. ☐
   C he got homesick. ☐

You now have five minutes to check your answers.

B Text-based Tasks

Part 1

Where can you find these signs?
Example: B–Part 1: f) A

a)
Please Place Your Order Here!

A in a self-service restaurant
B at a hotel reception
C at the police station

b)
Please respect our neighbours and local residents and leave the premises and the area quietly.

A at a train station
B in a pub
C in a library

c)
SORRY – THIS TRAIL IS CLOSED
The route is dangerous due to land slips. It is not safe to walk on.

A in a forest
B on a motorway
C at a bus station

What information do these signs give you?

d)
For safety reasons, please do not leave your children unattended

A You have to look after your child at all times.
B You have to make sure that your child is left alone.
C Children can't play here for safety reasons.

e)
Cyclists have to limit their speed to 10 mph. Do not use this path in bad weather.

A You can only cycle here when the weather is bad.
B The speed limit during bad weather is 10 mph.
C Avoid this path during bad weather.

Part 2 – Part 5: text

The Most Popular Lonesome Cowboy

Almost everyone all over the world knows the comic-strip hero Lucky Luke. He is the one and only cowboy who is able to shoot faster than his own shadow.

Maurice de Bevere, also known as Morris, was a Belgian artist who created a lot of comic strips. As a child he was fascinated by western films and their heroes, so he decided to create his own western star who should have special skills. Lucky Luke was born – a lonesome cowboy, surrounded by an aura of mystery, a fearless guy who always tries to help people in trouble.

Lucky is not married and his best friend is an animal: his loyal horse Jolly Jumper. On horseback he crosses the American states and undergoes a lot of adventures. He is always there when a bank is robbed, a train is hijacked or a young lady is in danger. In most of his adventures he has to deal with four hilarious guys: the Daltons. In almost every story Lucky Luke has to find them because they always escape from one of the numberless prisons all over the country. And of course – in the end Lucky wins and brings them back to where they belong. Once his job is done, he always leaves the celebrations given in his honor and rides into the sunset, ready for new adventures, claiming no rewards.

Lucky Luke has been a comic-strip hero for more than 70 years now, and almost 90 titles have been published. They were translated into 30 languages and several hundred million copies have been sold. So Lucky Luke is one of the most successful legendary figures in the history of comic-strips.

But like in similar cases, there is much more than just the comic strips. A French broadcasting company produced an animated series for television – 26 episodes of 26 minutes each, based on the comics – and the western film hero Terence Hill played the 'Lonesome Cowboy' in ten Lucky Luke 'live' films.

The hero's huge popularity has also led to a huge and increasing number of merchandising stuff: you can buy his outfit (remember – the hat must be white!), soft toys, puzzles, games and other things: the 'Lonesome Cowboy' is even with you at school – on pencil cases and school bags!

5 pts | **Part 2**
Match each part of the text with the correct heading.
Example: B – Part 2: f) A

a) lines 1–8   A Lucky Luke on the screen
b) lines 9–18   B Lucky Luke's 'father'
c) lines 19–22   C Long-lasting mega-seller
d) lines 23–27   D Advertising Lucky Luke
e) lines 28–31   E Lucky Luke's heroic actions

5 pts | **Part 3**
Decide whether the statements are 'true', 'false' or 'not in the text'.
Example: B – Part 3: f) not in the text

a) Morris wanted to create an ordinary cowboy.
b) Lucky Luke avoids adventures.
c) He doesn't want anything for his help.
d) Lucky Luke comic strips are published in more than 70 countries.
e) There are movies as well as animation films about Lucky Luke.

5 pts | **Part 4**
Find the corresponding sentence parts or sentences in the text that mean the same.

a) The author liked cowboy movies when he was younger.
b) Lucky Luke rides through different parts of America.
c) Lucky Luke is able to catch the Daltons eventually.
d) Lucky Luke's comic strips are not the only product you can see.
e) As a student you can take Lucky Luke with you.

5 pts | **Part 5**
Complete the sentences by choosing the correct ending according to the text.
Example: B – Part 5: f) A

a) Morris de Bevere's cowboy had to have
   A extraordinary abilities.
   B a good sense of humor.
   C an ordinary face.

b) Lucky Luke always tries to
   A rob banks.
   B help in difficult situations.
   C hijack young ladies in trains.

c) The Four Daltons are Lucky Luke's
   A friends.
   B roommates.
   C opponents.

d) The success of the comic strips can be measured by about
   A 30 titles in 90 different languages.
   B 70 titles in 26 different languages.
   C 90 titles in 30 different languages.

e) Lucky Luke was filmed with real actors
   A 10 times.
   B 26 times.
   C 30 times.

C Use of Language

Part 1
Read the text and choose the correct word from the list.

Fido

1   During World War II, a lot of dogs **(a)** killed in military attacks. People's pets had to leave their families and live on the streets. One of the **(b)** famous street dogs from World War II is Fido. Fido
5   is a Latin word and means "faithful". In November 1941, **(c)** his way home from the bus stop, a brick worker near Florence, Italy, found Fido lying injured on a road. Not knowing who the dog belonged to Carlo Soriani **(d)** him home and helped him. After Fido recovered, he fol-
10 lowed Soriani to the bus stop every day. When the bus returned, Fido was always there to greet Soriani with great joy. That repeated for two years until December 1943, when Soriano died. Despite his friend's **(e)** Fido returned to the bus stop looking for Soriani every day for fourteen more years. Fido came to symbolize extreme loyalty. He died on June 9, 1958, **(f)** still waiting for
15 his master.

Foto: Sailko/Wikipedia, CC BY 3.0

a)	are	were	is
b)	more	much	most
c)	at	by	on
d)	took	found	gave
e)	dead	death	died
f)	while	if	because

Part 2
Find the opposites in the text.

a) lost
b) never

Part 3
Find the synonyms in the text.

a) well-known
b) hurt

Part 4

Choose two of the following words from the text and give a definition.

a) pets (line 2)
b) greet (line 11)
c) June (line 14)

2 pts

Part 5

You are interested in dogs. You want to find out more about owning a dog. You meet a dog owner. Ask three different questions.

3 pts

D Writing

20 pts

Part 1

8 pts

You are looking for a job in your summer holidays and have read a job advert offering a job as a waiter / waitress. Write an e-mail to the restaurant.

Include the following points:

- introduce yourself (e. g. name, age, interests, contact details) (2 pts)
- say why you want the job and why they should take you (3 pts)
- ask for job details (e. g. working times, salary, outfit) (2 pts)

Write at least **60** words. Count your words.

Part 2

12 pts

Write about a place that you've visited recently and liked very much.
The following ideas can help you.

| where / when / with whom? | What did you do there? | why? | What did it look like? |

idea box
holidays / abroad / family / friends / sightseeing / weather / food / …

Write at least **80** words. Count your words.

Hauptschulabschlussprüfung in Baden-Württemberg
Englisch 2021

2021-1

A Listening Comprehension

20 pts

Part 1

5 pts

You will hear five short conversations. There is one task for each conversation. You will hear each conversation twice. For tasks a)–e) mark A, B or C.

a) When will they visit Glasgow Zoo?

Tuesday	Wednesday	Friday
A ☐	B ☐	C ☐

b) Who will join Bobby for the pop concert?

Alex	Mo	Frank
A ☐	B ☐	C ☐

c) At what time will the young woman take the train?

4.20	5.15	6.00
A ☐	B ☐	C ☐

d) What will Pete and Kate buy for James' birthday?

a mug	a T-shirt	chocolate
A ☐	B ☐	C ☐

e) Whose room does Charley choose?

Tom's	Pete's	Robbie's
A ☐	B ☐	C ☐

Part 2

You will hear an advert for the Museum Context in Edinburgh.
You will hear the information twice.
For tasks a)–e) fill in the grid.

a)	Museum context is a	_____ shop
b)	you can buy	stuffed owls and chocolate _____
c)	shop's address	_____, Edinburgh
d)	the house was finished in	_____
e)	you'll soon feel like a witch or	_____

Part 3

You will hear a radio interview with some teens in Scotland. What does each person talk about?
You will hear the information twice. For tasks a)–e) write a letter, A–H, next to each person.

a) Francis ☐
b) Angus ☐
c) Keira ☐
d) Merida ☐
e) Rory ☐

A lake
B museum
C football match
D Highland festival
E castles and monuments
F TV show
G islands
H flight

Part 4

You will hear a conversation between two friends talking about their weekend plans. You will hear the conversation twice.
For tasks a)–e) mark A, B or C.

a) Steffi has some problems with
- A sights. ☐
- B words. ☐
- C places. ☐

b) Loch Lomond is a
- A hole. ☐
- B lake. ☐
- C ground. ☐

c) In Glen Coe, a lot of people
- A were killed. ☐
- B are soldiers. ☐
- C speak Gaelic. ☐

d) Hiking can be dangerous because of the
- A height. ☐
- B weather. ☐
- C summer. ☐

e) The word *fell* is used to describe
- A animals. ☐
- B Scottish people. ☐
- C landscapes. ☐

You now have five minutes to check your answers.

B Text-based Tasks

Part 1

Where can you find these signs? Write down the correct answer.
Example: B–Part 1: f) A

a) **Cattle crossing – be careful**
- A on a road
- B on a lake
- C underwater

b) **Might contain traces of soy**
- A in a forest
- B on a field
- C on a chocolate bar

c) **SINGLE ROAD TRACK – ALWAYS DRIVE CAREFULLY**
- A on a motorway
- B on a railway track
- C in the countryside

What information do these signs give you? Write down the correct answer.

d) **Don't step on the pitch – Flying sport equipment**
- A You can't perform a step-dance here.
- B Javelins or frisbees might fly around here.
- C Planes and helicopters might land here.

e) **Bagpipe makers offer:**
- **Scottish gifts**
- **Kilts to hire**

- A Scottish people should be careful with gifts.
- B You can borrow traditional Scottish clothes.
- C Bagpipes can be killed.

Part 2 – Part 5: text

Scotland's Highland Games

The Scottish Highland Games are a fun way to celebrate Scottish and Celtic traditional cultures. Originally founded as an athletics and sports competition, these games were called Highland Games
5 and are now well-known all over the world. There are a lot of Highland Games outside Scotland – even in Germany!
Hundreds of years ago the Scots wanted to test the power and strength of Scottish troops during the games. Over the centuries the Highland Games
10 turned into festivals for all Scottish people. Thousands of people wanted to watch the games. Dancing, pipe bands, drumming and food and drink were added – the Scottish Highland Games were born!
In Scotland, there are a lot of big families called *clans*. These clans have been a part of the Highland Games right from the start, with clan members going
15 head-to-head in different competitions. In modern times, their participation is more of a social and ceremonial meeting. Many clans set up tents and share information about Scottish history. Clans are famous for their *tartans*. This is the colour and the pattern of their *kilts* – the traditional skirts for men – that can be compared to the shirts football teams wear. Every clan has its own tar-
20 tan. Following this tradition, every competitor has to wear a kilt during the games.
What has to be done during the games? There are different field events with special Scottish names. One of them is the *fell-running* in which you have to run up a *fell*, the Scottish word for hill or mountain. On top of the hill the
25 runners have to take a little flag with their starting number and bring it back down to the finish line.
Besides square-dancing, hammer-throwing and weight for height (you have to lift heavy stones), *tossing the caber* is the most popular event. Many people think that the athletes have to throw the trunk of a tree (the caber) as far as
30 they can – but that's wrong! The aim is to throw the caber in such a way that it lands in a 12 o'clock position. The one who can make it the closest is the winner!
So, you see – Highland Games are always great fun and whenever there are Highland Games nearby – join them!

Abb: https://www.highland-games.eu/disziplinen-bei-den-dhg; Stand: 01.07.2020

Part 2

5 pts

Match each part of the text with the correct heading.
Write down the correct letter for each part.

a) lines 1–7   A Different events

b) lines 8–12   B Family traditions influence the Games

c) lines 13–21   C The distance doesn't count

d) lines 22–26   D A famous cultural event

e) lines 27–34   E The origin of the Games

Part 3

5 pts

Decide whether the statements are 'true', 'false' or 'not in the text'.
Write down the correct answer.

a) The Highland Games were originally created as a war simulation.

b) They wanted to see how fit the soldiers were.

c) Clan members open the games every year.

d) Some names of the events are different from the English expressions.

e) *Tossing the caber* means lifting heavy stones.

Part 4

5 pts

Find the corresponding line/lines in the text that mean the same.
Write down the correct letter.

a) The events are familiar to people all over the world.

b) Centuries later, not only sportsmen can take part in the games.

c) Clan members present cultural information.

d) To end the race, athletes carry their flags to the foot of the mountain.

e) Athletes must raise things of great weight.

lines 1–2 A	lines 4–5 B	lines 8–9 C	lines 9–10 D	line 13 E
lines 13–15 F	lines 16–17 G	lines 22–23 H	lines 24–26 I	lines 27–28 K

Part 5

Find the correct endings to complete the sentences according to the text. Write down the correct letter.

a) Nowadays, the Highland Games are

    A a worldwide event.

    B a Scottish event.

    C an English event.

b) Today, The Highland Games are

    A only a sports event.

    B more than a sports event.

    C only a food and drink festival.

c) From the very beginning, clan members

    A took part in the games.

    B only pitched tents.

    C were excluded from the games.

d) *Fell-running*

    A is a special word from England.

    B is like a race.

    C has to do with Scottish animals.

e) To win *tossing the caber* you need

    A the longest throw.

    B the most exact throw.

    C the highest throw.

5 pts

C Use of Language

Part 1
Read the text and choose the correct word for each gap.
Write down the correct word.

The Story of Street Art

1. Modern graffiti began in big cities in the United States in the 1970s. In New York, young people wrote **(a)** names, or 'tags', with pens on walls around the
5. city.
   One of the first 'taggers' **(b)** a teenager called Demetrius. His tag was TAKI 183. Demetrius wrote his tag on walls and in stations in New York. Other teenagers saw his tag and started writing their
10. tags too. Soon, there were tags on walls, buses and trains all **(c)** New York.
    Then, some **(d)** started writing their tags with aerosol paint. Their tags were bigger and more colourful. Aerosol paint graffiti **(e)** very popular in the 1970s and 1980s. It appeared on trains, buses and walls around the world.
    In the 1990s and 2000s, **(f)** graffiti artists started painting pictures. Some art-
15. ists' pictures were about politics. Other artists wanted to make cities beautiful and painted big, colourful pictures on city walls.

Robin Newton, https://learnenglishteens.britishcouncil.org/study-break/graded-reading/graffiti-street-art-level-1
Abb © Designpro Studio. Shutterstock

a)	its	there	their
b)	was	is	were
c)	about	over	of
d)	teenage	teenagers	youth
e)	get	became	become
f)	a lot of	much	very

Part 2
Find synonyms for <u>two</u> of the three words in the text and write them down.
a) noticed
b) after a short time
c) good-looking

Part 3
Find opposites for <u>two</u> of the three words in the text and write them down.

a) old
b) last
c) smaller

Part 4
Choose <u>two</u> of the following words from the text and give a definition.

a) teenager (line 9)
b) popular (line 12)
c) to paint (line 14)

Part 5
You are preparing a school presentation about Demetrius/TAKI 183.
You have got the chance to talk to him personally.
Ask <u>three</u> different questions to get further information.

D Writing

Part 1: E-mail

You have watched a documentary about the Highland Games in Scotland. You want to do a school presentation about it, so you write an e-mail to the producers asking for more details.

Include the following points:
- introduce yourself (e. g. name, age, contact details) (2 pts)
- reason for your mail/how you want to do the presentation (3 pts)
- ask for more information (e. g. material, films, internet links) (2 pts)

Write at least **60** words. Count your words.

Abb: https://www.highland-games.eu/disziplinen-bei- den-dhg; Stand: 01. 07. 2020

12 pts

Part 2: Best Holiday / Dream Holiday

Write about the best holiday you have ever had or your dream holiday.
The following ideas can help you.

| where / destination / country | means of transport / journey | when / how long | activities / sights |

idea box
holiday / abroad / family / friends / sightseeing / tickets / go by / sports / weather / food / …

Write at least **80** words. Count your words.

Hauptschulabschlussprüfung in Baden-Württemberg
Englisch 2022

2022-1

A Listening Comprehension

20 pts

Part 1

5 pts

You will hear five short conversations. There is one task for each conversation. You will hear each conversation twice. For tasks a)–e) mark A, B or C.

a) When will John's train leave?

9:00	9:30	9:20
A ☐	B ☐	C ☐

b) Which place in New York isn't Sean going to visit?

Brooklyn Bridge	Spring Creek Park	Louis Armstrong House
A ☐	B ☐	C ☐

c) How much is the umbrella?

£10	£20	£12
A ☐	B ☐	C ☐

d) Who is Prakash going to share a room with?

Jason	Brenda	Brian
A ☐	B ☐	C ☐

e) Which tests will be next week?

biology/English	English/maths	biology/maths
A ☐	B ☐	C ☐

Part 2

You will hear some information about the Fridays for Future movement.
You will hear the information twice.
For tasks a)–e) fill in the grid.

a)	movement began in (month/year)	_____ _____
b)	Greta Thunberg started:	global school _____ for the _____
c)	number of strikes in March 2019:	_____
d)	Greta's means of transport to NY:	by _____
e)	one reason for striking:	_____

Abbildung: https://fridaysforfuture.de/flyer-plakat-sticker/

Part 3

Listen to Mary and Jack talking about yesterday. What did Mary do at each time?
You will hear the information twice. For tasks a)–e) write a letter, A–H, next to each person.

a) 9:00 a.m. ☐
b) 10:00 a.m. ☐
c) 12:00 a.m. ☐
d) 1:30 p.m. ☐
e) 4:00 p.m. ☐

A worked shift
B walked the dog
C saw the doctor
D swam
E art lesson
F had lunch
G private lesson
H maths lesson

Part 4

Listen to a report about unusual British festivals. You will hear the report twice. For tasks a)–e) mark A, B or C.

a) The Burning of the Clavie
  A ☐ takes place on 10th January every year.
  B ☐ is an old tradition in the south of Scotland.
  C ☐ is like a bonfire which brings good luck.

b) On Shrove Tuesday
  A ☐ people in England have pancakes for dinner.
  B ☐ 25 people jump over one long rope.
  C ☐ people have pancake races and jump over ropes.

c) Cheese rolling is a race where people
  A ☐ dress up as cheese.
  B ☐ have to catch a cheese.
  C ☐ meet in summer.

d) In the World Snail Racing Championship, the snails
  A ☐ have to race to an outer circle.
  B ☐ are from a village in Norfolk.
  C ☐ can be eaten at the party after the race.

e) The World Gurning Championship
  A ☐ is a very modern competition.
  B ☐ is a contest where you make an ugly face.
  C ☐ can only be taken part in toothless.

You now have two minutes to check your answers.

25 pts **B Text-based Tasks**

5 pts **Part 1**

Where can you find these signs? Write down the correct letter.

a)
Return your trays here, please!

A cafeteria
B library
C tennis court

b)
This sink is for washing your hands only!

A attic
B bedroom
C school kitchen

c)
no running or playing in the locker room

A in a park
B in a museum
C on a football field

What information do these signs give you? Write down the correct letter.

d)
Please walk and use respectful voices

A You're only allowed to talk while walking.
B You mustn't run and shout.
C You have to leave respectfully.

e)
Supervision by parents is required for the use of this playground equipment

A Children can play when their parents are around.
B Parents have to bring the equipment.
C Parents must be supervised.

Part 2 – Part 5: text

The Legendary Little Leprechauns

Leprechauns are one of Ireland's most famous characters of Irish folklore. They have become well-known all over the world. Have you ever heard of Leprechauns? The Leprechauns are part of Irish mythology and folklore. They are known as the 'little people'. Once upon a time they invaded Ireland but had to live underground. Some even say they are the true natives of Ireland.

Leprechauns are only 2–3 feet tall, but they are very quick, highly intelligent and will do anything not to be caught! The Leprechauns can only be found in Ireland, in rural areas away from where people live. But people always try to catch them, because once you have caught one your 3 wishes will come true! So, in order to find safety, they hide in underground caves like rabbits.

Sometimes you can hear them before you see one. If you're ever out in the rural countryside and hear a tap, tap, tap, it's usually the sound of them hammering nails into the soles of a shoe. They are said to be very good shoemakers. Catching one of the little ones is no easy task and it's usually unsuccessful, because they're quick and smart. Moreover, they have magical powers and are able to vanish into thin air but they can be caught. It's believed that if you're lucky enough to catch a Leprechaun he'll grant you 3 wishes to be free again. But be careful: making the wrong wish could result in a lifetime of bad luck.

Because they are fiction, there are a lot of stories about them – and no one can judge whether they are true or not. For example, they like singing, a very Irish tradition. And in fact, Leprechauns are well-known for their love of Irish music and traditional dance. They often hold concerts that can last for days. They are expert musicians when it comes to playing the tin whistle, the fiddle and even the Irish harp.

But sometimes stories are not true: Many people say that Leprechauns are drunk all the time. But that's unfair – never mistake them for their Irish cousins, the Cluricauns, drunken creatures who love to cause chaos around Ireland during the night!

Adapted from: https://www.yourirish.com/folklore/legend-of-leprechauns; Stand: 01. 06. 2021
Abbildung: https://www.kindpng.com

Part 2

Match each part of the text with the correct heading.
Write down the correct letter for each part.

a) lines 1–7   A Choose wisely – your wishes might come true
b) lines 8–12   B Leprechauns are a myth
c) lines 13–20   C Don't mix up Leprechauns with anyone else
d) lines 21–26   D Leprechauns are real artists
e) lines 27–30   E How Leprechauns appear

Part 3

Decide whether the statements are 'true', 'false' or 'not in the text'.
Write down the correct answer.

a) Leprechauns are quite tall creatures.
b) You can hear the sound of their work.
c) Leprechauns love to perform classical songs.
d) Leprechauns play traditional Irish instruments very well.
e) Leprechauns cause trouble at night.

Part 4

Find the corresponding line/lines in the text that mean the same.
Write down the correct letter.

a) Ages ago, Leprechauns came to Ireland.
b) They are hunted by human beings for a special reason.
c) Sometimes your ears realize them faster than your eyes.
d) They have great knowledge about some musical instruments.
e) Their relatives are known for having bad habits and making trouble.

lines 8–9	lines 23–24	lines 21–22	line 13	lines 28–30
A	B	C	D	E
lines 10–11	lines 5–6	lines 25–26	lines 27–28	line 15
F	G	H	I	K

Part 5

Find the correct endings to complete the sentences according to the text. Write down the correct letter.

a) Leprechauns are
   A a part of the Irish coast.
   B an Irish legend.
   C another name for young Irish people.

b) It is said that Leprechauns live
   A in the countryside.
   B in Irish cities.
   C on underground trains.

c) When in danger, Leprechauns are able to
   A fly high in the air.
   B disappear without a trace.
   C live without air.

d) Stories about the Leprechauns
   A are true word for word.
   B cannot be confirmed.
   C cannot be told to children.

e) They are able to
   A make tin whistles and fiddles.
   B hold things for a long time.
   C perform songs and dances.

5 pts

C Use of Language

Part 1
Read the text and choose the correct word for each gap.
Write down the correct word.

The Giant's Causeway

1 Located on the northeast coast of Northern Ireland, the Giant's Causeway is an area of about 40,000 stone columns **(a)** are connected to each
5 other. In 2005, it was named as the fourth greatest **(b)** wonder in the United Kingdom. The tops of the stones form stepping stones that lead from the cliff foot and disap-
10 pear under the sea. **(c)** Stonehenge in England, no one really knows how this fantastic site was formed. The **(d)** stones of all are about 12 metres high and up to 28 metres thick in places. Legend says that once upon a time a giant **(e)** Fionn MacCumhaill built these stone steps to be able to walk over the sea to the north coast of Britain, because he wanted to start a fight with the Scottish
15 giant Benandonner. Fionn tricked him by dressing up like a baby. When Benandonner saw him, he thought: "If this is the baby giant, how tall might his father be!?" Benandonner surrendered and destroyed parts of the stones. That's why the Causeway **(f)** under the sea.

Photo source: Tony Webster; CC BY 2.0

a)	who	which	where
b)	natural	nature	naturally
c)	How	Like	So
d)	tallest	tall	taller
e)	call	calling	called
f)	disappear	disappears	disappearing

Part 2
Find opposites for <u>two</u> of the three words in the text and write them down.
a) terrible
b) dwarf
c) built up

Part 3

Find synonyms for <u>two</u> of the three words in the text and write them down.

a) zone
b) to cross
c) gave up

Part 4

Choose <u>two</u> of the following words from the text and give a definition.

a) a wonder (line 6)
b) to dress up (line 15)
c) a baby (line 15)

Part 5

In your dream you meet Fionn MacCumhaill. Ask him <u>three</u> different questions about his life as a giant.

D   Writing

Part 1: E-mail

You are interested in nature and therefore you are starting a three-week job on Mr Jameson's farm in Ireland. But before you can start your trip you have to write an e-mail to him.

Give information:
- introduce yourself (4 x 0,5 pts)
- your journey to the farm (1 pt)

Ask about:
- suitable clothes and equipment (2 pts)
- farm life and duties (2 pts)

© Can Stock Photo/lfcastro

Write at least **60** words. Count your words.

Part 2: A special place

12 pts

Write about a place you want to see one day. The following ideas can help you.

where	what	trip	fascination
• name	• city/town	• plane	• scenery
• country	• monument	• bus	• tradition
• location	• sight	• hike	• history
			• activity

Write at least **80** words. Count your words.

Hauptschulabschlussprüfung in Baden-Württemberg
Englisch 2023

2023-1

A Listening Comprehension

20 pts

Part 1

5 pts

You will hear five short conversations. There is one task for each conversation. You will hear each conversation twice. For tasks a)–e) tick (✓) A, B or C.

a) What kind of trip did Mike and Judy take?

city trip	walking holiday	journey to the sea
A ☐	B ☐	C ☐

b) When will school start tomorrow?

7:20	8:00	7:30
A ☐	B ☐	C ☐

c) In which sport did they **not** win any gold medals?

swimming	running	cycling
A ☐	B ☐	C ☐

d) What kind of accommodation is Mrs Schofield going to book?

single room lake view	double room mountain view	tent lake view
A ☐	B ☐	C ☐

e) How many free seats are there next to the elderly lady in the end?

two	one	three
A ☐	B ☐	C ☐

Part 2

You will hear some information about the Wembley Stadium Tour.
You will hear the information twice.
For tasks a)–e) fill in the grid.

a)	Wembley Stadium is located in:	
b)	attractions (name one):	
c)	first and last tour:	_____ a.m. / _____ p.m.
d)	days without tours (name one):	
e)	price for an adult's ticket:	

Abbildung: Richard Johnson/wikimedia, CC BY-SA 3.0

Part 3

Listen to five people who emigrated to Australia sharing their stories of culture shock. Which person has which story? You will hear the information twice.
For tasks a)–e) write a letter, A–H, next to each person.

a) Kartini ☐
b) Anna ☐
c) Uyen ☐
d) Mante ☐
e) Ronald ☐

A Australia's wildlife
B the climate
C children correct teachers
D people next door
E strict about time
F relaxed about money
G so many cuisines
H no 24/7 shopping

Part 4

Listen to a conversation about best and worst gifts. You will hear the report twice. For tasks a)–e) tick (✓) A, B or C.

5 pts

a) Samantha got a pair of socks
- A ☐ she liked a lot.
- B ☐ she didn't like at all.
- C ☐ that looked like a treasure.

b) Marc says that the football goal his dad gave him was
- A ☐ for his friends.
- B ☐ self-made.
- C ☐ expensive.

c) Most of the time the plastic unicorn was
- A ☐ locked away.
- B ☐ on display.
- C ☐ next to the desk.

d) Samantha's top was
- A ☐ brown and awful.
- B ☐ rough but nice.
- C ☐ cute and brown.

e) After some time, Samantha
- A ☐ threw the top away.
- B ☐ wore the top regularly.
- C ☐ drank coffee only in that top.

You now have 2 minutes to check your answers.

B Text-based Tasks

Part 1

Where can you find these signs? Tick (✓) the correct answer.

a) **SPEED LIMIT 15 WHEN CHILDREN ARE PRESENT**

- A ☐ on a road
- B ☐ in a playground
- C ☐ in a school

b) **Please don't litter. Help keep your community clean**

- A ☐ in a park
- B ☐ on a motorway
- C ☐ in a bathroom

c) **Come and celebrate with us this Sunday. Service is at 10:30 a.m.**

- A ☐ at a tennis court
- B ☐ at a church
- C ☐ at a garage

What information do these signs give you? Tick (✓) the correct answer.

d) **ORDER YOUR GROCERIES ONLINE! We are offering PICKUP & DELIVERY**

- A ☐ You can only drive there in a pickup.
- B ☐ You can buy your food on the internet.
- C ☐ You can get a special offer online.

e) **PLEASE SWIM ONLY BETWEEN THE RED AND YELLOW FLAGS. This beach is patrolled where these flags are displayed.**

- A ☐ The surfing area is between the flags.
- B ☐ Beaches are patrolled at various times.
- C ☐ The flags indicate the safest place to swim.

Part 2 – Part 5: text

Life in a circus – circus facts

1. Every child knows and loves a circus – tents, trapeze artists, lions, tigers, horses, clowns, fascinating tricks and the
5. smell of cotton candy in the air. Most circuses provide their own electrical power, large circuses have their own schools, cafés, stores, laundry
10. and even pastors for Sunday services.

But how is life in a circus? A circus is like a small town that moves from one place of exhibition to the next. In past years and still today, some circuses move every day. That's seven towns a week and two performances a day.
15. Others stay at one place for one or two weeks. From the opening in spring until the closing in fall there are usually no days off. You will rarely hear of a show person taking a sick day, the old saying "the show must go on" certainly applies to circus people.

Circus life is not an easy one. There are storms, cold, heat, mud, injury and
20. months away from home. Still, if you ask any life-long showman the question "Why do you do it and why not find another job?" he will answer: "I'll never give up show business! We do it for a love of the business, of the traditions, of the culture and a love of the circus."

And what about the children? Growing up in the circus means that every
25. member of the family is part of the circus right from the very beginning. Playtime often serves as a training for circus children's future careers. In addition, children have their own duties that must be performed daily. Circus children can't attend normal schools constantly. So often they are home-schooled by a parent or a designated person. Their progress is monitored
30. closely by a school authority.

There are dangers connected with being on the road like strong storms. A circus tent is no place to be in a thunderstorm or high winds. Showpeople have to monitor the weather closely and know when dangerous conditions may arise. When people watch a circus performer walking on a thin wire forty
35. feet above the ground, they may think there are many injuries and deaths due to performing mistakes, but that is far from the truth. Accidents are extremely rare.

Adapted from: https://www.circusesandsideshows.com/circuslife.html/; Zugriff am: 05. 01. 2022 (zu Prüfungszwecken bearbeitet)
Abbildung: Pixabay

Part 2

5 pts

Match each part of the text with the correct heading.
Write down the correct letter.

a) lines 1–11   A Never in one place for long

b) lines 12–18   B Circus life for children

c) lines 19–23   C Loving the show and tradition

d) lines 24–30   D Problems and accidents

e) lines 31–37   E A community of its own

Solution:
a) _____   b) _____   c) _____   d) _____   e) _____

Part 3

5 pts

Decide whether the statements are 'true', 'false' or 'not in the text'. Tick (✓) the correct answer.

		true	false	not in the text
a)	A circus always needs an energy supply from the place they stay at.	☐	☐	☐
b)	Showpersons rarely miss a show because they don't feel well.	☐	☐	☐
c)	Circus people often struggle with their way of life.	☐	☐	☐
d)	As children have their own jobs and responsibilities, they aren't happy.	☐	☐	☐
e)	Stormy weather is a problem for people in a circus.	☐	☐	☐

Part 4

5 pts

Find the corresponding line/lines in the text that mean the same.
Write down the correct letter.

Letter:

a) A circus is nearly always open, there are rarely any holidays. _____

b) Someone who has spent nearly all his life working for the circus. _____

c) By playing games, children learn for their future lives in the circus. _____

d) Visiting school on a regular basis is impossible for them. _____

e) Circus people must observe weather conditions carefully. _____

lines 27–28 A	lines 32–34 B	lines 1–6 C	lines 20–21 D	lines 6–11 E
lines 15–16 F	lines 21–22 G	lines 36–37 H	line 26 I	lines 12–13 K

Part 5

Tick (✓) the correct endings to complete the sentences according to the text.

a) When you go to a circus, you can usually
   - A ☐ learn tricks yourself.
   - B ☐ watch animals and artists.
   - C ☐ visit the trailers.

b) There are circuses that move
   - A ☐ daily.
   - B ☐ monthly.
   - C ☐ once a year.

c) Circus people have to face a lot of problems caused by
   - A ☐ shops.
   - B ☐ traffic.
   - C ☐ nature.

d) Children who live in a circus family
   - A ☐ can decide against life in a circus.
   - B ☐ can easily choose between different lifestyles.
   - C ☐ belong to the circus from the start.

e) Circus performers
   - A ☐ don't have accidents very often.
   - B ☐ do have a lot of accidents during their life.
   - C ☐ have severe accidents at the beginning of their careers.

5 pts

C Use of Language

Part 1

Read the text and choose the correct word for each gap.
Tick (✓) the correct word.

Growing up in a circus

1 My name is Olivia and I live in a circus. Our home is a trailer. – I can't imagine living _____ (a) a house and staying at the same place for ages. For me, being in another
5 town all the time is wonderful. We travel from mountains to cities, from the sea to the forest. I always _____ (b) my playmates around. We all come from different countries. I love my family and they are always around me. We live together, work together and eat together every day. We are never _____ (c) than a few hundred feet away from each other. My
10 parents look after me and the other children – nobody is left alone.
"What _____ (d) schooling?", you may ask. But guess what – we have our own teachers and they travel with us. From time to time, we are supposed to talk to a head teacher from a school nearby. But that isn't a problem for us.
15 In our circus life we have our own responsibilities – most of them daily. We help feeding the animals, we look after their cages, we help cleaning our wagons and of course we practise our own circus acts. We do it as _____ (e) parents do – we watch them very closely and one day we _____ (f) be showmen and showwomen – just like them!

a) ☐ on ☐ in ☐ with
b) ☐ had ☐ have ☐ has
c) ☐ less ☐ longer ☐ more
d) ☐ about ☐ if ☐ when
e) ☐ our ☐ their ☐ her
f) ☐ were ☐ will ☐ was

Part 2
Find opposites for two of the three words in the text and write them down.

a) the same _____

b) to answer _____

c) solution _____

2 pts

Part 3
Find synonyms for two of the three words in the text and write them down.

a) city _____

b) all the time _____

c) duties _____

2 pts

Part 4
Choose two of the following words from the text and give a definition.

a) forest (line 6)

_____

b) we are supposed to (lines 12/13)

_____

c) feeding (line 16)

_____

2 pts

Part 5
You have chance to talk to Olivia about her daily life at the circus.
Ask her three different questions.

a) _____

b) _____

c) _____

3 pts

D Writing

Die Lösungen für den Teil D sind auf separaten Papierbögen zu notieren.

Part 1: E-mail

You and your class want to visit a special magic show which will be in your town next month. Write an e-mail to the ticket service.

In your e-mail you should:
- say why you are writing (1 pt)
- introduce your class (e. g. school, age, number of students) (2 pts)
- ask for details (e. g. dates, price, reductions) (2 pts)
- ask for further information (e. g. duration, food & drinks) (2 pts)

Write at least **60** words. Count your words.

Abbildung: makrovector/freepik

Part 2: A day with your best friend

Write about a day you spent with your best friend last summer. The following ideas can help you.

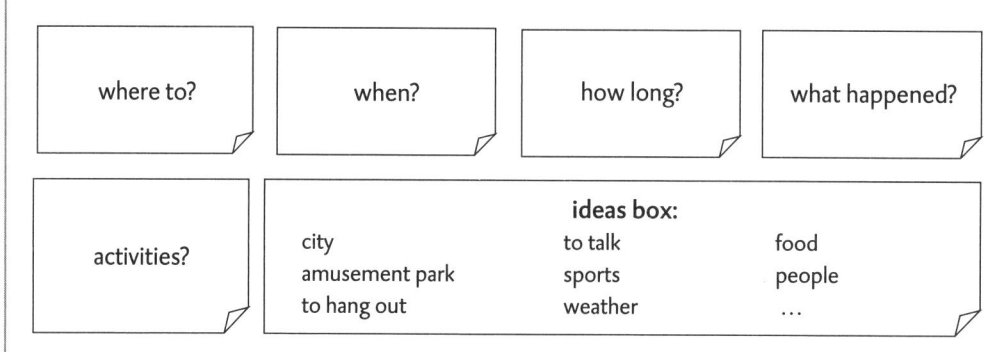

| where to? | when? | how long? | what happened? |

| activities? | ideas box: city / amusement park / to hang out / to talk / sports / weather / food / people / … |

Write at least **80** words. Count your words.

Hauptschulabschlussprüfung in Baden-Württemberg
Englisch 2024

2024-1

Um dir die Prüfung 2024 schnellstmöglich zur Verfügung stellen zu können, bringen wir sie in digitaler Form heraus.

Sobald die Original-Prüfungsaufgaben 2024 zur Veröffentlichung freigegeben sind, können sie als PDF auf der Online-Plattform MySTARK heruntergeladen werden (Zugangscode vgl. Umschlaginnenseite vorne im Buch).

Aktuelle Prüfung

www.stark-verlag.de/mystark

D Writing

Part 1

Hinweis: In formellen Mails solltest du darauf achten, keine Kurzformen wie „don't" oder „I'm" zu verwenden. Wichtig ist außerdem die Anrede und die Schlussformel, die höflich formuliert sein sollten. Da keine bestimmte Person genannt ist, beginnst du die E-Mail mit „Dear Sir or Madam" und beendest sie mit „Yours faithfully". Gehe auf alle Punkte ein, die in der Aufgabenstellung genannt werden und achte auf die Mindestanzahl an Wörtern.

Beispiellösung:

Dear Sir or Madam,

I am writing to buy some tickets for your magic show next month. We want to surprise our teacher with a trip to your show. We are 20 pupils aged 14 and 15 from Hermann-Merz-School.

Can you tell me the dates of your show and how much the tickets are? Do you offer discounts for school classes?

Are we allowed to bring our own food and drinks? Finally, I would like to know how long your show lasts and if there is a break in between.

I am looking forward to hearing from you.

Yours faithfully,

Gregor Benz   *(102 words)*

Part 2

Hinweis: Es ist ratsam, dass du dich an den Stichwörtern und Ideen in der Aufgabenstellung orientierst. Beachte die angegebene Mindestanzahl an Wörtern.

A day with my best friend

Last summer my friend Becky and I went camping on a camping site next to a beautiful lake. We travelled by train and bus to reach the place. After we put up our tent we walked to the lake and enjoyed the nice weather at the waterside, spending our time talking, swimming and sunbathing. When the sun went down we hired a paddleboat and spent some time on the water and watched the orange sky. Back at the shore we joined a live music event and danced all night long until we eventually went to our tent and fell asleep straight away. This trip felt like being on holiday!

(115 words)

Lösungen der Original-Aufgaben der Abschlussprüfung 2024

Um dir die Lösungen zur Prüfung 2024 schnellstmöglich zur Verfügung stellen zu können, bringen wir sie in digitaler Form heraus.
Sobald die Original-Prüfungsaufgaben 2024 freigegeben sind, können die dazugehörigen Lösungen als PDF auf der Plattform **MySTARK** heruntergeladen werden (Zugangscode vgl. Umschlaginnenseite vorne im Aufgabenband).

e) B
  Hinweis: "Showpeople have to monitor the weather closely ..." (Z. 32 f.)

Part 5

a) B
  Hinweis: "Every child knows and loves a circus – ... trapeze artists, lions, tigers, horses ..." (Z. 1 ff.)

b) A
  Hinweis: "... some circuses move every day." (Z. 13 f.)

c) C
  Hinweis: "There are storms, cold, heat, ..." (Z. 19)

d) C
  Hinweis: "... every member of the family is part of the circus right from the very beginning." (Z. 24 f.)

e) A
  Hinweis: "Accidents are extremely rare." (Z. 36 f.)

C Use of Language

Part 1

a) in
  Hinweis: living <u>in</u> a house

b) have
  Hinweis: Hier muss das Verb „have" in der 1. Person Singular im Simple Present stehen, da Olivia von sich in der Gegenwart berichtet.

c) more
  Hinweis: more than = mehr als

d) about
  Hinweis: What about schooling? = Was ist mit der Schulausbildung?

e) our
  Hinweis: Hier brauchst du den Possessivbegleiter „our" zum Possessivpronomen „we": our parents = unsere Eltern

f) will
  Hinweis: Hier muss das Futur stehen, da es um die Zukunft geht.

Part 2

a) different (line 7)
  Hinweis: "We all come from different countries."

b) (to) ask (line 11)
  Hinweis: "... you may ask."

c) problem (line 13)
  Hinweis: "But that isn't a problem ..."

Part 3

a) town (line 5)
  Hinweis: "... being in another town all the time ..."

b) always (lines 6/7)
  Hinweis: "I always have my playmates around ... I love my family and they are always around me."

c) responsibilities (line 15)
  Hinweis: "In our circus life we have our own responsibilities ..."

Part 4

Lösungsbeispiele:

a) an area with lots of trees and bushes
b) we have to / we should / we must / we are expected to / we are told to
c) giving food to a baby or an animal

Part 5

Lösungsbeispiele:

1. At what time do you have to get up in the morning? /
2. Would you like to attend a normal school? /
3. Do you have time to visit the places you stay at? /
4. What is your favourite trick? /
5. Is there any job you would like to do outside the circus? /
6. Has anybody of your family ever had a bad accident? /
7. How can you make friends with other people?

a) A
Hinweis: "I just loved them …" (Z. 5 f.)

b) B
Hinweis: "My dad made it himself." (Z. 10)

c) A
Hinweis: "… I was so embarrassed that I hid it in my wardrobe, so nobody would see it. But every time she came to our house, I took it out …" (Z. 21 ff.)

d) A
Hinweis: "… a very close friend once bought me a top in brown, it was so ugly." (Z. 25 ff.)

e) A
Hinweis: "Later I used it to mop up some coffee and then I just threw it out." (Z. 32 f.)

B Text-based Tasks

Part 1

a) A
Hinweis: speed limit = Geschwindigkeitsbegrenzung

b) A
Hinweis: Please don't litter = Bitte keinen Müll wegwerfen/auf den Boden werfen

c) B
Hinweis: service = Gottesdienst

d) B
Hinweis: to order online = im Internet bestellen

e) C
Hinweis: The beach is patrolled where these flags are displayed = Der Strand wird überwacht, wo diese Fahnen zu sehen sind

Part 2

a) E
Hinweis: "Most circuses provide their own electrical power, large circuses have their own schools, cafés, stores, laundry and even pastors for Sunday services." (Z. 6 ff.)

b) A
Hinweis: "A circus is like a small town that moves from one place of exhibition to the next … some circuses move every day." (Z. 12 ff.)

c) C
Hinweis: "We do it for a love of the business, of the traditions, of the culture and a love of the circus." (Z. 22 f.)

d) B
Hinweis: "And what about the children? Growing up in the circus means that every member of the family is part of the circus right from the very beginning." (Z. 24 f.)

e) D
Hinweis: "There are dangers connected with being on the road like strong storms." (Z. 31 f.), "Accidents are extremely rare." (Z. 36 f.)

Part 3

a) false
Hinweis: "Most circuses provide their own electrical power …" (Z. 6 f.)

b) true
Hinweis: "… 'the show must go on' certainly applies to circus people." (Z. 17 f.)

c) false
Hinweis: "Still, if you ask any life-long showman the question 'Why do you do it and why not find another job?' he will answer: 'I'll never give up show business!'" (Z. 20 ff.)

d) not in the text

e) true
Hinweis: "A circus tent is no place to be in a thunderstorm or high winds." (Z. 31 f.)

Part 4

a) F
Hinweis: "… there are usually no days off." (Z. 16)

b) D
Hinweis: "… if you ask any life-long showman …" (Z. 20)

c) I
Hinweis: "Playtime often serves as a training for circus children's future careers." (Z. 26)

d) A
Hinweis: "Circus children can't attend normal schools constantly." (Z. 27 f.)

Part 3

Listen to five people who emigrated to Australia sharing their stories of culture shock. Which person has which story? You will hear the conversation twice. For tasks a)–e) write a letter, A–H, next to each person.

Kartini: Hi, my name is Kartini Mustafa. I grew up in Malaysia where the average temperature ranges between 21 and 32 degrees. So, the winter here is a nightmare, to be honest. Half the time, I'm in a jacket, shivering, whereas in Malaysia, I was always warm.

Anna: Hello, my name is Anna. Although the US and Australia have a lot in common, I do notice some differences. One of my first days here in Australia, I remember, I got up at 5 or 6 a.m., and I just decided to walk out and go and get some food. But nothing was open. No one was out. It blew my mind.

Uyen: Hi, my name is Uyen and I am originally from Vietnam. In the village back home, I was used to walking across and talking to neighbours. But here, the doors are always closed and the gates into the gardens are locked. You almost have to make an appointment to see people.

Mante: Hello, my name is Mante and I'm from Ghana. One of the big things I had to get used to after moving to Australia was how punctual people are. If they say, "2 p.m.", you should be there at 2 p.m.

Ronald: Hi, my name is Ronald Lee and I am originally from Hong Kong. Once during math class, my son pointed out that the teacher made a mistake in one step. You can't do that in Hong Kong. Here in Australia, they encourage students to be brave and speak up in front of other people. That really is a positive thing.

Adapted from: https://www.abc.net.au/news/2021-09-18/australian-migrants-culture-shock/100364028; Zugriff am 04. 10. 2022

a) B
   Hinweis: "… Malaysia where the average temperature ranges between 21 and 32 degrees. So, the winter here is a nightmare, to be honest." (Z. 2 ff.)

b) H
   Hinweis: "… at 5 or 6 a.m. … nothing was open." (Z. 10 ff.)

c) D
   Hinweis: "… I was used to walking across and talking to neighbours." (Z. 15 f.)

d) E
   Hinweis: "… how punctual people are." (Z. 22 f.)

e) C
   Hinweis: "… my son pointed out that the teacher made a mistake … they encourage students to be brave and speak up in front of other people." (Z. 27 ff.)

Part 4

Listen to a conversation about best and worst gifts. You will hear the conversation twice. For tasks a)–e) tick A, B or C.

Marc: Samantha, we're talking about gifts and presents. What are the best and worst presents you have ever got?

Samantha: Hi Mark! Well, my mum made a pair of socks. They had little flowers on each side. I just loved them and wore them every day when I was a kid. I thought that was so special. I still have them in my little box of treasures.

Marc: The best present I was ever given was a football goal. My dad made it himself. I got it for my birthday and all my friends played football together, that was great.

Samantha: Yeah, that sounds nice. And how about a gift you didn't like?

Marc: I don't know if it is OK to say that I had a bad gift or something. But yes, once I did get a very big unicorn made of plastic from a friend who loved things like that. She gave me this massive toy and I didn't know what to do with it.

Samantha: How awkward! So …

Marc: Well, I was so embarrassed that I hid it in my wardrobe, so nobody would see it. But every time she came to our house, I took it out and put it next to my desk. But I hated it.

Samantha: Sounds horrible … For me, a very close friend once bought me a top in brown, it was so ugly. The texture was rough, and it just didn't look nice at all. When I saw it first I knew I would never wear it. But I felt bad about it.

Marc: So what did you do with it?

Samantha: Actually, I wore it once, when my friend came round. Later I used it to mop up some coffee and then I just threw it out.

Adapted from: https://learnenglishteens.britishcouncil.org/skills/listening/intermediate-b2-listening/unusual-british-festivals; Stand 01. 05. 21

Receptionist: Wait, the computer is showing a lake view, but only single rooms.

65 **Mrs Schofield:** No, thanks. Any doubles with mountain view?

Receptionist: Oh yes, we have a double room on the second floor with a really splendid view of the mountains.

70 **Mrs Schofield:** Fine. We'll go for that one.

Task e)
How many free seats are there next to the elderly lady in the end?

Young lady: Excuse me, are these two seats vacant? I'm looking for a seat for my daughter and me.

Elderly lady: Oh, I'm afraid there is only one as this friendly young man is sitting here next to me.

75 **Young lady:** Of course, I see. Well, let's have a look. I'm pretty sure there are more empty seats further on. Have a nice day then.

Elderly lady: But wait … sorry, I see, the young man has chosen another seat over there. Seems as if the
80 seat next to that good-looking lady is more interesting than this one here.

Young lady: Great, so you don't mind if we sit down?

a) C
  ✎ *Hinweis:* "…they wanted to spend a few days at the seaside." (Z. 8 f.)

b) B
  ✎ *Hinweis:* "…she agreed that we meet at eight…" (Z. 28 f.)

c) C
  ✎ *Hinweis:* "…Ian Thorpe. He's a very famous swimmer. He has won so many gold medals." (Z. 36 ff.), "What did she win the gold medal in?"– "…she's a runner." (Z. 45 ff.)

d) B
  ✎ *Hinweis:* "…we have a double room…with a really splendid view of the mountains." – "Fine. We'll go for that one." (Z. 67 ff.)

e) A
  ✎ *Hinweis:* "…I'm afraid there is only one…" (Z. 73), "But wait…the young man has chosen another seat over there." (Z. 78 f.)

Part 2

You will hear some information about the Wembley Stadium Tour. You will hear the information twice. For tasks a)–e) fill in the grid.

Wembley Stadium Tour

1 Why not take the unforgettable Wembley Stadium Tour? Visit this popular stadium in London and feel the spirit of the most famous football matches ever. Go behind the scenes and experience all the exciting
5 attractions like England's changing rooms and the players' tunnel to the lawn. Walk in the footsteps of legends and stand triumphantly in front of The Cup and feel like a matchwinner.

Until your dream of playing at Wembley comes true,
10 the only way to experience all this and more is to book your Wembley Stadium Tour now.

Our opening times: The first tour departs at 10 a.m. and the last one at 3:30 p.m. The Wembley Stadium Tour operates every day with the exception of the
15 25th and 26th of December and 1st of January. Please check our website for tour availability and book in advance to avoid disappointment.

Please note that there are flat routes from parking area to entrance and you will find full wheelchair access
20 to the building. In addition, we offer conference rooms, meeting rooms and event facilities.

The prices are as follows: It's £ 15 for children and £ 22 for adults. Group discounts are available for parties of 25 or more people.

Adapted from: https://www.visitlondon.com/things-to-do/place/ 4114851-wembley-stadium-tour/; Zugriff am 01. 05. 2022

a) London
  ✎ *Hinweis:* "…this popular stadium in London…" (Z. 2)

b) changing rooms, players' tunnel, The Cup
  ✎ *Hinweis:* "…all the exciting attractions like England's changing rooms and the players' tunnel…" (Z. 4 ff.), "…stand triumphantly in front of The Cup…" (Z. 7)

c) 10, 3:30
  ✎ *Hinweis:* "The first tour departs at 10 a.m. and the last one at 3:30 p.m." (Z. 12 f.)

d) 25th (of) December/25 December, 26th (of) December/26 December, 1st (of) January/ 1 January / Christmas, New Year
  ✎ *Hinweis:* "…operates every day with the exception of the 25th and 26th of December and 1st of January." (Z. 14 f.)

e) £ 22
  ✎ *Hinweis:* "…It's £ 15 for children and £ 22 for adults." (Z. 22 f.)

Abschlussprüfung 2023

A Listening Comprehension

Allgemeiner Hinweis: Lies dir alle Aufgaben zuerst genau durch, damit du weißt, worauf du beim Zuhören achten musst. Sieh dir die Lösungen erst an, wenn du die Aufgaben bearbeitet hast. Höre dir einen Text noch einmal an, wenn deine Antwort nicht richtig war. Falls du etwas nicht verstanden hast, kannst du dir den Hörverstehenstext auch durchlesen.

Part 1

You will hear five short conversations. There is one task for each conversation. You will hear each conversation twice. There is one question for each conversation.
For tasks a)–e) tick A, B or C.

Task a)
What kind of trip did Mike and Judy take?

Sally: Look at these pictures of our walking trip to Yorkshire, aren't they cool?
Paul: Yes, there are some really good ones. Why didn't Mike and Judy join us?
Sally: Mike and Judy preferred to go to Brighton, remember?
Paul: Didn't they go to London?
Sally: No, I think they wanted to spend a few days at the seaside.
Paul: I see. Are they coming next time when we go to the Lake District in July?
Sally: I'm not so sure. They don't enjoy hiking that much ...

Task b)
When will school start tomorrow?

Jonny: When does school start tomorrow?
Amber: Stupid question, Jonny, it starts as usual. Eight o'clock.
Jonny: But Ms Cunningham mentioned this special project in the morning and told us to be there at 7:20, didn't she?
Amber: But that was before we talked about our really long day tomorrow, 'cos we're planning to go to the museum with our history club in the afternoon.
Jonny: As far as I know, Ms Cunningham wasn't very much impressed by your programme for tomorrow. I remember she suggested 7:30 as a compromise.
Amber: Anyway, in the end she agreed that we meet at eight – just as usual. Everybody begged for a later start as it is going to be a long, long day.
Jonny: Thanks, Amber, now I know when to come to school.

Task c)
In which sport did they not win any gold medals?

Cheryl: Hey Nick, I've never actually been to Australia. Can you tell me about any famous people that live there?
Nick: Well, one famous person is Ian Thorpe. He's a very famous swimmer. He has won so many gold medals.
Cheryl: Oh, really?
Nick: In maybe four Olympics. I think he won about fourteen to twenty gold medals.
Cheryl: In swimming? I thought you guys are really famous for athletics.
Nick: Yes, we are. There's another famous person by the name of Cathy Freeman. She's the first Aboriginal Australian to win an Olympic gold medal.
Cheryl: What did she win the gold medal in?
Nick: In the 400 meters sprint, she's a runner.
Cheryl: Wow, I didn't know that.

Adapted from: https://elllo.org/english/1051/1061-Nick-Famous-Aussies.htm; Zugriff am 12.11.2021

Task d)
What kind of accommodation is Mrs Schofield going to book?

Receptionist: Good afternoon, River Crossing Lodge. May I help you?
Mrs Schofield: Yes. I'd like to book a room, please.
Receptionist: What kind of room would you like, madam?
Mrs Schofield: Er ... double with bath. Could you give me a room with a view of the lake?
Receptionist: Certainly, madam. I'll just check what we have available ... I'm afraid, no lake views anymore for the doubles. I could offer you a tent next to the lake.
Mrs Schofield: Gosh, a tent, my husband and I are in our seventies. We'll skip the lake view then.

D Writing

Part 1

Hinweis: Achte in formellen Mails darauf, besonders höflich zu sein und auch keine Kurzformen wie „don't" oder „I'm" zu verwenden. Denke auch an die Anrede und die Schlussformel. Da hier ein Ansprechpartner (Mr Jameson) genannt ist, musst du mit „Yours sincerely" schließen. Gehe auf alle Punkte ein, die in der Angabe genannt werden und achte auf die geforderte Mindestanzahl an Wörtern. Die erreichbaren Punkte sind in der Beispiellösung in Klammern angegeben.

Beispiellösung:

Dear Mr Jameson,

My name is Henri *(0,5)*. I am 15 years old *(0,5)* and from Germany *(0,5)*. As I like being outdoors and working with animals *(0,5)*, I would love to do the job on your farm. I would fly to Dublin and take a bus to your place *(1)*.

Do I need special clothes for the farm work or are jeans and T-shirt OK *(1)*? Is there any equipment I should buy in advance *(1)*? It would also be interesting to know what kind of jobs I would have to do and what a typical day on the farm looks like *(2)*.

Yours sincerely,

Henri Baumann   *(100 words)*

Part 2

Hinweis: Bei dieser Aufgabe kannst du deiner Fantasie freien Lauf lassen – es kann dir jedoch helfen, wenn du dich an den vorgegebenen Stichwörtern orientierst. Beachte auch die angegebene Mindestzahl an Wörtern.

A special place

I can't wait to visit my uncle and his family in England. They live in Billericay which is east of London in the county of Essex. They own a small but pretty house with a huge garden in the middle of a forest. My uncle Peter works in a town nearby, which has some small shops, a shopping centre and a new cinema. When I visit them I can even go to London by train, which would take me about one hour. As I'm a fan of the British Royals, visiting Buckingham Palace is on my top 3 list of things to see and do. London has so much to offer!   *(118 words)*

Part 5

a) B
   Hinweis: "The Leprechauns are part of Irish mythology and folklore." (Z. 3 f.)

b) A
   Hinweis: "…can only be found…in rural areas…" (Z. 9 f.)

c) B
   Hinweis: "…are able to vanish into thin air…" (Z. 17 f.)

d) B
   Hinweis: "…they are fiction…" (Z. 21)

e) C
   Hinweis: "…they like singing…and traditional dance." (Z. 22 ff.)

C Use of Language

Part 1

a) which
   Hinweis: "…columns which are connected to each other." („…Steinsäulen, die miteinander verbunden sind.") = Relativsatz, eingeleitet mit dem Relativpronomen „which", das für Sachen gebraucht wird („who" nur für Personen).

b) natural
   Hinweis: Das Adjektiv „natural" (= „natürlich"), beschreibt das Nomen „wonder" näher („Naturwunder").

c) Like
   Hinweis: "Like Stonehenge in England…" = „Wie Stonehenge in England…"

d) tallest
   Hinweis: "the tallest" („die größten") = Superlativ (3. Steigerungsform) von „tall"

e) called
   Hinweis: "called" = „genannt" (oder: „mit Namen", „namens")

f) disappears
   Hinweis: "disappear" = „untergehen/verschwinden"; bezieht sich auf „causeway", daher „disappears" (3. Person Singular)

Part 2

a) fantastic
   Hinweis: "…fantastic site…" (Z. 11)

b) giant
   Hinweis: zum Beispiel: "…once upon a time a giant…" (Z. 12)

c) destroyed
   Hinweis: "…destroyed parts of the stones." (Z. 17)

Part 3

a) area
   Hinweis: "…an area of about…" (Z. 3)

b) to walk over
   Hinweis: "…walk over the sea." (Z. 13)

c) surrendered
   Hinweis: "Benandonner surrendered…" (Z. 17)

Part 4

Lösungsbeispiele:

a) a miracle / something magic / something amazing or magical that happens to somebody

b) to put on a costume to become/look like somebody else / to put on special clothes

c) a (very little) human being who is younger than one year / a very young child

Part 5

Lösungsbeispiele:

1. Were you already a giant when you were born? /
2. What is it like to be a giant? /
3. How tall are you? /
4. Do you have human friends? /
5. How much do you eat? /
6. Do you do any sports? /
7. Why did you start a fight? /
8. How long did it take you to build the causeway?

c) B
Hinweis: "...round cheeses...sent rolling down a hill and people run after them and try and catch them." (Z. 22 ff.)

d) A
Hinweis: "The snails have to race from an inner circle to an outer circle..." (Z. 29 f.)

e) B
Hinweis: "...a competition to pull the ugliest face." (Z. 34 f.)

B Text-based Tasks

Part 1

a) A
Hinweis: tray = Tablett

b) C
Hinweis: sink = Waschbecken

c) B
Hinweis: locker = Schließfach

d) B
Hinweis: "You mustn't run and shout" („Man darf nicht rennen und schreien") = "Please walk and use respectful voices"

e) A
Hinweis: supervision = Aufsicht, is required = wird benötigt

Part 2

a) B
Hinweis: "The Leprechauns are part of Irish mythology and folklore." (Z. 3 f.)

b) E
Hinweis: "...they hide in underground caves like rabbits." (Z. 12)

c) A
Hinweis: "...if you're lucky enough to catch a Leprechaun he'll grant you 3 wishes to be free again. But be careful: making the wrong wish could result in a lifetime of bad luck." (Z. 18 ff.)

d) D
Hinweis: "They are expert musicians...playing the tin whistle, the fiddle and even the Irish harp." (Z. 25 f.)

e) C
Hinweis: "...never mistake them for their Irish cousins, the Cluricauns..." (Z. 28 f.)

Part 3

a) false
Hinweis: "They are known as the 'little people'..." (Z. 4 f.); "Leprechauns are only 2–3 feet tall..." (Z. 8)

b) true
Hinweis: "...it's usually the sound of them hammering nails..." (Z. 14 f.)

c) not in the text

d) true
Hinweis: "...tin whistle, the fiddle and even the Irish harp." (Z. 25 f.)

e) false
Hinweis: "...the Cluricauns...cause chaos around Ireland during the night!" (Z. 29 f.)

Part 4

a) G
Hinweis: "Once upon a time they invaded Ireland but had to live underground."

b) F
Hinweis: "But people always try to catch them, because once you have caught one your 3 wishes will come true!"

c) D
Hinweis: "Sometimes you can hear them before you see one."

d) H
Hinweis: "They are expert musicians when it comes to playing the tin whistle, the fiddle and even the Irish harp."

e) E
Hinweis: "But that's unfair – never mistake them for their Irish cousins, the Cluricauns, drunken creatures who love to cause chaos..."

appointment at the doctor's for an allergy test at 9 a.m. but they rang me up and asked me to come an hour later. So, I used the time and went for a swim first. I was lucky because the swimming centre opens at 9.

Jack: I see. So, did you go straight to school after the doctor's appointment?

Mary: Err, sort of. Please don't tell anyone, but I had to walk my sister's dog right after the doctor. My sister had to work shift and I helped her out. So, I didn't arrive at school till lunchtime. Let's just say it took some time to get there.

Jack: *(laughing)* OK, OK, I understand. But arriving at 12 gave you enough time for lunch before the maths lesson at 1:30, right?

Mary: Ah, don't remind me about the maths lesson. Mr Parker was 30 minutes late yesterday and apart from the feeling that the lesson lasted forever, I didn't understand a single word. I guess I'm more the creative type.

Jack: Mary, I know that you prefer art but only doing that won't give you a final degree, will it?

Mary: I know, which is why I decided to take private lessons after school.

Jack: That might be helpful. When are you starting?

Mary: I already have, yesterday afternoon at 4.

Jack: Sounds like you had a really busy day yesterday.

Mary: You could say that.

a) D
 Hinweis: "… the swimming centre opens at 9." (Z. 10 f.)

b) C
 Hinweis: "… allergy test at 9 a.m. but they rang me up and asked me to come <u>an hour later</u>." (Z. 7 ff.)

c) F
 Hinweis: "But arriving at 12 gave you enough time for lunch …" (Z. 19 f.)

d) H
 Hinweis: "… lunch before the maths lesson at 1:30, right?" (Z. 20 f.)

e) G
 Hinweis: "… to take private lessons …" (Z. 29 f.), "… yesterday afternoon at 4." (Z. 32)

Part 4

Listen to a report about unusual British festivals. You will hear the report twice. For tasks a) – e) mark A, B or C.

Today, I'm going to talk about unusual British festivals. A lot of these are not exactly festivals, but strange races or competitions. Some of them are very old and some are modem.

So, let's start in January in the north of Scotland with the Burning of the Clavie. This is a whisky barrel which is set on fire and carried through the streets as a bonfire. It's an old tradition which always takes place on 11th of January. The bonfire brings good luck for the coming year and people used to keep bits of burnt wood as protection against evil spirits.

Now, to the north of England. On Shrove Tuesday in February, also known as Pancake Day, a special Pancake Bell is rung in Scarborough. Everyone goes down to the beach where they jump over long ropes, up to fifteen people to one rope. They also have pancake races. This is quite common in the UK – running with a frying pan and tossing a pancake at the same time.

Another kind of race takes place in spring – cheese-rolling. In Gloucestershire, in the south-west of England, round cheeses in round boxes are sent rolling down a hill and people run after them and try and catch them. The hill is very steep, so people often fall over – if you take part in this you need to be very fit and wear your oldest jeans.

From people-racing to animals, very tiny animals. The World Snail Racing Championship takes place in a village in Norfolk. The snails have to race from an inner circle to an outer circle and the winner gets a lot of lettuce. There's a party and barbecue for the snail owners and observers.

Another fun contest is The World Gurning Championship in Cumbria. It is a competition to pull the ugliest face. It sounds funny but this is an ancient tradition from 1267. The man who won the title of best gurner the most often had all his teeth taken out so he could make terrible faces more easily.

So, that's just a taste of a few of our old and more modern traditions. Would you like to take part in any of them?

Adapted from: https://learnenglishteens.britishcouncil.org/skills/listening/intermediate-b2-listening/unusual-british-festivals; Stand 01. 05. 21

a) C
 Hinweis: "… the bonfire brings good luck …" (Z. 9 f.)

b) C
 Hinweis: "… they <u>jump over long ropes</u>, up to <u>fifteen people</u> to one rope. They also have <u>pancake races</u> …" (Z. 15 ff.)

Jason: OK, I see. Brian's room is quite nice. He's got lots of space.
Mum: Good idea! Let's talk to your older brother.
Jason: Oh wait, Brian is such a night owl! Prakash won't get any sleep in Brian's room. I think it's best to stick to my first idea.

Task e)
Which tests will be next week?
Mr. Pepper: Good morning, everyone. Sorry, I'm late. I had a chat with your English teacher, Mrs Martin. She forgot to tell you that she will be on a training course for the rest of the week and therefore needs to change the date of your English test.
Victoria: Oh no, Mr Pepper. Really? This will be the third test apart from maths and biology next week.
Mr. Pepper: Well, Victoria. I know you weren't here yesterday, because I had to change the maths test as well. Maths will be the week after the next. So, plenty of time to prepare for it, don't worry,
Victoria: That's good news, thanks, Mr Pepper.
Mr. Pepper: No problem, Victoria.

a) C
   🖊 Hinweis: "You should leave at 9 and take the 9.20 train." (Z. 8 f.)

b) A
   🖊 Hinweis: "Brooklyn Bridge? I'm sorry, but Brooklyn Bridge connects Manhattan with Brooklyn, so Queens would be the wrong borough..." (Z. 13 ff.)

c) C
   🖊 Hinweis: "They are £12 now, they were £ 10 two weeks ago." (Z. 43)

d) A
   🖊 Hinweis: Jason: "So, I suggest he stays with me." (Z. 53 f.), Jason: "...I think it's best to stick to my first idea." (Z. 64 f.)

e) A
   🖊 Hinweis: "...and therefore needs to change the date of your English test." (Z. 69 f.); "...the third test apart from maths and biology next week." (Z. 71 f.); "...I had to change the maths test as well. Maths will be the week after the next." (Z. 74 f.): Also bleiben in der nächsten Woche nur noch der Biologie- und der Englisch-Test.

Part 2

You will hear some information about the Fridays for Future movement. You will hear the information twice. For tasks a)–e) fill in the grid.

Fridays for Future is a global climate strike movement. It started in August 2018, when 15-year-old Swedish student Greta Thunberg began a school strike for the climate. Instead of going to school, she sat outside the Swedish Parliament, demanding urgent action on the climate crisis. This marked the beginning of global school strikes for the climate. In March 2019 more than one million people gathered in 2,200 strikes organised in 125 countries.
In August 2019, Greta Thunberg travelled to New York City on a two-week journey by sailboat to continue her work and call for people's attention. She participated in school strikes planned in the US on 20 September, and soon after she spoke at the UN Climate Summit on 23 September 2019, in New York City. Many people ask why millions of children and adults across the world are taking the time to strike: don't they have school, work or other responsibilities? The answer is simple: they strike for their future and for their children's future. They strike because there is still time to change.

Adapted from: https://fridaysforfuture.org.com; Stand 01.08.21

a) August 2018
   🖊 Hinweis: "It started in August 2018 ..." (Z. 2)

b) strike(s), climate
   🖊 Hinweis: "...Greta Thunberg began a school strike for the climate." (Z. 3 f.)

c) 2,200
   🖊 Hinweis: "...more than one million people gathered in 2,200 strikes ..." (Z. 8 f.)

d) (sail)boat
   🖊 Hinweis: "...travelled to New York City on a two-week journey by sailboat ..." (Z. 10 f.)

e) (their) future /(their) children's future
   🖊 Hinweis: "...they strike for their future and for their children's future." (Z. 19 f.)

Part 3

Listen to Mary and Jack talking about yesterday. What did Mary do at each time? You will hear the conversation twice. For tasks a)–e) write a letter, A–H, next to each person.

Jack: Hey Mary. How's it going?
Mary: Hi Jack. Fine, thanks. And you?
Jack: Not too bad. I didn't see you yesterday at school. Everything alright?
Mary: Yes, it was such a crazy day yesterday. I was at school, but only in the afternoon. I had an

Abschlussprüfung 2022

A Listening Comprehension

🖉 *Allgemeiner Hinweis: Lies dir alle Aufgaben zuerst genau durch, damit du weißt, worauf du beim Zuhören achten musst. Sieh dir die Lösungen erst an, wenn du die Aufgaben bearbeitet hast. Höre dir einen Text noch einmal an, wenn deine Antwort nicht richtig war. Falls du etwas nicht verstanden hast, kannst du dir den Hörverstehenstext auch durchlesen.*

Part 1

You will hear five short conversations. There is one task for each conversation. You will hear each conversation twice. There is one question for each conversation.
For tasks a)–e) mark A, B or C.

Task a)
When will John's train leave?
John: Linda, do you know how to get to Central Park? I've never been there before.
Linda: Take the train. It's the quickest way to get there. It only takes about half an hour. Do you have an appointment?
John: I'm going to meet my friends at 10 a.m., so I'll take the train at 9:30.
Linda: That's a busy time. You should leave at 9 and take the 9:20 train.
John: OK, I'll do so. Thanks, Linda.

Adapted from: https://www.thoughtco.com/dialogue-giving-directions-1211300; Stand: 4th January 2021

Task b)
Which place in New York isn't Sean going to visit?
Sean: Hi there, could you get me to Queens? I'd like to see the Brooklyn Bridge.
Taxi driver: Brooklyn Bridge? I'm sorry, but Brooklyn Bridge connects Manhattan with Brooklyn, so Queens would be the wrong borough of New York.
Sean: Sorry, my mistake. You see, I'm going to meet some friends in Spring Creek Park this evening, which definitely is in Queens. I thought it would be a good idea to visit something there first.
Taxi driver: How about the Louis Armstrong House?
Sean: Sounds good! Let's do that.
Taxi driver: Buckle up, please. Here we go!

Task c)
How much is the umbrella?
Kelly: You know, Susan, having a day off during the week is great. Especially when we can go shopping together like now.
Susan: You're right. This doesn't happen too often. But oh no! Look, it's starting to rain. Kelly, did you bring an umbrella?
Kelly: Ah, I wanted to, but left it on the kitchen table, I'm afraid. And the rain's really getting stronger now. Shall we look somewhere to buy one?
Susan: Good idea. I've got a £20 note in my pocket. That should be enough, shouldn't it?
Kelly: Well, yes. There's this shop around the corner that sells everything for £10. I've seen umbrellas there recently. Let's go there!
Susan: Alright. I think I know the shop. We're nearly there. Hurry up, Kelly, I'm getting wet.
Kelly: Here it is! And in front of the shop – umbrellas in all colours. Can I have the red one?
Susan: 'Course you can. Prices have gone up though. They are £12 now, they were £10 two weeks ago. Never mind. We need one now.
Kelly: Thanks, Susan. Let's pay and get on with our shopping tour.

Task d)
Who is Prakash going to share a room with?
Mum: Jason, when is Prakash, you know, your exchange student from India, arriving?
Jason: Hm, good question, mum. He should be here around 8 p.m.
Mum: Well, then it's definitely time to make up your mind which room he's in.
Jason: Yeah, you're right. So, I suggest he stays with me.
Mum: Oh Jason, you've got the tiniest room of all. That's not very comfortable.
Jason: True. What about Brenda's room?
Mum: No, Jason, no. I don't want boys and girls mixed up, sorry.

D Writing

Part 1

Hinweis: In formellen Mails solltest du darauf achten, höflich zu sein und auch keine Kurzformen wie „don't" oder „I'm" zu verwenden. Vergiss auch die Anrede und die Schlussformel nicht. Da hier kein Ansprechpartner/keine Ansprechpartnerin genannt ist, musst du mit „Yours faithfully" schließen. Gehe auf alle Punkte ein, die in der Angabe genannt werden und achte auf die geforderte Mindestanzahl an Wörtern.

Beispiellösung:

Dear Sir or Madam,

I am writing to ask for some information about your documentary about the Highland Games. My name is Tom Schmidt from Germany and I am 13 years old. I have to do a school presentation about the Highland Games and I would like to use some interesting material from your film. Maybe you can send me some links which might be helpful for my research.

I am looking forward to your answer.

Yours faithfully,

Tom Schmidt   *(80 words)*

Part 2

Hinweis: Bei dieser Aufgabe bist du relativ frei, in dem was du schreibst – es ist jedoch ratsam, sich an den angegebenen Stichwörtern und Ideen zu orientieren. Beachte auch die angegebene Mindestzahl an Wörtern.

My dream holiday

I would love to fly to a little island in the Caribbean where it is hot and the sun always shines. On the island there are a lot of palm trees and exotic – but not dangerous – animals.

There would also be a fridge which automatically refills with all my favourite food and drinks. I could do stand-up paddling in the ocean to exercise and to get a nice suntan quickly.

After two weeks, however, I would get homesick and fly back home to my family and friends.

(90 words)

c) A
Hinweis: "These clans have been a part of the Highland Games right from the start …" (Z. 13 f.)

d) B
Hinweis: "… you have to run up a fell …" (Z. 23 f.)

e) B
Hinweis: "… throw the caber in such a way that it lands in a 12 o'clock position." (Z. 30 f.)

C Use of Language

Part 1

a) their
Hinweis: their names = ihre Namen

b) was
Hinweis: Hier muss das Simple Past von „to be" in der 3. Person Singular stehen

c) over
Hinweis: all over New York = überall in New York

d) teenagers

e) became
Hinweis: Auch hier muss das Simple Past stehen (became = wurde), da über die Vergangenheit berichtet wird.

f) a lof of
Hinweis: „Graffiti artists" sind eine zählbare „Menge", daher wäre „much" hier falsch.

Part 2

a) saw
Hinweis: "… teenagers saw his tag …" (Z. 9)

b) soon
Hinweis: "Soon, there were tags on walls …" (Z. 10)

c) beautiful
Hinweis: "… to make cities beautiful …" (Z. 15)

Part 3

a) young
Hinweis: "In New York, young people wrote …" (Z. 3)

b) first
Hinweis: "One of the first 'taggers' was a teenager …" (Z. 6)

c) bigger
Hinweis: "Their tags were bigger and more colourful." (Z. 12)

Part 4

Lösungsbeispiele:

a) teenager: a young person / someone between 13 and 19 (years)

b) popular: A person is popular if he/she is liked by many people.

c) to paint: When you paint you put colour on a wall, for example.

Part 5

Lösungsbeispiele:

- What does your tag "TAKI 183" mean? /
- How did you get the idea for your tag? /
- When did you start spraying? /
- Did your parents know about your hobby? /
- How do you feel when you see your tag all over the city? /
- Have you ever been afraid of being caught by the police? /
- Has anybody ever caught you while you were writing your tag?

d) B
Hinweis: "It seems to be an easy hiking tour – but you must be careful because it can get very foggy very quickly …" (Z. 27 ff.)

e) C
Hinweis: "… a fell is a hill …" (Z. 34)

B Text-based Tasks

Part 1

a) A
Hinweis: cattle = das Vieh

b) C
Hinweis: traces of soy = Spuren von Soja

c) C
Hinweis: „Single road tracks" sind schmale Landstraßen, die lediglich für ein einziges Fahrzeug breit genug sind.

d) B
Hinweis: pitch = Spielfeld

e) B
Hinweis: to hire = (aus-)leihen, mieten

Part 2

a) D
Hinweis: "… celebrate Scottish and Celtic traditional cultures." (Z. 2); "well-known all over the world" (Z. 5)

b) E
Hinweis: "Hundreds of years ago … Over the centuries …" (Z. 8 ff.)

c) B
Hinweis: "… there are a lot of big families called clans. These clans have been a part of the Highland Games right from the start …" (Z. 13 f.)

d) A
Hinweis: "There are different field events with special Scottish names." (Z. 22 f.)

e) C
Hinweis: "Many people think that the athletes have to throw the trunk of a tree (the caber) as far as they can – but that's wrong! The aim is to throw the caber in such a way that it lands in a 12 o'clock position." (Z. 28 ff.)

Part 3

a) false
Hinweis: "Originally founded as an athletics and sports competition …" (Z. 3 f.)

b) true
Hinweis: "… the Scots wanted to test the power and strength of Scottish troops during the games …" (Z. 8 f.)

c) not in the text

d) true
Hinweis: z. B. „fell-running": fell = hill, mountain (Z. 23 f.)

e) false
Hinweis: "… throw the trunk of a tree (the caber) …" (Z. 29)

Part 4

a) B
Hinweis: "… well-known all over the world." (Z. 5)

b) D
Hinweis: "… turned into festivals for all Scottish people." (Z. 10)

c) G
Hinweis: "Many clans … share information about Scottish history." (Z. 16 f.)

d) I
Hinweis: "… take a little flag … and bring it back down to the finish line." (Z. 25 f.)

e) K
Hinweis: "… you have to lift heavy stones …" (Z. 27)

Part 5

a) A
Hinweis: "… well-known all over the world." (Z. 5)

b) B
Hinweis: "Dancing, pipe bands, drumming, and food and drink were added …" (Z. 11 f.)

and the Glenfinnan Monument on the west coast of Scotland. It was amazing.

Presenter: Thank you, Angus, now what about you, Keira, are you also a Bravehearts fan?

Keira: That's boy stuff – I did a tour on a boat and visited some of the little islands off the Scottish west coast. I loved Portree, a town on the Isle of Skye. It was so relaxing, I just sat there for hours watching the boats leaving the harbour and returning from their fishing trips.

Presenter: Ah, lovely, and you Merida?

Merida: I was near Balmoral in the Highlands to see the strong men – men in kilts throwing logs, lifting heavy stones and dancing. What a show – I often watch the Highland Games on TV, but being so close to such strong men is a completely different thing! It was great!

Presenter: Last but not least, here is Rory.

Rory: I really love mystic and strange stories – and I do know that there are no monsters on lakes, but I couldn't resist joining a bus tour to the shores of Loch Ness and waiting for Nessie to come up ... and ... nothing happened, of course, but it was a nice trip with a nice girl ...

Adapted from: http://learnenglishteens.britishcouncil.org/skills/listening/elementary-a2-listening/work

a) C
   🖋 *Hinweis: "... I succeeded in buying a ticket for the match." (Z. 8 f.)*

b) E
   🖋 *Hinweis: "I went to Eilean Donan Castle, visited the Sterling buildings and the Glenfinnan Monument ..." (Z. 16 ff.)*

c) G
   🖋 *Hinweis: "... I did a tour on a boat and visited some of the little islands ..." (Z. 22 f.)*

d) D
   🖋 *Hinweis: "I was near Balmoral in the Highlands ... Highland Games ..." (Z. 29 ff.)*

e) A
   🖋 *Hinweis: "... bus tour to the shores of Loch Ness ..." (Z. 38 f.)*

Part 4

You will hear a conversation between two friends talking about their weekend plans. You will hear the conversation twice. For tasks a) – e) mark A, B or C.

Steffi: Hi, Ian, could you help me, please? I don't understand some words in this brochure about the sights and places here in Scotland.

Ian: Sure. I know it's sometimes hard to understand 'cause we use Gaelic words instead of English. How can I help you?

Steffi: I want to go on a trip to the Highlands and the first stop will be Loch Lomond. Sounds like a German word – *Loch* – which means 'hole' in English.

Ian: Oh, really, that's funny! It's like a big, big hole in the ground filled with water. 'Loch' is Gaelic and means 'lake'. Loch Lomond is a very nice place in the Lowlands and sometimes, in summer, you can go swimming there.

Steffi: But not in spring, surely! The next strange words are *glen* and *ben*. These sound like boys' names!

Ian: Yeah, might be, but in this case *glen* is another word for valley. There are a lot of *glens* in the Highlands and some have a very tragic history. In Glen Coe, for example, a lot of Scottish people died during the battles with the king's army.

Steffi: And who is Ben Nevis?

Ian: It's not a person – Ben Nevis is the highest mountain here in Scotland, but not only in Scotland, it's the biggest in the UK! It is 1345 metres high and you shouldn't go there in winter. It seems to be an easy hiking tour – but you must be careful because it can get very foggy very quickly!

Steffi: OK, I'm not interested in hiking. One last word – what does *fell* mean? It's another word that we use in German! It's the German word for the fur of an animal.

Ian: Oh no, a *fell* is a hill and there is a lot of *fell-running* in Scotland.

Steffi: That's even worse than hiking! Thanks a lot, Ian for your help!

Ian: You're welcome, have a nice trip!

Adapted from: http://www.elllo.org/english/1101/1108-Camp-Warren.htm

a) B
   🖋 *Hinweis: "I don't understand some words in this brochure ..." (Z. 1 f.)*

b) B
   🖋 *Hinweis: "'Loch' is Gaelic and means 'lake'." (Z. 11 f.)*

c) A
   🖋 *Hinweis: "... a lot of Scottish people died during the battles with the king's army." (Z. 21 f.)*

Pete: Of course, no problem, Charley. You can stay in Tom's room.

Charley: Thank you so much, but doesn't Tom have to get up early to get to work?

Pete: Ah, you're right. Well, you could sleep in my room, but I'm already sharing it with Jake.

Charley: Oh no, you know, Jake and me – not the best idea, sorry Pete.

Pete: Then I can offer you Robbie's room.

Charley: Your younger brother's? I know his jokes and pranks, but that's much better than getting up so early.

a) C
  🖉 *Hinweis: "… Friday afternoon would be possible." (Z. 13 f.); "… so we'll come at the end of this week." (Z. 18)*
b) B
  🖉 *Hinweis: Mo: "… I'll come with you." (Z. 31)*
c) A
  🖉 *Hinweis: "There's one at 4.20 …" (Z. 35); "That's quite a long trip …" (Z. 38); "I think I'll have to take the early but longer one." (Z. 48 f.)*
d) A
  🖉 *Hinweis: "… one of these 'I love Scotland' mugs." (Z. 52 f.); "Let's go for the 'I love Scotland' souvenir!" (Z. 59)*
e) C
  🖉 *Hinweis: "I can offer you Robbie's room …" – "… I know his jokes and pranks, but that's much better than getting up so early." (Z. 70 ff.)*

Part 2

You will hear an advert for the Museum Context in Edinburgh. You will hear the information twice. For tasks a)–e) fill in the grid.

The Museum Context in Edinburgh

Just in time for the 20th anniversary of the publication of *Harry Potter and the Philosopher's Stone*, the Museum Context, a gift shop for all Harry Potter fans, has opened in Edinburgh. But it's far more than a shop, it's a playground for them all. Museum Context offers an incredible shopping experience. Curiosities range from stuffed Hedwig owls and Potter mugs to chocolate frogs and everything and anything else in between. You can also find clothes in Gryffindor, Ravenclaw, Slytherin and Hufflepuff house colours – of course all made in Scotland.

You will find Museum Context in one of the most beautiful streets in Edinburgh, Victoria Street. The house was built between 1829 and 1834 and has an interesting fact: some people say it was the inspiration for J. K. Rowling to invent the stories about Harry Potter.

So, come in and enjoy the atmosphere of Harry Potter's world! You'll soon begin to feel like a witch or wizard. Don't miss it!

Adapted from: [https://theculturetrip.com; Stand 01. 08. 20]

a) gift
  🖉 *Hinweis: "… a gift shop for all Harry Potter fans …" (Z. 3)*
b) frogs
  🖉 *Hinweis: "… Potter mugs to chocolate frogs and everything …" (Z. 7 f.)*
c) Victoria Street
  🖉 *Hinweis: "… in Edinburgh, Victoria Street." (Z. 13)*
d) 1834
  🖉 *Hinweis: "… was built between 1829 and 1834 …" (Z. 14)*
e) wizard
  🖉 *Hinweis: "… feel like a witch or wizard." (Z. 19 f.)*

Part 3

You will hear a radio interview with some teens in Scotland. What does each person talk about? You will hear the interview twice. For tasks a)–e) write a letter, A–H, next to each person.

Presenter: Today we are talking to five teens who spent two weeks here in Scotland and are asking them about their favourite activities and places. Welcome Francis, where did you spend your time?

Francis: I have dreamt of attending the Old Firm in Glasgow since I was a little boy, and I was the luckiest boy on earth when I succeeded in buying a ticket for the match. It was great fun – and the best thing was – Celtic Glasgow won the match!

Presenter: Lucky you! Hi Angus, what was your favourite activity here in Scotland?

Angus: Well, I'm not so much into football, but I'm very interested in that medieval stuff. I really enjoyed visiting all these ancient places – you know, Rob Roy fighting against the English, ay! I went to Eilean Donan Castle, visited the Sterling buildings

Abschlussprüfung 2021

A Listening Comprehension

Allgemeiner Hinweis: Lies dir alle Aufgaben zuerst genau durch, damit du weißt, worauf du beim Zuhören achten musst. Sieh dir die Lösungen erst an, wenn du die Aufgaben bearbeitet hast. Höre dir einen Text noch einmal an, wenn deine Antwort nicht richtig war. Falls du etwas nicht verstanden hast, kannst du dir den Hörverstehenstext auch durchlesen.

Part 1

You will hear five short conversations. There is one task for each conversation. You will hear each conversation twice. There is one question for each conversation.
For tasks a)–e) mark A, B or C.

Task a)
When will they visit Glasgow Zoo?

Jenny: Hello, this is the Glasgow Zoo. You're talking to Jenny. What can I do for you?

Greg: Hi Jenny, this is Greg speaking. I'd like to visit the zoo with my class and I wonder if you could tell me more about the entrance fees for school classes.

Jenny: No problem, tomorrow is Tuesday. Well, the entrance fee for a school class on Tuesdays is 15 pounds per student.

Greg: Oh, thank you, so I think …

Jenny: Wait a second. If you come on Friday afternoon it will be 2 pounds cheaper per person.

Greg: Oh, that's an offer worth thinking about – Friday afternoon would be possible.

Jenny: Or you could come on Wednesday morning. I can offer you the same price!

Greg: Unfortunately, we have a school assembly on Wednesday, so we'll come at the end of this week. Thanks a lot!

Task b)
Who will join Bobby for the pop concert?

Bobby: Hi Mo, would you like to come with me to the pop concert in the Royal Concert Hall this evening?

Mo: I'd like to, but my football team is going to the Karaoke contest down in the pub – but what about Alex?

Bobby: Oh, didn't he tell you? His brother Frank bought two tickets for the rugby match in Glasgow tonight. I'm sure he won't want to come.

Mo: Let me think. I haven't been to a pop concert for a long time. I'll tell my mates that I'll join them next week and I'll come with you. Can you pick me up?

Task c)
At what time will the young woman take the train?

Woman: Excuse me, sir? When's the next train to Aberdeen?

Clerk: There's one at 4.20, but it stops at nearly every station, so it takes two hours, but it's only 15 pounds.

Woman: Oh, that's quite a long trip. Is there an alternative?

Clerk: Let me see, there is one at 5.15 from Glasgow's main station, but you have to change trains in Edinburgh or there's one at 6 o'clock. You don't need to change.

Woman: Fine, then I'll take the 6 o'clock one. How much is it?

Clerk: Both the 5.15 and the 6 o'clock trains are 45 pounds.

Woman: Oh no, that's far too expensive. I think I'll have to take the early but longer one. Thanks!

Task d)
What will Pete and Kate buy for James' birthday?

Pete: It's James' birthday tomorrow and we need a present for him.

Kate: What about one of those "I love Scotland" mugs? I like them. Or do you think we should buy a shirt with the Scottish flag?

Pete: A shirt? Great idea, let's buy it!

Kate: But we don't know which size to get, so what about special Harry Potter chocolate?

Pete: Well, he hates chocolate but he really enjoys his coffee. Let's go for the "I love Scotland" souvenir!

Task e)
Whose room does Charley choose?

Charley: Hi Pete, one question. Can I stay overnight after your party? It's a long way home for me.

Part 2

Hinweis: Bei dieser Aufgabe sollst du über einen Ort schreiben, an dem du vor Kurzem warst und wo es dir gefallen hat. In den Kästen findest du Ideen, die du für deinen Text verwenden kannst. Schreibe in ganzen Sätzen und versuche, sie durch Konjunktionen miteinander zu verbinden. Achte darauf, dass dein Text mindestens 80 Wörter umfasst. Die folgende Lösung ist ein Beispiel.

Last weekend I visited my friend Tina, who lives in the south of Bavaria. I stayed at her parents' house, which is located next to a beautiful forest. Tina and I enjoyed our daily walks through the forest, which looked like a fairy tale. The weather during my stay was perfect for those hiking trips. One day we also rode by bike to a lake nearby, where Tina taught me how to fish, but I enjoyed swimming in the lake afterwards more than catching fish! All in all, it was a nice, adventurous short trip and I would love to visit Tina there again one day. *(106 words)*

d) C
   Hinweis: "... almost 90 titles have been published. They were translated into 30 languages ..." (Z. 20)

e) A
   Hinweis: "... ten Lucky Luke 'live' films." (Z. 26 f.)

C Use of Language

Part 1

a) were
   Hinweis: Es handelt sich hier um einen Passivsatz im „simple past", der mit „were" (Plural „dogs") + „past participle" gebildet wird.

b) most
   Hinweis: „Famous" wird mit „more" und „most" gesteigert: "One of the most famous street dogs ..." *= „Einer der berühmtesten Straßenhunde ..."*

c) on
   Hinweis: feststehende Wendung: "on his way"

d) took
   Hinweis: "took him home" *= „nahm ihn mit nach Hause"*

e) death
   Hinweis: Hier musst du das Substantiv wählen.

f) while
   Hinweis: „while" = „während"

Part 2

a) found
   Hinweis: Z. 7

b) always
   Hinweis: Z. 11

Part 3

a) famous
   Hinweis: Z. 4

b) injured
   Hinweis: Z. 7

Part 4

Lösungsbeispiele:

a) A pet is an animal like a dog or cat which lives in your home.

b) It means saying hello to someone you meet.

c) It is the month after May.

Part 5

Lösungsbeispiele:

- How often do you take your dog for a walk?
- Is the equipment you need for a dog expensive?
- Can a dog stay alone for a certain time?

D Writing

Part 1

Hinweis: Hier musst du eine Bewerbungs-E-Mail von mindestens 60 Wörtern an ein Restaurant schreiben. Gehe auf alle drei genannten Punkte ein. Die Stichpunkte in Klammern sind Vorschläge, die du in deinem Text verwenden kannst. Formuliere höflich und schreibe keine Kurzformen wie „I'm", sondern Langformen wie „I am". Da du den Namen der Ansprechpartnerin/des Ansprechpartners nicht kennst, nimmst du als Anrede „Dear Sir or Madam". Der Schluss lautet dann „Yours faithfully". Die folgende Lösung ist ein Beispiel.

Dear Sir or Madam,

On your website I noticed your advert offering a job as a waiter. My name is Dirk, I am 15 and taking my final exams this year.

I have already had some work experience in a restaurant as a waiter and I enjoyed it. I am a friendly, reliable and communicative person who likes working with other people.

Maybe there is some more information you can give me: I would like to know about the salary and the working hours, and if I would have to wear special clothes.

I am looking forward to hearing from you.

Yours faithfully,

Dirk Brecht   *(105 words)*

c) A
   Hinweis: "...and we went on hikes." (Z. 19)
d) C
   Hinweis: "I spent hours <u>trying to find the perfect stick</u> to roast marshmallows on." (Z. 29 f.)

e) B
   Hinweis: "There weren't so many rules." (Z. 36 f.)

B Text-based Tasks

Part 1

a) A
   Hinweis: order = Bestellung
b) B
   Hinweis: premises = hier: Räumlichkeiten
c) A
   Hinweis: trail = Weg, Pfad (z. B. im Wald)
d) A
   Hinweis: unattended = unbeaufsichtigt
e) C
   Hinweis: Der Weg darf bei schlechtem Wetter gar nicht benutzt werden.

Part 2

a) B
   Hinweis: "Maurice de Bevere, also known as Morris ... decided to create his own western star ... Lucky Luke was born." (Z. 4 ff.)
b) E
   Hinweis: In diesem Abschnitt werden Beispiele für Lucky Lukes Abenteuer genannt, die er immer erfolgreich besteht.
c) C
   Hinweis: "...comic-strip hero <u>for more than 70 years</u> ... <u>several hundred million copies</u> have been sold." (Z. 19 ff.)
d) A
   Hinweis: "...animated series for television ... Lucky Luke 'live' films." (Z. 24 ff.)
e) D
   Hinweis: "...huge and increasing number of <u>merchandising stuff</u>..." (Z. 28 f.)

Part 3

a) false
   Hinweis: "...western star who should have special skills." (Z. 6 f.)

b) false
   Hinweis: "...undergoes a lot of adventures." (Z. 10 f.)
c) true
   Hinweis: "...claiming no rewards." (Z. 17 f.)
d) not in the text
   Hinweis: Die Zahl 70 bezieht sich darauf, wie lange es die Comicfigur Lucky Luke schon gibt.
e) true
   Hinweis: "...animated series for television ... Lucky Luke 'live' films." (Z. 24 ff.)

Part 4

a) As a child he was fascinated by western films [...]
   Hinweis: Z. 5
b) On horseback he crosses the American states [...]
   Hinweis: Z. 10
c) [...] in the end Lucky wins and brings them back to where they belong.
   Hinweis: Z. 15 f.
d) [...] there is much more than just the comic strips.
   Hinweis: Z. 23
e) The 'Lonesome Cowboy' is even with you at school [...]
   Hinweis: Z. 30 f.

Part 5

a) A
   Hinweis: "...should have <u>special skills</u>." (Z. 6 f.)
b) B
   Hinweis: "...to help people in trouble." (Z. 8)
c) C
   Hinweis: "...he has to deal with ... the Daltons ... in the end Lucky Luke wins and brings them back to where they belong." (Z. 12 ff.)

have a toothache. Sometimes it's very hard work but it's great to help people when they have a problem. It's so important to look after your teeth.

Susan: I'm Susan and I work in a hospital in the city centre. It's a very big hospital. I help the doctors with the patients. I hand out medicine and look after patients when they feel ill. I love my job but I don't like the uniform and sometimes I have to work at night.

Jeremy: My name is Jeremy. My job is very difficult but I like it because I love travelling. I take people to different places on holiday. Most of the time I stay in Europe flying to places like Spain, Greece and Italy. The most difficult thing about my job is when the weather is bad. Snow and thunderstorms are the worst. The best thing about my job is visiting all the different places.

Vincent: Hi. I'm Vincent. I work during my summer holidays when I'm not at university. Oxford has thousands of tourists in the summer, so it's easy to find a job there. I show tourists all the Oxford sights and then we go down to the river. We do a short trip on a boat. The tourists love the boat trip but last summer one tourist fell into the water! I love meeting people from all over the world.

Adapted from: http://learnenglishteens.britishcouncil.org/skills/listening/elementary-a2-listening/work

a) E
   🖊 *Hinweis: "We sell clothes and accessories…" (Z. 3 ff.)*

b) F
   🖊 *Hinweis: "…going to the doctor…when they have a toothache." (Z. 10 f.)*

c) H
   🖊 *Hinweis: "I help the doctors with the patients." (Z. 15 f.)*

d) C
   🖊 *Hinweis: "I take people to different places… flying to places like Spain…" (Z. 21 ff.)*

e) A
   🖊 *Hinweis: "I show tourists all the Oxford sights…" (Z. 31 f.)*

Part 4

You will hear a radio interview about summer camps. You will hear the interview twice. For tasks a)–e) mark A, B or C.

Millie: This is radio 102.2. Today, we're talking about summer camps. My guest in the studio is Matthew Waddle. Matthew, did you ever go to a summer camp when you were a kid?

Matthew: Hi, Millie! Yes, I did. I went to a summer camp every second year.

Millie: What did you do there?

Matthew: Well, different things like archery.

Millie: Archery?

Matthew: Yeah, with bows and arrows. We had a target and we tried to hit it. I was really bad at it. I remember it was quite difficult and I hurt my arm with the bow. But later we did distance shooting as well and I was pretty good at that.

Millie: Wow. Congratulations. OK, besides archery what were the other games you played or sports you did?

Matthew: Well, we learned how to paddle a canoe, we swam and we went on hikes. And we learned how to navigate through the forest with a compass.

Millie: What did you guys do at night? Did you play games or have campfires?

Matthew: Yes, we always had a campfire at night. We sang some songs and told ghost stories. But my favorite thing to do at the campfire was roasting marshmallows.

Millie: That's the best.

Matthew: I spent hours trying to find the perfect stick to roast marshmallows on.

Millie: That sounds yummy.

Matthew: Yes, it really was!

Millie: OK. Final question, was it hard to be away from your family?

Matthew: No, not at all. I remember feeling free and more independent away from my parents. There weren't so many rules.

Millie: You weren't homesick at all?

Matthew: No, I never got homesick. Each year when my parents came to pick me up I really didn't want to go home.

Millie: OK, thanks for being on the show, Matthew.

Matthew: Thanks too. It's been a pleasure.

Adapted from: http://www.elllo.org/english/1101/1108-Camp-Warren.htm

a) B
   🖊 *Hinweis: "I went to a summer camp every second year." (Z. 5 f.)*

b) C
   🖊 *Hinweis: "…we did distance shooting as well and I was pretty good at that." (Z. 13 f.)*

Task e)
Which piece of clothing is in the washing?

Bryce: Mum, any idea where my white sports T-shirt is? I need it for PE tomorrow.

Mother: It might be in the washing. Just go and have a look downstairs love.

Bryce: It isn't in the washing. And neither is the grey one. There are only dark-coloured clothes in the washing, mum.

Mother: Oh, yes. You're right. I completely forgot about that. You said your black pullover needed to be washed, so I did that last night before I went to bed.

Bryce: Right, but this still doesn't explain where my white and grey T-shirts are.

Mother: I wouldn't be surprised if you found them somewhere in your room. The place really is a mess.

Bryce: Alright, alright. I got the message.

a) C
  Hinweis: "So, I could visit grandma <u>the day after tomorrow</u>." (Z. 14 f.)

b) A
  Hinweis: "It's 6 o'clock now and the shop closes in half an hour." (Z. 18 f.)

c) C
  Hinweis: "…I couldn't resist buying this lamp and an armchair last week." (Z. 42 f.)

d) C
  Hinweis: "…<u>both Harry and William</u> said we could stay at their house for the night instead." – "…we <u>decided against Harry's place</u>…" (Z. 58 ff.)

e) B
  Hinweis: "There are only <u>dark-coloured clothes</u> in the washing…" (Z. 68 f.)

Part 2

You will hear some information about Drake, a Canadian rapper. You will hear the information twice. For tasks a)–e) fill in the grid.

If you think of rap music, you might think of tattoos, bad habits and bad language. But there are other examples as well. Aubrey Drake Graham was born in 1986 in Toronto and is known as Drake. He is a Canadian rapper, singer, songwriter, record producer and actor. In 2018 he released a music video in which he spent almost $ 1 million on people in Miami. The song is called "God's Plan". The message at the start of the video says: "The budget for this video was $ 996,631.90. We gave it all away. Don't tell the label!" The video clip shows Drake handing out money to struggling families, toys to children, scholarships to students and checks to a women's shelter and a youth club in Miami. Before its release, Drake called the video "the most important thing I have ever done in my career." Drake holds several Billboard chart records. He is one of the world's best-selling music artists, with more than 95 million records sold globally. "God's Plan" held the top spot on the Billboard Hot 100 singles chart for more than 10 weeks.

Drake gives away almost $1 million in 'God's Plan' music video, REUTERS vom 16.02.2018, https://uk.reuters.com/article/us-music-drake/drake-gives-away-almost-1-million-in-gods-plan- music-video-idUKKCN1G 02/M

a) 1986
  Hinweis: "…was born in 1986…" (Z. 3 f.)

b) singer/songwriter/record producer/actor
  Hinweis: "He is a Canadian rapper, singer, songwriter, record producer and actor." (Z. 4 ff.)

c) God's Plan
  Hinweis: "The song is called 'God's Plan'." (Z. 7 f.)

d) money/toys/scholarships/checks
  Hinweis: "The video clip shows Drake handling out <u>money</u> to struggling families, <u>toys</u> to children, <u>scholarships</u> to students and <u>checks</u> to a women's shelter and a youth club in Miami." (Z. 11 ff.)

e) 95 million
  Hinweis: "…with more than 95 million records sold globally." (Z. 18 f.)

Part 3

Listen to five people talking about their jobs. Which person has which job? You will hear the information twice. For tasks a)–e) write a letter, A–H, next to each person.

Fiona: My name is Fiona. I work on Saturdays and in the school holidays. Saturdays are busy because that's when everyone goes shopping. We sell clothes and accessories for men, women and children. I work in the children's department. I really like children a lot but my job can be crazy sometimes.

Michael: Hi, I'm Michael. I like my job, but lots of people don't like coming to see me because they hate going to the doctor, especially when they

Abschlussprüfung 2020

A Listening Comprehension

Allgemeiner Hinweis: Lies dir alle Aufgaben zuerst genau durch, damit du weißt, worauf du beim Zuhören achten musst. Sieh dir die Lösungen erst an, wenn du die Aufgaben bearbeitet hast. Höre dir einen Text noch einmal an, wenn deine Antwort nicht richtig war. Falls du etwas nicht verstanden hast, kannst du dir den Hörverstehenstext auch durchlesen.

Part 1

You will hear five short conversations. There is one task for each conversation. You will hear each conversation twice. There is one question for each conversation.
For tasks a)–e) mark A, B or C.

Task a)
When will Ernest visit his grandma?

Mum: Hello Ernest! Grandma called while you were at school. She asked when you are going to visit her.
Ernest: I wanted to visit her this week.
Mum: Maybe you can even manage to go and see her today. She's really looking forward to seeing you.
Ernest: No, today won't be possible. It's football practice this afternoon.
Mum: Right. I forgot about that … So how about tomorrow after school?
Ernest: Tomorrow … Well, I think I'll need the time to study for the English test.
Mum: That's true!
Ernest: But the rest of the week is free. So, I could visit grandma the day after tomorrow.
Mum: Alright. I'll let her know.

Task b)
What time does the shop close today?

Mum: Miles, could you go to the little corner shop and get me some milk and eggs, please? It's 6 o'clock now and the shop closes in half an hour.
Miles: Sure, Mum. No problem. But I thought the shop is open until 8. Didn't you tell me about the longer opening times the other day?
Mum: That's only on Thursdays. The shop closes earlier during the rest of the week. Jack, the shop owner, says that it isn't worth staying open because of all the supermarkets in town.
Miles: He's probably right. Anyway, I'm off now. Milk and eggs, anything else?
Mum: No, that's all. Thanks, dear.

Task c)
What's new in the house?

Laura: Hey, Marcus. It's great that you've finally come to visit us.
Marcus: Yes, thanks for the invitation, Laura. I love your house, it's so big and you've decorated it really well. Is the carpet new?
Laura: No, we've had this carpet for years and we want to buy a new one sometime soon. Same with the sofa here – but there are some things you just don't want to let go.
Marcus: I know exactly what you mean. But, from time to time you need something new, don't you?
Laura: I know, I know. There is a new furniture shop in town and I couldn't resist buying this lamp and an armchair last week.
Marcus: Oh, nice! I think I should go there myself. I've been looking for a new kitchen table but haven't found one that fits in my kitchen yet.

Task d)
Where did Peter sleep last night?

Dad: Good morning, Peter. How was the party? Were you able to get some sleep?
Peter: Mornin', Dad! Yes, but not before 2 o'clock in the morning.
Dad: Why's that? Was it too noisy at Steven's house?
Peter: The problem was that we couldn't stay there for the night. Steven's parents came back home from their hiking trip around midnight. His mum got sick so they returned earlier.
Dad: I see. Why didn't you give me a call? I could have picked you up.
Peter: Yes, I know. But both Harry and William said we could stay at their house for the night instead.
Dad: So you went to Harry's?
Peter: No, we decided against Harry's place because it was too far away.

Manteltaschen ist. Unterbreite Frau Potter einen Vorschlag, wie du deinen Mantel zurückbekommen könntest. Achte auf Höflichkeitsformen bei Anrede und Verabschiedung. Abschließend zählst du deine Wörter. Es müssen mindestens 60 sein.

From: *(your e-mail address)*
To: potterbnb@dover.co.uk
Subject: Coat left behind

Dear Mrs Potter,
My name is *(your name)* and I was your guest from Tuesday, 11th May to Wednesday, 12th May. Unfortunately, I left my coat behind in your entrance hall. It is a black wool coat size S with big white buttons. I am not sure about the label, but I think it's MAX. In the left pocket there are tissues and some chewing gum. I will be in Dover again next Monday on my way home. Would you mind keeping the coat till I come to pick it up?
Thank you very much in advance.

Yours sincerely,
(your name)   *(99 words)*

Part 3

11. false
   Hinweis: "...since the arrival of mobile phones, nobody really needs public telephones..." (Z. 5 ff.)
12. true
   Hinweis: "...more and more red phone boxes are taking on a new life..." (Z. 11 f.); "...use it for something completely different." (Z. 15 f.)
13. true
   Hinweis: "...help has to come quickly and that can be a problem in the countryside." (Z. 19 f.)
14. not in the text
15. false
   Hinweis: "...10 of the boxes are being used as mini art galleries..." (Z. 22 f.)

Part 4

16. C
   Hinweis: they are surrounded by... = sie sind umgeben von...
17. A
   Hinweis: to order = befehlen
18. B
   Hinweis: Der Satz beinhaltet eine indirekte Rede. Da der Hauptsatz in der Vergangenheit steht ("...he was told that..."), muss im Nebensatz der sog. backshift ("left") erfolgen. Auch handelt es sich hier um einen if-Satz Typ II, in dem im Bedingungssatz das simple past steht.
19. A
   Hinweis: not in any way = in keiner Weise
20. D
   Hinweis: change of scene = „Tapetenwechsel"

Part 5

21. C
   Hinweis: "...wants to rebuild a very high office building into 254 flats..." (Z. 3 f.)
22. A
   Hinweis: "There are minimum standards for homes in Great Britain...they do not apply..." (Z. 6 ff.)
23. A
   Hinweis: "...there is only little space to walk around." (Z. 14 f.)
24. B
   Hinweis: "...or £ 180,000 to buy." (Z. 18 f.)
25. C
   Hinweis: "...comments on the council's website like: 'This shouldn't be legal – it's inhuman!'" (Z. 21 f.)

III. Writing

Part 1 – Letter

Hinweis: Nachdem du die Lücken gefüllt hast, solltest du den Text noch einmal durchlesen, um zu überprüfen, ob deine Lösungen richtig sind bzw. einen Sinn ergeben.

sorry/bad/sad/unhappy – was – stay/be/remain – nice/kind/friendly – than – meal – able/allowed – patients/people/children – great/super/nice/cool/awesome – on

Part 2 – Dialogue

Hinweis: Statt Fragen kannst du auch treffende Aussagesätze formulieren, die ebenfalls als richtige Antwort gewertet werden.

1. Where do you want to go (to)? / Where are you flying to?
2. When is your flight? / What time do you fly? / What time are you flying?
3. You can see/find the gate on the (display) boards.
4. There is one on the right next to the kiosk.
5. I can show you the board if you like. / Shall I show you the board?
6. I'm flying to Los Angeles to visit some relatives.
7. Thanks/Thank you. Have a good flight.

Part 3 – E-mail

Hinweis: Deine Aufgabe ist es hier, eine E-Mail an Frau Potter, die Besitzerin eines B&B, zu schreiben. Du hast dort übernachtet und deinen Mantel vergessen. Beschreibe in wenigen Sätzen, wann und wo du den Mantel vergessen hast, wie er aussieht und was in den

Part 5

You will hear some young people discussing what they plan on doing after leaving school. Which person has which plan? You will hear the report twice. For questions 21 to 25 write a letter, A–H, next to each person.
[pause]

Presenter: Hi folks. Any plans after leaving school? Working, studying or travelling? We talked to five teens about their plans for the future and here are their answers:

Nala: Hi, my name is Nala. I'm 17 and will finish school in a few weeks. I still haven't decided what to do after my exams but I love children and travelling. I thought I could combine the two and look for a job as an au-pair somewhere abroad. I hope that will work out.

Patrick: I'm Patrick. A lot of my friends want to study but that's just not my thing. I'll be glad when school is over and I can earn my own money. I like working with my hands and I'm very creative. So this is why I'll train to be a carpenter.

Owen: My name is Owen and I guess I'm a bit of a freak *(laughs)*. I've been working as a DJ in various clubs in the area for three years now. Music is my life. I want to open my own club, organize events, promote bands etc. I've managed to get an internship with a radio station in London. So you will definitely be hearing from me!

Christine: My name is Christine and I'm 18 years old. Honestly, I haven't got a clue what to do after school. My parents suggested doing a voluntary social year. But the problem is that I wouldn't have much money then. At the moment I'm working as a waitress at the weekends, so I guess I'll just carry on doing different jobs until I've made up my mind about the future.

Lennox: Hey, I'm Lennox. I've just bought my plane ticket to Australia. For years and years I've wanted to do this, travelling around Australia and earning some money at the same time. I've got a job on a sheep farm near Brisbane and I can't wait to go.
[pause]

21. C
    Hinweis: "... look for a job as an au-pair ..." (Z. 8 f.)
22. A
    Hinweis: "... I'll train to be a carpenter." (Z. 15); carpenter = *Schreiner*in*
23. D
    Hinweis: "I've managed to get an internship with a radio station ..." (Z. 20 f.)
24. G
    Hinweis: "... I'll just carry on doing different jobs ..." (Z. 28 f.)
25. H
    Hinweis: "... travelling around Australia and earning some money at the same time." (Z. 33 f.)

II. Reading Comprehension

Part 1

1. B
    Hinweis: life vest = *Rettungsweste*
2. A
    Hinweis: stage = *Bühne*
3. C
    Hinweis: private property = *Privatgrundstück*. Private Grundstücke werden oft mit einem elektrischen Einfahrtstor gesichert.
4. B
    Hinweis: In einer Bücherei sind in der Regel keine Getränke erlaubt.
5. A
    Hinweis: priority = *Vorrang*, passengers = *Fahrgäste*
6. C
    Hinweis: petrol = *Benzin*, garage = *hier: Autowerkstatt*

Part 2

7. C
    Hinweis: break = *hier: Ferien, Urlaub*; trip = *Ausflug*
8. A
    Hinweis: appointment = *Termin, Vereinbarung*, visitor = *Besucher*in*
9. C
    Hinweis: must not = *nicht dürfen*
10. A
    Hinweis: limit = *Grenze*

a little bit and enjoy your free-time.
Karen: Yeah, I'll do that! What are you cooking? It smells good.
Mum: I am baking cakes. This here is one of your favourites. It's a chocolate cake.
Karen: It looks really delicious. And I can see muffins over there too.
Mum: Yes. Your brother Wayne has to take something to school on his birthday tomorrow. So, those muffins are for him. Don't you dare touch them.
Karen: Can I have a piece of chocolate cake then?
Mum: Yes, but only a small one as we are having dinner in an hour.
Karen: Hmmmm. That's yummy! Is baking difficult, mum?
Mum: No, not really. Anybody can learn. It's just a question of practice.
Karen: If that's true then I want to learn to bake too.
Mum: Well, that shouldn't be a problem. We could make an apple pie together when you get home from school tomorrow if you like.
Karen: No we can't. It's Wayne's birthday tomorrow. What about Saturday afternoon, let's say 3.30?
Mum: Fine. I'll have everything ready for our baking session.

[pause]

11. B
   Hinweis: "I thought you would be home earlier today." (Z. 2f.) – "I could have been." (Z. 4)

12. A
   Hinweis: "...I did very well on the test." (Z. 8)

13. B
   Hinweis: "Wayne has to take something to school..." (Z. 20f.); "...those muffins are for him." (Z. 22)

14. A
   Hinweis: "It's just a question of practice." (Z. 29f.)

15. C
   Hinweis: "What about Saturday afternoon, let's say 3.30?" (Z. 36)

Part 4

Mike is a fitness coach at a gym. He is presenting the sports centre to a group of people. You will hear the presentation twice.
For questions 16 to 20 mark A, B or C.
Look at questions 16 to 20 now.

[pause]

Now listen to the presentation.

Hi everybody, my name's Mike and I'm the head fitness coach here. As you can see, the main gym is really big and we have lots of brand-new machines. Here you can do running, cycling and weights. If you want a closer look at the machines, we can come back later. Oh, by the way, you can only come in here with trainers on. So, no outdoor shoes, please.
OK, here we have the swimming pool. There are certain times of the day when we have swimming classes and water aerobics. There is always a lifeguard in attendance who will also offer informal swimming tips. Over there you have the changing rooms and lockers, and on the right are the bathrooms and showers. We have our own shop here, where you can buy sportswear and sports drinks.
We are slightly more expensive than other gyms in the area because we're open 24 hours and we offer a very wide range of activities. The timetables of the extra classes such as boxing, taekwondo and quite a few others, as well as swimming classes, diving and water aerobics are in our brochure. You can also have a look at our website and check the timetables there. If you like you can speak to the receptionist about the best combination of activities for you.

adapted from: http://learnenglishteens.britishcouncil.org/skills/listening-skills-practice/sports-centres

[pause]

16. B
   Hinweis: "Here you can do running, cycling and weights." (Z. 4)

17. A
   Hinweis: "...you can only come in here with trainers on." (Z. 6f.)

18. A
   Hinweis: "There is always a lifeguard in attendance..." (Z. 10f.)

19. C
   Hinweis: "...slightly more expensive...we offer a very wide range of activities." (Z. 16ff.)

20. B
   Hinweis: "The timetables...are in our brochure...look at our website..." (Z. 18ff.)

Question 5
When will the football match be over?

Max: This is just the best game ever! Look at that, two goals in the last ten minutes – great.

Thomas: Yes, you're right and there's only one minute to go. Looks like Arsenal will really win the cup this time.

Max: Might well be. But I'm sure the game will take a bit longer 'cos the goalkeeper was fouled in the second half and the game was interrupted for a few minutes.

Thomas: Look, it says five minutes extra time on the scoreboard now.

Max: Oh, let's hope they can keep the score …

[pause]

1. B
   Hinweis: "…I put it in my school bag instead…" (Z. 13)
2. B
   Hinweis: "Then why don't you try exercise number 7a?" (Z. 25 f.)
3. C
   Hinweis: "…at half past twelve?" – "…a return ticket, please." (Z. 43 f.)
4. C
   Hinweis: "…I saw the same laptop…it was £ 50 cheaper there." (Z. 55 f.)
5. A
   Hinweis: "…there's only one minute to go." (Z. 61 f.) – "…it says five minutes extra time…" (Z. 68)

Part 2

You will hear some information about poetry slams. You will hear the information twice. Listen and complete questions 6 to 10.

[pause]

Poetry slams

A poetry slam is a competition where poets read or perform their work to a live audience.

Poetry slam was invented in 1986 by Marc Smith when the first slam took place at the Green Mill Jazz Club in Chicago.

The first national poetry slam took place in 1990 in San Francisco. Since then thousands of poetry slams have been held across the country and around the world, including youth slams like Brave New Voices.

Many slam poets have even gone on to careers as professional writers, actors, and hip-hop artists. The 2019 National Poetry Slam will take place in Oakland, California.

The rules of poetry slam are quite simple: each poet has three minutes to perform their poem. The poem must have been written by the person performing it. The poet is not allowed to use costumes or musical instruments. Five judges are randomly selected from the audience. Each judge gives the poems a score from 0–10 points.

adapted from: https://prezi.com/1rej-uw8wus9/history-rules-of-the-poetry-slam/

[pause]

6. 1986/Chicago
   Hinweis: "…was invented in 1986…at the Green Mill Jazz Club in Chicago." (Z. 3 ff.)
7. national
   Hinweis: "The first national poetry slam took place in 1990 in San Francisco." (Z. 6 f.)
8. actors
   Hinweis: "…careers as professional writers, actors, and hip-hop artists." (Z. 10 f.)
9. 3 min./minutes
   Hinweis: "…each poet has three minutes to perform their poem." (Z. 14 f.)
10. (musical) instruments
    Hinweis: "The poet is not allowed to use costumes or musical instruments." (Z. 17 f.)

Part 3

You will hear a conversation between Karen and her mum in the kitchen. You will hear the conversation twice.

For questions 11 to 15 mark A, B or C.

Look at questions 11 to 15 now.

[pause]

Now listen to the conversation.

Karen: Hi mum, I'm home.

Mum: Hi sweetie! You're quite late. I thought you would be home earlier today.

Karen: I could have been. But I was talking to Hannah at the bus station and we forgot about the time.

Mum: I can imagine that. Chatterboxes! How was school? How did you do on the test?

Karen: School was OK and I did very well on the test. Mum, I was so worried about it but now I feel great.

Mum: I'm very glad to hear that. You've studied so hard during the last few days. Now you can relax

Abschlussprüfung 2019

I. Listening Comprehension

⚑ *Allgemeiner Hinweis: Lies dir alle Aufgaben zuerst genau durch, damit du weißt, worauf du beim Zuhören achten musst. Sieh dir die Lösungen erst an, wenn du die Aufgaben bearbeitet hast. Höre dir einen Text noch einmal an, wenn deine Antwort nicht richtig war. Falls du etwas nicht verstanden hast, kannst du dir den Hörverstehenstext auch durchlesen. Vergiss in der Prüfung auf keinen Fall, im Listening- und im Reading-Teil deine Antworten richtig in das Answer Sheet zu übertragen. Nur die dort eingetragenen Lösungen zählen in der Prüfung!*

Part 1

You will hear five short conversations. You will hear each conversation twice. There is one question for each conversation.
For questions 1 to 5 mark A, B or C.
[pause]

Question 1
Where did Clara put her mp3 player?

1 **Clara:** Mum, have you seen my mp3-player? I've looked everywhere and can't find it.
Mum: Oh no, not again! Have you looked on your bedside table?
5 **Clara:** Yes, of course. It's not there.
Mum: Did you listen to music while you were doing your homework? It could still be on your desk.
Clara: Yes, I did, but I must have put the mp3 player somewhere else. It isn't on my desk.
10 **Mum:** Maybe you put it in your pocket so that you'll have it on the bus tomorrow morning …
Clara: Aaah, now I remember. I wanted to put it in my pocket. But then I put it in my school bag instead 'cos I haven't decided which jacket to wear tomor-
15 row. Thanks, mum!
[pause]

Question 2
Which exercise should Henrietta do next?

Henrietta: Excuse me, Mrs Brown, could you help me please?
Mrs Brown: Of course, Henrietta. What is it?
Henrietta: I can't decide which exercise to do next.
20 **Mrs Brown:** Let me see … you could go on with exercise number 4.
Henrietta: Exercise 4 … oh, I think this is too easy for me.
Mrs Brown: I see. You're looking for something more
25 challenging. Then why don't you try exercise number 7a?
Henrietta: OK, 7a … but what about 7b?
Mrs Brown: You need a partner to do 7b, but there's nobody free at the moment.
[pause]

Question 3
What ticket does the woman buy?

30 **Dorothee:** Excuse me. I need to go to Brighton today and would like to know when the next train leaves from this station.
Ticket seller: There are several trains to Brighton today. The next one leaves at 11.45 a.m.
35 **Dorothee:** Oh, but that's in four minutes and I haven't got a ticket yet. Is there a later one?
Ticket seller: There's one leaving at 12.30 but you'll have to change trains at Southampton. The one after that is a direct train and leaves at 1.55 p.m.
40 **Dorothee:** Oh, I don't want to wait here so long and I don't mind changing trains.
Ticket seller: No problem, one single ticket for you then for the train at half past twelve?
Dorothee: No, a return ticket, please.
[pause]

Question 4
What is the man complaining about?

45 **Man:** Hello there, I bought this laptop here last week and I would like to give it back.
Shop assistant: Is there a problem with it, sir? Is it damaged?
Man: No, that's not the problem.
50 **Shop assistant:** Well, maybe you're not happy with the colour. We've got this laptop in different colours in stock.
Man: Actually, I don't think the colour is too bad.
Shop assistant: So why do you want to return it then?
55 **Man:** Well to be quite honest, I saw the same laptop in another shop and it was £50 cheaper there.
Shop assistant: Right, in that case we'll give you the difference back and you can keep your laptop.
[pause]

4. A friend of mine visited/was at the 'Dr Who Experience' two years ago.
5. What a pity!/What a shame! I hope there are other interesting things on the tour.
6. Yes, please. How much is the ticket?
7. How long/For how long is the ticket valid?/How long/For how long can I use the ticket?

Part 3 – E-mail

Hinweis: Hier musst du eine E-Mail von mindestens 60 Wörtern an eine Ferienorganisation schreiben. Beschreibe in wenigen Sätzen, welches Land du und deine Freunde besuchen wollen. Nenne einen geeigneten Zeitraum und die Aufenthaltsdauer. Schildere, für welche Aktivitäten ihr euch interessiert und erkundige dich nach möglichen Unterkünften und deren Preisen. Formuliere höflich und verwende keine Kurzformen wie „I'm". Da kein Ansprechpartner angegeben ist, kannst du als Anrede „Dear Sir or Madam" verwenden. Der Schluss lautet dann „Yours faithfully". Die folgende Lösung ist ein Beispiel.

From: (your name)
To: info@ct-summercamps.co.uk
Subject: Summer camp in Scotland

Dear Sir or Madam,

I am looking for a youth summer camp in Scotland at the beginning of August. We are five boys aged 13 and 14 and we would like to spend a week in the Highlands. We are good at mountain biking and we also love hiking. It would also be great if we could learn fishing.

Can you send us a list of possible accommodation plus prices? I hope you can find a suitable camp for us.

Yours faithfully,

(your name) *(84 words)*

5. C
   Hinweis: priority = Vorrang; „priority seats" sollen für bestimmte Fahrgäste (= „passengers") freigemacht werden, z. B. Menschen mit Behinderung und Schwangere.
6. B
   Hinweis: check-out = Kasse

Part 2

7. B
   Hinweis: Man soll die Augen auf die Straße richten, um nicht vom Weg abzukommen.
8. D
   Hinweis: at their own risk/on your own responsibility = *auf eigene Gefahr*
9. C
   Hinweis: gift = Geschenk; es steht zwar nicht auf dem Schild, dass in dem Geschäft Postkarten und T-Shirts gekauft werden können, aber sie könnten auch als Geschenke/Souvenirs im Angebot sein.
10. A
    Hinweis: Hier gibt dir schon das Bild einen Hinweis auf die richtige Lösung; „what their dogs leave behind" bezieht sich auf die „Hinterlassenschaft" der Hunde.

Part 3

11. not in the text
12. true
    Hinweis: „... they light up when they see Petie." (Z. 7 f.)
13. true
    Hinweis: „... has been a therapeutic horse since 1997." (Z. 10)
14. not in the text
15. false
    Hinweis: „... back to his farm ... he likes to chase other horses ... 'Petie is an angel at the hospital, but at home he's a little devil!'" (Z. 17 ff.)

Part 4

16. B
17. D
    Hinweis: hopefully = hoffentlich
18. A
19. B
    Hinweis: didn't sink = verneinte Form im Simple past von „sink"
20. C
    Hinweis: „boats <u>are made</u> of ..." = „Boote <u>werden</u> aus ... <u>gemacht</u>" (Passiv)

Part 5

21. A
    Hinweis: „... the oldest traces of human life were found in Africa." (Z. 1 f.); traces = Spuren
22. B
    Hinweis: „Hikers discovered the oldest human footprints ..." (Z. 4)
23. A
    Hinweis: „Holes were revealed ... that looked like human footprints." (Z. 12 f.)
24. C
    Hinweis: „Technicians then presented the images ... at the British Museum ..." (Z. 16 f.)
25. B
    Hinweis: „Now scientists can reconstruct the way of living of the first humans in Northern Europe much better and gain a more detailed insight." (Z. 20 ff.)

III. Writing

Part 1 – Letter

Hinweis: Nachdem du den Brief vervollständigt hast, solltest du ihn noch einmal durchlesen, um zu überprüfen, ob deine Lösungen einen Sinn ergeben.

time/stay/week – made/got/found – There – start/begin – subjects/courses – take/catch/get – club/centre – daughter/girl/child – understand – fine/OK/well/good/alright

Part 2 – Dialogue

Hinweis: Wenn du statt Fragen Aussagesätze formulierst, werden diese als richtig gewertet, wenn sie den auf Deutsch formulierten Inhalt richtig wiedergeben.

1. I am / I come from Germany and I'd like to spend a day in Cardiff.
2. How often do the buses run?
3. Which sights can you recommend?

18. true
   Hinweis: "...trees, oil and water can be preserved longer." (Z. 14)
19. true
   Hinweis: "...it can even inspire your friends or others to start recycling too." (Z. 17 f.)
20. false
   Hinweis: "We have just a small window of opportunity and this window is closing rapidly." (Z. 22 f.)

Part 5

You will hear a radio report on the top five sights in New York. Which feature belongs to each sight? You will hear this report twice. For questions 21 to 25 write a letter, A–H, next to each sight.
[pause]

1 **Presenter:** Back on Radio Big Apple 95.6. If you are thinking about traveling to New York: it's an amazing city! And if you're not sure about which sights to visit – we can help you! Here are the top
5   five New York attractions:
   Number one and top of the list is the Empire State Building. It was built in just 410 days and opened in 1931. It is 381 meters high and one of the world's tallest buildings. The views from its out-
10   door and indoor decks are spectacular, especially at sunset.
   Top sight number two is the famous Times Square. It's a major crossing in midtown Manhattan. There are yellow cabs, skyscrapers, colors,
15   lights and billboards everywhere. Over 460,000 pedestrians walk through Times Square on a busy day. Some call it "the center of the universe".
   Attraction number three is the Statue of Liberty. The statue is on Liberty Island and made of cop-
20   per. It was built by Gustave Eiffel – the man who also designed the Eiffel Tower. The female figure is an impressive symbol of justice, law and freedom.
   Recommendation number four is Central Park. It
25 is the most-visited urban park in the USA. The park roads are used by a lot of joggers, bikers and inline-skaters. You can play baseball, volleyball and tennis in the park or go ice-skating in winter. And you can even go to a live concert or to the
30 theater.
   The fifth and last attraction is an absolute must-see as well. It is the Museum of Modern Art, better known in its short form of MoMA. Since its opening in 1929 it has collected almost 200,000 works
35 of art including paintings, sculptures, architecture, photography and electronic media. Its galleries show works by such great artists as Picasso and Van Gogh.
   Have we aroused your interest? So, just give it a
40 go, come and visit the Big Apple!
[pause]

21. G
   Hinweis: "...the Empire State Building. It was built in just 410 days..." (Z. 6 f.)
22. C
   Hinweis: "Over 460,000 pedestrians walk through Times Square on a busy day." (Z. 15 ff.)
23. A
   Hinweis: "The statue is on Liberty Island..." (Z. 19)
24. F
   Hinweis: "...used by a lot of joggers, bikers, and inline-skaters. You can play baseball, volleyball and tennis in the park or go ice-skating in winter." (Z. 26 ff.)
25. B
   Hinweis: "...it has collected almost 200,000 works of art including paintings,...photography." (Z. 34 ff.)

II. Reading Comprehension

Part 1

1. A
   Hinweis: Das Schild befindet sich wahrscheinlich in der Nähe eines Bauernhofs, auf dem Enten gehalten werden.
2. C
   Hinweis: bridge = *Brücke*
3. C
   Hinweis: railings = *Geländer*
4. A
   Hinweis: restroom *(Am. Englisch)* = *Toilette*

Paula: No, the 18th.
Simone: I'm sorry … but the 18th would be five nights.
Paula: Ooooh, yes! You're right. Sorry!
Simone: No problem. So that's five nights and you'll be checking out on the 18th?
Paula: Yes, that's it. By the way, how much are the rooms?
Simone: Well, the rates depend on the type of room. For the nights you'll be staying, we have the single suite, the studio and a standard room available. Or … no, sorry … I see that the studio is not available on 13 June.
Paula: Okay. So how much is the single suite?
Simone: It is £ 124.90, plus tax, per night.
Paula: Oh wow! That's a lot! And how much is the standard room?
Simone: The standard room is £ 49, plus tax.
Paula: OK, I'll take the standard room, please.
Simone: Good. May I have your name, please?
Paula: Paula Robinson.
Simone: Paula Robinson … Great. OK, and how will you be paying?
Paula: Do you take credit cards?
Simone: Yes, we do. Can I have your credit card number, please?
Paula: Just a moment, please … That's, uh … 5497 5358 0577 9539.
Simone: OK, let me confirm that number: 5497 5358 0577 9539. Is that right?
Paula: Yes, that's right.
Simone: OK, I've got you booked in for 13 June. Is there anything else I can do for you?
Paula: No, that's all. Thanks.
Simone: OK. Thank you. Have a good day.

Adapted from: http://www.sloweasyenglish.com/hotel-reservations-english-conversation-lesson; Stand: 22. 06. 2017

[pause]

11. A
   Hinweis: "… you'll be checking out on the 18th?" (Z. 17 f.) – "Yes, that's it." (Z. 19)

12. B
   Hinweis: "… but the 18th would be five nights." (Z. 14 f.) – "… You're right. Sorry!" (Z. 16)

13. B
   Hinweis: "… the studio is not available on 13 June." (Z. 24 f.)

14. B
   Hinweis: "It is £ 124.90, plus tax, per night." (Z. 27)

15. C
   Hinweis: "That's … 5497 5358 0577 9539." (Z. 39 f.)

Part 4

You will hear a climate expert talking about recycling. You will hear the report twice. For questions 16 to 20 mark 'true' or 'false'.
Look at questions 16 to 20 now.
[pause]
Now listen to the report.

Deciding the Future of the Earth

Do you love the planet you live on? Do you love the trees, the rivers and the lakes, the blue sky and the wildlife? But what if you woke up tomorrow and it was all gone? Well, global warming has the power to really make this happen in the future. This is why we must change something. One step to changing the future is to recycle. Recycling not only saves the Earth, it saves you money, too. You throw away fewer things, which means you need to empty the trash bin less often. And another good thing about recycling is that air and water pollution are reduced and that not as many raw materials are destroyed. For example, trees, oil and water can be preserved longer. Recycling is a small act that can have a huge effect. It can show others that you care about the environment. If you do it, it can even inspire your friends or others to start recycling too. If everyone starts with something as small as recycling then maybe we can heal our planet and save our future. It is an action that needs to be taken immediately. Climate change is for real. We have just a small window of opportunity and this window is closing rapidly. There is not a moment to lose. So let's start recycling – now!

Adapted from: http://www.teenink.com/opinion/environment/article/136428/Deciding-the-Future-of-the-Earth/; 01.10.2009

[pause]

16. true
   Hinweis: "… and it was all gone?" (Z. 4 f.), "… global warming has the power to … make this happen …" (Z. 5 f.)

17. false
   Hinweis: "… you need to empty the trash bin less often." (Z. 10 f.)

Travel agent: Just a moment ... there are three planes going to Southampton that day. Two in the morning and one in the afternoon.
Customer: What time do they take off?
Travel agent: The two flights in the morning go at quarter past eight and quarter to eleven. The plane in the afternoon takes off at 4.35.
Customer: 4.35 in the afternoon ... no, that's too late for me. Can you book me in for the 10.45 flight?
Travel agent: Sure ... Oh, I just see that there are only business class tickets left. They cost almost double. Would you like a business class ticket?
Customer: No, thank you. In that case I'll take the other morning flight.
[pause]

1. B
   ✏ Hinweis: "Oh, you've got milkshakes as well!" (Z. 6f.), "I'll have strawberry ..." (Z. 10)
2. A
   ✏ Hinweis: "... help him look for a new sweatshirt." (Z. 17)
3. B
   ✏ Hinweis: "No, Billy wasn't interested, so they asked Tommy instead and he agreed." (Z. 35f.)
4. C
   ✏ Hinweis: "... we're going on a one-week hiking-trip in the Black Forest." (Z. 51f.);
   Black Forest = Schwarzwald
5. A
   ✏ Hinweis: "The two flights in the morning go at <u>quarter past eight</u> and quarter to eleven." (Z. 62f.), "Can you book me in for the 10.45 flight?" (Z. 66), "No, thank you. In that case I'll take <u>the other morning flight</u>." (Z. 70f.)

Part 2

You will hear some information about a high school in Britain. You will hear the information twice. Listen and complete questions 6 to 10.
[pause]

Welcome to the Hastings Castle High School hotline. Thank you for calling. Please listen to the following five options: Press number one on your phone to report a pupil's absence. Press two to report a staff member's absence. Press three to speak to the office. Press four for further information. Press five to hear these options again. You have chosen FOUR – further information: Our school hours are from Monday to Thursday from 8.45 a.m. to 3.50 p.m. On Friday school ends at 12.10. If you want to talk to the headmaster, please call 01424-77390. Our school uniform consists of a plain white shirt with a tie and black trousers or a black skirt. Footwear must be dark, black trainers are acceptable. At lunchtime you should use the dining hall to eat, including packed lunches. Food is not allowed in the classrooms. We expect our students to respect each other, the teachers and all other staff. We wish you a nice day. Good bye.
[pause]

6. office
   ✏ Hinweis: "Press three to speak to the office." (Z. 5)
7. 12.10
   ✏ Hinweis: "On Friday school ends at 12.10." (Z. 9f.)
8. 77390
   ✏ Hinweis: "If you want to talk to the headmaster, please call 01424-77390." (Z. 10f.)
9. shirt, black
   ✏ Hinweis: "... uniform consists of a plain white <u>shirt</u> with a tie and <u>black</u> trousers or a black skirt." (Z. 11ff.)
10. food
    ✏ Hinweis: "Food is not allowed in the classrooms." (Z. 16)

Part 3

You will hear a telephone conversation between a hotel clerk and a tourist. You will hear the conversation twice.
For questions 11 to 15 mark A, B or C.
Look at questions 11 to 15 now.
[pause]
Now listen to the conversation.

Simone: Hello, Central Hotel, Simone speaking. How can I help you?
Paula: Hi. My name is Paula and I'm looking for a hotel room.
Simone: Sure. When would you like to check in?
Paula: Do you have any rooms available for 13 June?
Simone: Yes we do. For how many people?
Paula: Just for me. I am travelling alone.
Simone: Alright. And for how many nights will that be?
Paula: I was thinking about four nights.
Simone: So you'll be checking out on 17 June, then?

Abschlussprüfung 2018

I. Listening Comprehension

Allgemeiner Hinweis: Lies dir alle Aufgaben zuerst genau durch, damit du weißt, worauf du beim Zuhören achten musst. Sieh dir die Lösungen erst an, wenn du die Aufgaben bearbeitet hast. Höre dir einen Text noch einmal an, wenn deine Antwort nicht richtig war. Falls du etwas nicht verstanden hast, kannst du dir den Hörverstehenstext auch durchlesen. Vergiss in der Prüfung auf keinen Fall, im Listening- und im Reading-Teil deine Antworten richtig in das Answer Sheet zu übertragen. Nur die dort eingetragenen Lösungen zählen in der Prüfung!

Part 1

You will hear five short conversations. You will hear each conversation twice. There is one question for each conversation.
For questions 1 to 5 mark A, B or C.
[pause]

Question 1
What does the woman order at the bar?
Tender: Hi there. Something to drink?
Woman: Yes, please. Can you recommend anything non-alcoholic?
Tender: Well, we've got fresh fruit juices or really nice cocktails. I can show you on the menu.
Woman: Thank you, let's have a look ... Oh, you've got milkshakes as well!
Tender: Yes, we do. We've got strawberry, vanilla, chocolate or toffee flavour in stock.
Woman: I'll have strawberry then, please.
Tender: Comin' right up.
[pause]

Question 2
What was Sally doing this morning?
Mother: Sally, this place is a mess. What have you been doing all day? I thought you wanted to wash the dishes and tidy up this morning.
Sally: Oh Mum, please don't be angry. I really wanted to do the washing up, but then Mat called and asked me to help him look for a new sweatshirt. I couldn't say no, could I?
Mother: Well, I guess not. Still, have you at least posted my letters as you promised?
Sally: Ah, no, but there is still time before the post office closes. I'm on my way now. Bye!
[pause]

Question 3
Who is the new frontman?
Kyle: Hey Darius! What's up?
Darius: Hi Kyle! How are you?
Kyle: Alright, thanks. Have you heard the news about the school band? They've got a new frontman.
Darius: A new frontman? I thought James was the frontman.
Kyle: Yes, he was. But he is going to move house and change school next week. So they need a new frontman before their next concert in June.
Darius: I see. Yes, that makes sense 'cos they need to practice a lot. So, who is the new frontman then? Billy?
Kyle: No, Billy wasn't interested, so they asked Tommy instead and he agreed.
Darius: Yeah, he's quite a good singer. But I still think it would have been better if Billy were in the band.
[pause]

Question 4
Where will Danny spend his summer holidays?
Tom: Hi Danny! Good to see you. What's new?
Danny: Hello Tom! Just imagine! My parents want to take me on a holiday trip to Europe this summer.
Tom: Wow, that's cool! Where are you going then?
Danny: They let me choose between Spain, Slovenia and Germany.
Tom: My brother says Slovenia is great. He went there on a mountain bike trip last year.
Danny: I'm not so much into biking.
Tom: I see. So, where are you going?
Danny: Even though Spain is warm in summer and I like sunshine I decided against it. We love hiking and we're going on a one-week hiking-trip in the Black Forest.
Tom: Wow!
[pause]

Question 5
What time will the customer travel?
Travel agent: Good morning, Sir. How can I help you?
Customer: Good morning. I need a cheap one-way flight from Belfast to Southampton on 4 September.

C Use of Language

Part 1

a) a lot of

b) ago

c) from

d) enough
   Hinweis: Auch wenn „nicht viel Nahrung" ebenfalls einen Sinn ergeben würde, stimmt „many" nicht, weil hier eine Verneinung und ein unzählbares Substantiv vorliegen = not much food.

e) always

f) because

Part 2

a) gain
   Hinweis: Z. 8

b) more
   Hinweis: Z. 10

c) late
   Hinweis: Z. 14

Part 3

a) a lot of
   Hinweis: Z. 7

b) close to
   Hinweis: Z. 16

c) look for
   Hinweis: Z. 17

Part 4

Lösungsbeispiele:

a) bin: a container in which you put rubbish

b) to chase: someone runs after you and tries to catch you.

c) to lock: you can use a key to lock a door, for example, so that it can't be opened.

Part 5

Lösungsbeispiele:
– How many polar bears are there in Canada?
– What age can polar bears reach?
– Why are polar bears white?

D Writing

Part 1

Hinweis: Hier verfasst du eine Nachricht an einen Brieffreund, in der du ihm von deinen Urlaubsplänen berichtest. Achte darauf, dass du in deinem Text auf alle inhaltlichen Vorgaben eingehst. Halte dich auch an die angegebene Textlänge. Der folgende Text ist ein Lösungsbeispiel.

Hi Jason,

You asked me about my holiday plans. In August, I'm going to visit my aunt, uncle and cousins in Australia. My brother is coming with me. Aunt Lisa and Uncle Dan live in Sydney. I would like to see the Opera House and walk on Harbour Bridge. I would also like to go surfing at Bondi Beach and go on a trip to the Outback – and I would love to see kangaroos!

Take care!

(your name) *(76 words)*

Part 2

Hinweis: Hier sollst du mit Hilfe der Vorgaben einen Text von mindestens 80 Wörtern über deinen Lieblingsstar schreiben.

My favourite star is not a singer or YouTuber, but a student from Sweden. Her name is Greta Thunberg. She was born in January 2003. In 2018, she started the "Fridays for Future" strikes to fight for climate protection. Millions of students have already taken part in the strikes. Greta and the students want to put pressure on people to stop destroying our planet and they want politicians to do much more to protect the climate. I think Greta is a special person because what she does is great! *(89 words)*

B Text-based Tasks

Part 1

a) C
   Hinweis: hazard = Gefahr
b) C
   Hinweis: to display = zeigen, sichtbar machen
c) B
   Hinweis: unless = außer wenn
d) A
   Hinweis: not permitted = not allowed
e) B
   Hinweis: to steer = steuern

Part 2

a) – C
b) – A
c) – E
d) – B
e) – D

Part 3

a) false
   Hinweis: "Rainwater is collected in large containers and sent through a system that waters the rooftop garden." (Z. 9 f.)
b) true
   Hinweis: "The roof is filled with green life that appeals to insects." (Z. 10 f.)
c) true
   Hinweis: "'… we're trying just to see which variety grows the best in a green roof setting.'" (Z. 24 f.)
d) not in the text
e) true
   Hinweis: "She says she's been surprised by the garden's output. 'My biggest surprise was that we produced 4,250 pounds of produce the first year …'" (Z. 33 f.)

Part 4

a) C
   Hinweis: "(Water is a necessity of life.) Rain, especially, helps plants grow and stay green." (Z. 1)
b) E
   Hinweis: "Rainwater is collected in large containers and sent through a system that waters the rooftop garden." (Z. 9 f.)
c) F
   Hinweis: "… rooftops are just (unused) space …" (Z. 14 f.)
d) H
   Hinweis: "… UDC's Master Gardener program. It seeks to improve cities and make them beautiful by training people to become Master Gardeners." (Z. 31 ff.)
e) B
   Hinweis: "(… food can be grown on a rooftop.) 'This is the future for food'." (Z. 37 f.)

Part 5

a) C
   Hinweis: "But too much rain – especially in cities – can lead to flooding." (Z. 2)
b) A
   Hinweis: "The garden holds many kinds of plants to help absorb rainwater …" (Z. 7 f.); absorb = soak up
c) B
   Hinweis: "In cities, 'you don't have that many spaces to choose from and so rooftops are just (unused) space,' …" (Z. 12 ff.)
d) C
   Hinweis: "'We have the same experiment running with tomatoes as we do with strawberries, so we're doing variety trials …'" (Z. 23 f.)
e) C
   Hinweis: "This is the future for food." (Z. 37 f.)

a) C
  Hinweis: "Yellowstone's hotels always celebrate Christmas in August with Christmas trees and decorations." (Z. 10 ff.)

b) B
  Hinweis: "A long time ago there was a heavy snow storm in summer – it can happen ..." (Z. 15 f.)

c) C
  Hinweis: "Have you got any other good stories from Yellowstone? They're more fun than just talking about animals and geysers." (Z. 25 ff.)

d) B
  Hinweis: "In 1914, one robber stopped 25 stagecoaches ..." (Z. 39 f.)

e) A
  Hinweis: "Come on, Greg, the good guys always win!" (Z. 45)

Part 4

John: My name's John and I'm 35. I've got a very stressful job, and I hardly ever go on holiday, but when I find the time, I only want to relax, so my wife and I usually go to a luxurious boutique hotel on Vancouver Island that doesn't allow small children. We go for long walks in the woods, get massages, go to the sauna and enjoy the fantastic food there.

Olivia: Hi, I'm Olivia and I'm a student at the University of British Columbia. I'm 21 and I love travelling, but I don't want to be seen as a tourist. Since I don't have much money, I usually go couchsurfing when I'm abroad. It's a great and cheap way to meet locals, make new friends and explore places far away from the typical tourist paths.

Hailey: I'm Hailey and I'm 25 years old. I wouldn't like to go couchsurfing. I think it's dangerous to stay at the house of someone you don't know. I love travelling, but I don't earn much money, so I always stay at youth hostels. I always choose a small hostel so that there's a cosy atmosphere and travellers get in touch with each other easily.

Carter: Hello, my name's Carter and I'm 16. In my summer vacation I usually go camping with my friends. I love hiking and fishing and being outside 24/7, so I wouldn't like to spend my holidays in any other way. My parents, in contrast, usually go on city trips together with their friends from the golf club.

Josh: Camping is great, isn't it? I'm Josh and I'm 15. My parents bought a large mobile home five years ago, so we always go camping. I like sleeping in the comfy bed of the mobile home, whereas my younger brother always sleeps in a tent. We always go to the same campsite, which is great, because we meet the same people every year.

a) John – D
  Hinweis: "... go to a luxurious boutique hotel ..." (Z. 4)

b) Olivia – F
  Hinweis: "... I usually go couchsurfing when I'm abroad. It's a great and cheap way to meet locals ..." (Z. 12 ff.)

c) Hailey – A
  Hinweis: "... I always stay at youth hostels. I always choose a small hostel ..." (Z. 19 ff.)

d) Carter – B
  Hinweis: "... I usually go camping with my friends. I love hiking and fishing and being outside 24/7 ..." (Z. 24 ff.)

e) Josh – C
  Hinweis: "My parents bought a large mobile home five years ago, so we always go camping. I like sleeping in the comfy bed of the mobile home ..." (Z. 31 ff.)

Part 2

On November 11, 1926, a 3,900 km long highway was established in the United States. It was not the first American highway. It was not the longest either. And it might not have been the fastest. But the road inspired musicians, writers and filmmakers. It appealed to explorers and dreamers. It's known as the Route 66. The road cuts through cornfields, deserts, mountains and unusual red rock formations of the west. As the scene outside the car window changes, so, too, do the people and cultures found along the road.

It was disaster that fuelled the road's early success. A series of powerful dust storms in the 1930s destroyed a huge amount of farmland across the prairie states. Hundreds of thousands of mostly poor farm workers and their families began to leave. The migrants headed west on Route 66, hoping the path would lead to a better life in California, the land of opportunity. Exploring the open road has long been an important part of the American experience. And Route 66 became even more popular as the car culture exploded in the 1940s and 50s. However, by the 1960s, large parts of Route 66 were not fit for driving.

The U.S. government built bigger highways, with faster speed limits and fewer traffic lights. These new interstates bypassed small towns, the heart of Route 66. Many of these small towns had depended on Route 66 for business and income. The economies of bypassed small towns suffered. When the traffic stopped on Route 66, so did many of the towns themselves.

Abridged and adapted from: Ashley Thompson and Caty Weaver: Route 66: 'The Highway that's The Best', in: Voice of America Learning English

a) The highway wasn't the first, the longest or the **fastest**.
   Hinweis: "And it might not have been the fastest." (Z. 4)

b) The dust storms happened during the **1930s**.
   Hinweis: "A series of powerful dust storms in the 1930s …" (Z. 12 f.)

c) The people who left wanted **a better** life in California.
   Hinweis: "… hoping the path would lead to a better life in California …" (Z. 17 f.)

d) The 1940s and 50s saw the rise of the **car** culture.
   Hinweis: "… the car culture exploded in the 1940s and 50s." (Z. 21 f.)

e) The new highways were faster and didn't have many **traffic lights**.
   Hinweis: "… highways, with faster speed limits and fewer traffic lights." (Z. 24 f.)

Part 3

Greg: Hi Sina, how was your trip?
Sina: It was really great – Yellowstone National Park is huge and there's a lot to see there.
Greg: Old Faithful, I guess, and a few buffalo.
Sina: Actually, they're called bison. And, they're big. At Christmas we opened our cabin door and there was one looking at us. I didn't know what to do.
Greg: Wait a minute – I thought you went in August.
Sina: We did *(laughs)* … but it was Christmas there – honest. Let me explain: Yellowstone's hotels always celebrate Christmas in August with Christmas trees and decorations.
Greg: Why do they do that? It's weird.
Sina: There are two stories really – I like the first one. A long time ago there was a heavy snow storm in summer – it can happen – and some visitors to the Park couldn't leave their hotel for many days, so, they decided to have some fun and pretend it was Christmas.
Greg: I think I would have done that, too. And the other story?
Sina: It's boring. It's just about the people who work in the Park – so let's forget it. I like the snow one best.
Greg: Have you got any other good stories from Yellowstone? They're more fun than just talking about animals and geysers.
Sina: Oh, Greg! Bison, wolves and bears are cool and the geysers are great, but … I did hear another story.
Greg: Go on, tell me … is it more snow or Easter eggs in December?
Sina: Now you're just being silly. No, it's about robbers.
Greg: Robbers? Real cowboys … the Wild West, and all that?
Sina: I knew you'd like this story … and it's true! A long time ago visitors came by stagecoach and sometimes they were robbed. In 1914, one robber stopped 25 stagecoaches and robbed 165 passengers. He took over $ 1,000 – and lots of jewellery, too.
Greg: Wow, that's some story … did they catch the robber?
Sina: Come on, Greg, the good guys always win!

Aufgabe im Stil der Prüfung

Allgemeiner Hinweis: Lies dir alle Aufgaben und Texte zuerst genau durch, damit du weißt, worauf du beim Bearbeiten achten musst. Sieh dir die Lösungen erst an, wenn du alles bearbeitet hast. Außer in Teil A (Hörverstehen) darfst du in der Prüfung auch ein Wörterbuch benutzen. Schlage jedoch nur für das Verständnis wichtige Wörter nach, da du sonst zu viel Zeit verlierst. Beachte, dass du in den Teilen A–C deine Antworten direkt auf dem Aufgabenblatt notieren bzw. ankreuzen sollst. In Teil D schreibst du deine Lösungen auf ein extra Blatt.

A Listening Comprehension

Part 1

Question 1
Where does Tom want to go on holiday?
Jane: Where should we go on holiday this year, Tom?
Tom: I don't want to go to a city again. We went to one last year.
Jane: I'd like to go to Japan – we haven't been there yet.
Tom: I'm not sure I want to go there. I'd like to go somewhere different.
Jane: Like where? South Africa? Australia?
Tom: A safari in South Africa sounds fun. I'll see what's on the internet about it.

a) C
Hinweis: "A safari in South Africa sounds fun. I'll see what's on the internet about it." (Z. 9 f.)

Question 2
What does the man need?
Man: Excuse me, please. Can you help me?
Woman: Of course. Are you lost?
Man: No, I'm not. I just need some change for the ticket machine. It just takes coins or cards and I've only got a £ 5 note.
Woman: I'm sorry, I can't change that. Ask in the shop over there.
Man: Thank you, I'll do that.

b) B
Hinweis: "I just need some change for the ticket machine." (Z. 13 f.)

Question 3
How many minutes late is the train today?
Tina: I hate this train at the moment. Every day it arrives at a different time.
George: What time should it arrive?
Tina: At 6.33. But yesterday it was 10 minutes late, on Monday it was 13 minutes early and today it's 30 minutes late! Who knows when it will come tomorrow!
George: It's very annoying, isn't it?
Tina: Yes, it is, ... especially when you use it every day to get to work.

c) C
Hinweis: "... today it's 30 minutes late!" (Z. 23 f.)

Question 4
What did the bird take?
Phil: Hi, Julia. I'm going to Whitby tomorrow with my class.
Julia: That'll be fun.
Phil: Hope so, ... and I'm going to have some fish and chips and an ice cream.
Julia: Whitby has the best fish and chips in the world.
Phil: And the worst seagulls! Last year I was eating my fish and chips outside and one flew down and stole my fish! I only had my chips left!
Julia: A flying thief ... how cool is that!

d) B
Hinweis: "... and stole my fish!" (Z. 36 f.)

Question 5
Which question is difficult?
Teacher: Good morning everyone. So, how far did we get yesterday?
Sam: We'd just finished question 14 on page 40.
Teacher: That's right ... and today we're going to do questions 15 and 16.
Sam: Can I say something first?
Teacher: Of course, Sam, go on.
Sam: Most of us had a problem with number 14 ... I don't think anyone has got it right.
Teacher: Oh dear ... let's look at it again then before we do something new.

e) A
Hinweis: "Most of us had a problem with number 14 ... I don't think anyone has got it right." (Z. 46 f.)

German tourist: Noch eine Frage: Können wir im Hotel auch Karten für das Musical „Lion King" kaufen?
You: **They have one more question: can they also buy tickets for the "Lion King" musical at the hotel?**
Receptionist: I'm afraid we don't sell theater tickets. You can buy them at the theaters on Broadway or at the ticket office on Times Square.
You: **Leider verkaufen sie keine Theaterkarten im Hotel, aber Sie können sie in den Theatern am Broadway oder im Ticketbüro am Times Square kaufen.**
German tourist: Danke für den Tipp.

Aufgabe 9

Beispiellösung:

English tourist: Hello, could you help me, please? I would like to have this T-shirt in blue.
You: **Die Dame/Der Herr möchte dieses T-Shirt gerne in Blau haben.**
Shop assistant: Ja, klar, hier bitte.
You: **Sure. Here you are.**
English tourist: Thank you. Where can I put it on?
You: **Wo kann er/sie es anprobieren?**
Shop assistant: Da drüben sind die Umkleidekabinen.
You: **The changing rooms are over there.**
English tourist: Thank you. *(A while later)* This T-shirt is too big. Can I have it in a size smaller?
You: **Das T-Shirt ist zu groß. Haben Sie es auch eine Größe kleiner?**
Shop assistant: Sicher, hier ist Größe S.
You: **Sure, here is size S / a smaller one.**
English tourist: Thanks. That should fit now.
You: **Danke, das sollte jetzt passen.**
Shop assistant: Möchten Sie noch etwas?
You: **Would you like anything else?**
English tourist: I'll take these two postcards as well. Do you sell stamps?
You: **Er/Sie nimmt auch diese zwei Postkarten. Verkaufen Sie auch Briefmarken?**
Shop assistant: Ja, verkaufen wir auch.
You: **Yes, they sell them/those too.**
English tourist: Great. Thank you!

Candidate B: At 4 pm and 8 pm.
Candidate A: Do have special prices for students?
Candidate B: Yes, we do. You pay only £4 per ticket as a student.
Candidate A: Can I buy snacks and drinks?
Candidate B: Yes you can buy soft drinks, popcorn and several other snacks.
Candidate A: Do you sell film posters?
Candidate B: Yes, we have them on sale.
Candidate A: Do you have any special offers?
Candidate B: On Tuesdays you get a ticket, a soft drink and a snack for £7.50.
Candidate A: Thank you for the information.

Aufgabe 7

Hinweis: Mithilfe der Vorlagen könnt ihr zu dritt eine Sprachmittlungssituation üben. Die Person, die sprachmitteln muss, bekommt die Vorlage nicht zu sehen. Die beiden anderen nehmen die Rolle der Lehrkraft (spricht Englisch) bzw. des Mitprüflings (spricht Deutsch) ein und lesen jeweils ihren Text vor. Bei den folgenden Aufgaben können die Rollen gewechselt werden, sodass alle einmal sprachmitteln müssen.

Beispiellösung:

German tourist: Entschuldigen Sie, ich würde hier gerne ein Fahrrad mieten. Können Sie mir helfen?
You: Ja, gerne. (An den Angestellten/die Angestellte:) The lady/gentleman would like to rent a bike.
Assistant: Yes, of course. How long would he/she like to rent the bike for?
You: Natürlich. Für wie lange möchten Sie das Fahrrad leihen?
German tourist: Ich möchte gerne eines für zwei Tage mieten. Wie viel kostet das?
You: He/She would like to rent one for two days. How much would that be/cost?
Assistant: That would be € 30.
You: Das würde 30 € kosten.
German tourist: Das passt. Kann ich mir gleich eines aussuchen?
You: That would be OK: can he/she choose one right now?
Assistant: Yes, sure. We have a lot of different bikes on offer. Where would he/she like to ride the bike – in the city or in the countryside?
You: Sie haben viele verschiedene Fahrräder im Angebot. Möchten Sie in der Stadt fahren oder auf dem Land?
German tourist: Ich würde nur in der Stadt fahren. Welches Rad kann er/sie mir empfehlen?
You: He/She would only ride the bike in the city. Which bike can you recommend?
Assistant: This nice red city bike, for example.
You: Dieses schöne rote Stadtrad, zum Beispiel.
German tourist: Ja, das sieht schön aus. Kann ich es ausprobieren?
You: He/She likes it. Can he/she try it?
Assistant: Yes, of course. Go ahead.
You: Ja, natürlich. Probieren Sie es aus.
German tourist: Dankeschön.

Aufgabe 8

Beispiellösung:

German tourist: Hallo, mein Name ist Elisabeth Schmidt. Ich habe für meinen Mann und mich ein Zimmer reserviert.
You: Mrs Schmidt has booked a room for herself and her husband.
Receptionist: Yes, Mrs Schmidt … Your reservation is from August 15th to 18th. Could I have your passports and your credit card, please?
You: Er/Sie hat Ihre Reservierung vom 15. bis 18. August bestätigt und möchte nun Ihre Pässe und die Kreditkarte sehen.
German tourist: Hier sind unsere Pässe und die Kreditkarte.
You: Here they are.
Receptionist: Thank you very much.
You: Vielen Dank.
German tourist: Können Sie uns morgen um 7 Uhr aufwecken?
You: Can you wake them up at 7 am, please?
Receptionist: Sure, we can do that. Here's your key. Your room number is 223.
You: Ja, das können sie machen. Hier ist Ihr Schlüssel und Ihre Zimmernummer ist 223.
German tourist: Dankeschön. Wo und wann können wir denn das Frühstück zu uns nehmen?
You: Where and when can they have breakfast?
Receptionist: Breakfast is served from 7 to 10 am. The breakfast room is on the first floor.
You: Frühstück gibt es von 7 bis 10 Uhr. Der Frühstücksraum ist im Erdgeschoss.

Aufgabe 4

Hinweis: Teile deinen Vortrag nun in Einleitung, Hauptteil und Schluss:
In der Einleitung nennst du dein Thema und warum du es gewählt hast. Versuche im Hauptteil deinen Vortrag gut zu strukturieren. Finde auch sinnvolle Übergänge zwischen den einzelnen Abschnitten. Am Ende deines Vortrags kannst du z. B. deine eigene Meinung erwähnen bzw. eine Empfehlung geben. Der Schluss kann aber auch in einem Satz eine Zusammenfassung des Gesagten enthalten.
Übe nun deinen Vortrag mehrmals und versuche dabei, immer weniger auf deinen Text zu schauen und immer freier zu sprechen. Abschließend kannst du dein Referat einem Freund/einer Freundin oder der Familie vortragen.

Beispiellösung:

Einleitung:
Today I'd like to tell you something about the "Harry Potter" books. I started reading them when I was ten years old and I have finished all of the seven books by now. I really love the characters and the story is thrilling!

Hauptteil:
The main characters are Harry Potter, Ron Weasley and Hermione Granger. They are friends and they are pupils at Hogwarts, a school for wizards. Harry's parents were killed by Voldemort, an evil wizard, when he was only a baby. From then on he had to live with his aunt, uncle and cousin, who treated him badly. On his eleventh birthday Harry finds out that he is a wizard and is taken to Hogwarts, where he finds a new home. Harry, however, is in danger: Voldemort tries to gain power again and kill Harry, because he was not able to kill him when he was a baby because Harry's mother protected him. From then on Harry has to fight his biggest enemy and often gets into really dangerous situations, but he's very brave and his friends help him. As the story continues you learn more and more about Harry's parents and what happened in the past. The story also grows darker and darker, so it isn't for the fainthearted – but, fortunately, the good side wins!
However, it's not only the thrilling story I like but also the fact that the books are about friendship and love. There are also a lot of lovable or funny characters at Hogwarts, such as Hagrid, the gamekeeper, or some of the ghosts.

Schluss:
I can really recommend reading the books. You can identify with Harry and his friends and the story contains so many details that you can read the books over and over again without getting bored.

(294 words)

Aufgabe 5

Hinweis: Anhand der vorgegebenen Karten mit den „Prompts" kannst du mit einem Freund/einer Freundin oder jemandem in deiner Familie schon einmal die Prüfungssituation einüben. Eine von euch stellt die Fragen auf ihrer Karte, der andere hat die Karte mit den entsprechenden Informationen und beantwortet die Fragen. Versucht, das Gespräch so natürlich und flüssig wie möglich zu führen.

Beispiellösung:

Candidate A: Hello, this is … I would like to rent a bike with your company. What kind of bikes do you offer?
Candidate B: Oh, we have a huge choice of bikes.
Candidate A: Great! How long can you rent a bike for?
Candidate B: From several hours to one week.
Candidate A: What are the prices?
Candidate B: It's £ 9 a day per person.
Candidate A: I see. Do you have special offers?
Candidate B: Yes, we offer special family rates. You pay only £ 60 for four people for one week.
Candidate A: What about an insurance?
Candidate B: Insurance is included in the price and it covers damage and theft.
Candidate A: Do you have any more information?
Candidate B: Yes, we can give you the addresses of small hotels that have storage places for bikes.
Candidate A: Great. Thank you!

Aufgabe 6

Hinweis: Im zweiten Dialog der Prüfung tauscht ihr die Rollen: wer zuerst die Fragen gestellt hat, antwortet nun und umgekehrt. Achtet wieder darauf, dass euer Gespräch so natürlich wie möglich ist.

Beispiellösung:

Candidate A: Hello. I'd like to know if you're showing any new films?
Candidate B: Yes, the new films are *Squirrels Gone Nuts 2* and *All About You*.
Candidate A: When do you show them?

Kompetenzbereich: Speaking

Allgemeiner Hinweis: Du findest hier Aufgaben zu allen Bereichen der Kommunikationsprüfung. Lies die Aufgabenstellungen genau durch, dann bist du auch in der Prüfung schon darauf vorbereitet, wie die einzelnen Teile, v. a. das dialogische Sprechen und die Sprachmittlung, ablaufen.

Aufgabe 1

Hinweis: Überlege dir bis zu sechs Stichpunkte, auf die du in deinem Vortrag zum Thema „Holidays" eingehen möchtest. Du kannst in einem Brainstorming deiner Fantasie dabei freien Lauf lassen. Erst im zweiten Schritt (Aufgabe 2) musst du deine Ideen strukturieren und ausformulieren.

Beispiellösung:

Mindmap "Holidays": Spain, without parents, volleyball, made Spanish friends, beach, sea

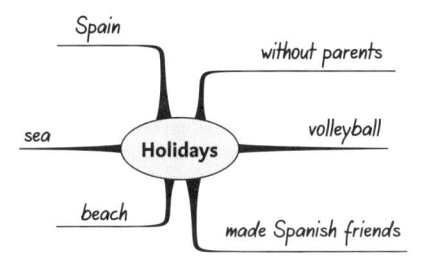

Aufgabe 2

Hinweis: Hier musst du deinen Vortrag nun in Einleitung, Hauptteil und Schluss einteilen.
In der Einleitung nennst du dein Thema und warum du es gewählt hast. Versuche im Hauptteil deinen Vortrag gut zu strukturieren. Finde auch sinnvolle Übergänge zwischen den einzelnen Abschnitten. Am Ende deines Vortrags kannst du z. B. eine abschließende Bewertung abgeben. Der Schluss kann aber auch in einem Satz eine Zusammenfassung des Gesagten enthalten.
Übe nun deinen Vortrag mehrmals und versuche dabei, immer weniger auf deinen Text zu schauen und immer freier zu sprechen. Zum Schluss kannst du dein Referat einem Freund/einer Freundin oder der Familie vortragen.

Beispiellösung:

Einleitung:
I'm going to tell you about my last holiday because it was the first one I've had without my parents. I went to Spain with my volleyball team and it was one of the best holidays I've ever had!

Hauptteil:
On the first day we visited Barcelona. It's a really beautiful city. Then we went to the Costa Brava, where we stayed at a nice little hotel at the beach. The sand was almost white and really soft. It was very hot and the sun was shining every day, so we ate a lot of ice-cream to cool off a bit! We spent most of the time at the beach, where we also played beach volleyball. One day some Spanish teenagers asked us to play with them. That was so much fun! After a couple of games we found out that we were staying at the same hotel and we became good friends. Before we left for the airport, we started a WhatsApp group so that we could stay in touch with each other. It would be great to see them again!

Schluss:
So I really enjoyed my holiday in Spain! It was great to travel with a group and to meet new people. Next year my volleyball team are going to Italy or maybe Portugal – and I'll definitely join them again!

(219 words)

Aufgabe 3

Hinweis: Überlege dir bis zu sechs Stichpunkte/ Themen, auf die du in deinem Vortrag zum Thema „Harry Potter" eingehen möchtest. Lasse dabei in einem Brainstorming deiner Fantasie freien Lauf. Erst im zweiten Schritt (Aufgabe 4) musst du deine Ideen strukturieren und ausformulieren.

Beispiellösung:

Mindmap "Harry Potter": fan since age ten, read all the books, read the books!, topics: friendship + love, lovable and funny characters, thrilling story

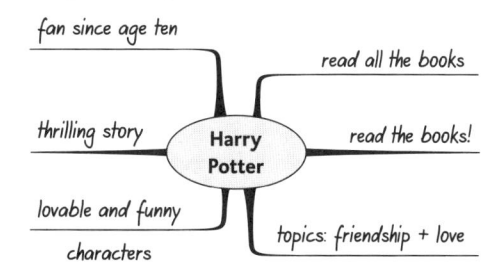

Beispiellösung:

Hi Danny,

How are you? My name is Tobias Schmidt, I'm 15 years old and I'm in Year 9 at a *Gemeinschaftsschule*. When you are here I'll show you my favourite places in Stuttgart. That's where I live with my mum, Sarah, and my little sister, Lena.

What about your family – do you have any brothers and sisters?

What can we do in Dublin? Maybe we could go to the St. Patrick's Day Festival?

Take care,
Tobi *(77 words)*

Aufgabe 6

Hinweis: Dies ist eine förmliche E-Mail. Achte deshalb auf die richtige Anrede und den korrekten Schluss. Da du den Namen des Ansprechpartners/der Ansprechpartnerin nicht kennst, musst du hier „Dear Sir or Madam" und „Yours faithfully" verwenden. Kurzformen wie „I'd" oder „don't" solltest du vermeiden. Gehe auf alle Punkte ein, und versuche, mindestens 60 Wörter zu schreiben.

Beispiellösung:

Dear Sir or Madam,

My name is Paul Maier, I am 16 years old and I am leaving school in June. In the summer I would like to do some volunteer work in England. Working with children or disabled people would be great. I have already done some work experience at a school for children with special needs, which was very interesting. Maybe you can find something similar for me in July and August? Could you also offer accommodation during my stay?

I am looking forward to hearing from you soon.

Yours faithfully,
Paul Maier *(95 words)*

Aufgabe 7

Hinweis: Hier verfasst du eine E-Mail an einen Brieffreund/eine Brieffreundin. Baue alle geforderten Angaben ein. Beachte, dass du in ganzen Sätzen schreibst und mindestens 60 Wörter verwendest.

Beispiellösung:

Dear Liam,

How are you? You are going to Italy this summer? I was there last year and it was fabulous. I went with my grandparents for a week in August. The weather was warm and sunny and we went to see a lot of tourist attractions, like the Leaning Tower of Pisa and the Colosseum in Rome. In Rome, we stayed in a small hotel in the centre. It was very loud at night and the rooms were pretty expensive!

If you like, I can send you some pictures of the trip.

See you soon,
Tina *(97 words)*

Aufgabe 8

Hinweis: Bei dieser Aufgabe sollst du über deinen perfekten Ort zum Leben schreiben. Hierfür kannst du die Ideen in den Kästen verwenden. Achte auf vollständige Sätze und versuche, sie durch Konjunktionen miteinander zu verbinden. Der Text muss mindestens 80 Wörter umfassen.

Beispiellösung:

What do I think is the perfect place to live? That is easy to answer. I love the sun and warm temperatures, like in Spain or Greece, so that I can wear shorts and a T-shirt most of the time. It would be great to live in a big house by the sea with my family and friends. We could relax at the beach and have a swim or have breakfast outside in the morning. I also fancy a place with lots of things to do like sports or exciting trips to the countryside. The best thing would be to combine both options.

(103 words)

Aufgabe 9

Hinweis: Deine Aufgabe ist es hier, einen Text über deinen Traumberuf zu verfassen, wobei du mindestens 80 Wörter verwenden sollst. Die Fragen und Wörter in den Kästen helfen dir beim Schreiben.

Beispiellösung:

I have always wanted to be a vet. I live on a farm with a lot of animals such as pigs, cows, geese, rabbits and chicken. My father is a vet and he often lets me help him and I can do a lot on my own. I think it is great to help sick animals to get well again. I love animals! As a vet you have to work hard and sometimes very long hours. The pay is not so good either, but nevertheless I would love to become a vet!

(92 words)

Kompetenzbereich: Writing

Allgemeiner Hinweis: Für den Bereich „Writing" ist es hilfreich, dass du die Arbeitsschritte und Tipps zum Verfassen eines Textes zu Beginn des Kapitels genau durchliest und dementsprechend vorgehst. Wenn du dich daran hältst, wird es dir nicht schwerfallen, einen guten, flüssigen Text zu schreiben.

Aufgabe 1

Hinweis: Hier musst du noch keinen vollständigen Text schreiben, sondern die unterstrichenen Wörter z. B. durch Adjektive näher beschreiben. So trainierst du, deine Texte anschaulicher und abwechslungsreicher zu gestalten.

Beispiellösungen:

a) The **small/beautiful/old** house at the end of the street is ours.
b) Mum told me to give away my **old** T-shirts.
c) Jack loves sitting in his room and listening to **loud/beautiful** music.
d) Take off your **dirty** shoes!
e) I live in a **small/beautiful**/an **old** village.
f) Sarah wore a **light** blue dress at her birthday party.
g) We travelled a lot during our **summer** holidays.

Aufgabe 2

Hinweis: Konjunktionen helfen dir, Sätze elegant zu verknüpfen und nicht nur aneinanderzureihen. Es ist hilfreich, wenn du sie mit Beispielsätzen in deine Vokabelkartei bzw. -datei aufnimmst.

a) I took an umbrella with me this morning **because** it was raining.
b) **When** I'm 18 years old I will move out.
c) I'd love to visit New York, **but** I don't have enough money.
d) **Although** Jack had studied a lot, he did not pass the exam.
e) Claire washes the dishes **while** she is talking to her best friend on the phone.

Aufgabe 3

Hinweis: Die Wendungen zu Beginn des Kapitels helfen dir, diese Aufgabe zu lösen. Es ist hilfreich, wenn du sie auswendig lernst.

a) Dear (Aunt) Mary — Best wishes/Love
b) Dear Mrs Smith — Yours sincerely
c) Dear/Hi Luke — Best wishes/(Love) Cheers
d) Dear Mr O'Brien — Yours sincerely/ Kind regards
e) Dear Grandma and Granddad — Best wishes/Love
f) Dear Sir or Madam — Yours faithfully

Aufgabe 4

Hinweis: Schreibe hier eine Antwort auf einen Post. Schritt für Schritt wird dir dabei auf Englisch vorgegeben, auf welche Aspekte du antworten sollst.

Beispiellösung:

Dear Jack,

I read your post about musicals and I disagree with you. Musicals are not boring.
I went to see "The Phantom of the Opera" in Oberhausen and I enjoyed it a lot. The music was wonderful and the story was exciting.
Musicals are never boring. Everybody should go and see one!

Kind regards,

(your name)

Aufgabe 5

Hinweis: Da du hier eine persönliche E-Mail verfasst, musst du nicht in einem förmlichen Stil schreiben, sondern kannst z. B. auch Kurzformen verwenden. Lies dir genau durch, was du in deiner Mail an Danny schreiben und was du ihn fragen sollst.

c) Zoe is jealous that her brother is going to take a trip.
d) Zoe's aunt promises that she can visit them soon too.

Test 1: London

Part 1

a) people
  Hinweis: „people" = „Leute/Menschen"; „peoples" = „Völker"
b) everyone
  *Hinweis: „for everyone" = „für jeden*jede"*
c) for
d) where
  Hinweis: In dem Relativsatz geht es um einen Ort: „where the Queen lives" = „wo die Queen wohnt"
e) next
  Hinweis: Hier passt nur „next", da ein „to" folgt: „next to" = „neben"
f) discover
  Hinweis: „to discover" = „entdecken"

Part 2

a) big
  Hinweis: Z. 1
b) always
  Hinweis: Z. 5

Part 3

a) fantastic
  Hinweis: Z. 8
b) lots of
  Hinweis: Z. 4

Part 4

Lösungsbeispiele:

a) (almost) everyone has heard of it / known of by lots of people
b) interesting or famous buildings or places visited by a lot of tourists / tourist attractions
c) not cheap / costing a lot of money

Part 5

Lösungsbeispiele:

– When was London founded?
– How much is a ride on the London Eye?
– What else can you do in London?

Test 2: The Grand Canyon

Part 1

a) largest
  Hinweis: Der korrekte Superlativ von „large" („groß") ist „largest".
b) than
  Hinweis: „more than" = „mehr als"
c) Because of
  Hinweis: „because of" = „wegen"
d) different
e) takes
  Hinweis: „it takes several hours" = „man braucht mehrere Stunden"
f) place
  Hinweis: „the only place" = „der einzige Ort"

Part 2

a) often
  Hinweis: Z. 12
b) above
  Hinweis: Z. 20

Part 3

a) may
  Hinweis: Z. 13
b) see
  Hinweis: Z. 22

Part 4

Lösungsbeispiele:

a) very old
b) to give money to someone when you buy something
c) very big / large

Part 5

Lösungsbeispiele:

– How old is the Grand Canyon?
– Is the Grand Canyon the biggest canyon in the United States?
– When is the best time to visit the Grand Canyon?

Aufgabe 31

Hinweis: Die hier geforderten Zukunftsformen findest du ebenfalls im Kapitel „Zeiten – tenses".

a) I <u>am going to meet</u> Jessie for dinner on Saturday.
   Hinweis: geplante Handlung

b) On Monday, I <u>am going to go</u> to the hairdresser's at 3 p.m.
   Hinweis: geplante Handlung

c) After that I <u>am going to buy</u> a birthday present for my brother.
   Hinweis: geplante Handlung

d) He <u>will turn</u> 12 next Sunday.
   Hinweis: Die Tatsache, dass jemand 12 Jahre alt wird, kann man nicht planen oder beeinflussen.

e) I hope the weather <u>will be</u> good on Sunday.
   Hinweis: Du kannst das Wetter nicht beeinflussen, also kann dies keine geplante Handlung sein.

Aufgabe 32

Hinweis: Diese Aufgabe ist etwas schwieriger, weil keine Zeitform vorgegeben ist. Signalwörter wie „yesterday" können dir helfen, die richtige Lösung zu finden. Wenn du dir unsicher bist, dann lies in der Kurzgrammatik noch einmal den Abschnitt zu den Zeiten durch.

a) I <u>felt</u> very sick yesterday, so I went to bed early. Now <u>I am feeling</u> much better.

b) "I <u>haven't been</u> to the cinema for ages. Thank you so much for the ticket!"

c) My little brother <u>was</u> born in 2010.

d) My parents <u>have been married</u> for 20 years.

e) I <u>am going to travel</u>/<u>am travelling</u> to Australia for three weeks in January. I can't stand the winter here any longer.

f) "Jenny, <u>have you eaten</u> my cake?! There's nothing left!"

g) My parents <u>gave</u> me these headphones for my birthday last week.

Aufgabe 33

Emma: <u>Do you have</u>/<u>Have you got</u> tickets for the Rihanna concert?

Shop assistant: No, I'm sorry. We <u>sold</u> the last one yesterday.

Emma: What a pity! But what about the open air festival which <u>takes place</u> in August?

Shop assistant: Yes, we <u>still have</u> tickets for the festival.

Aufgabe 34

Hinweis: Hier musst du sowohl das passende Relativpronomen („who" für Personen und „which" für Dinge) finden, als auch den Relativsatz, der sich sinnvoll auf den Hauptsatz bezieht.

1	2	3	4	5
who	who	which	which	who
D	C	E	B	A

Aufgabe 35

Hinweis: Wenn bei der indirekten Rede das einleitende Verb, z. B. „wrote", in der Vergangenheit steht, musst du darauf achten, dass das Verb im Nebensatz eine Zeitstufe zurückversetzt wird. Auch die Pronomen, Orts- und Zeitangaben müssen geändert werden. Im Grammatik-Kapitel „Indirekte Rede – reported speech" findest du eine genaue Übersicht über die Veränderungen von der direkten zur indirekten Rede.

a) Sam writes that he is going to Spain this year.

b) Jason wrote that his bus arrived at 8 p.m.

c) Emily and Jessica told me that they had had a test the week before.

d) Daniel wrote that he was going to buy a new smartphone the next day.

e) Lisa wrote me that her sister was not at home.

f) Mum told me that she had left for Dublin to go shopping.

g) Jackie mentioned that her brother worked in New York.

Aufgabe 36

Hinweis: Die englischen Wortstellungsregeln kannst du noch einmal im Grammatik-Kapitel „Wortstellung – word order" nachlesen.

a) Paul is going to visit his aunt and uncle in California.

b) They invited him to spend the summer with them.

and say sorry to her. You will stay behind after school and clean up the classroom." Jack is very angry and says, "It wasn't me!" He points at Tim: "He did it – it was all his fault!" Mrs Brown turns to the whole class and says, "All of you saw them / him take the jacket and throw it out of the window, and did any of you help Maggie? No, you didn't. I have decided that you will all stay behind after school and clean up the classroom. Maggie, you go to Lisa's house straight after school, return the jacket to her and explain what we / they did at school today. And now, everyone, please show me your homework!"

Aufgabe 25

Hinweis: Hier musst du die einzelnen Satzteile so zusammenfügen, dass sie einen Satz im Passiv ergeben. Wie das Passiv gebildet wird, kannst du dir im entsprechenden Kapitel in der Kurzgrammatik noch einmal durchlesen.

a) The message is written by Laura.
b) The last ticket was bought by Sarah.
c) The window has been closed by Paul.
d) The hamburger was eaten by Lisa.
e) The pen is given to Jack by Tony.

Aufgabe 26

Hinweis: Präpositionen musst du auswendig lernen (am besten zusammen mit dem jeweiligen Verb). In der Kurzgrammatik findest du eine Liste mit häufigen Präpositionen.

a) The teacher is sitting at the table.
b) Jessica has never been to Australia.
c) What do you think of my new dress?
d) The new boy in our class is from Singapore.
e) I am waiting for you at the bus stop.

Aufgabe 27

Hinweis: Lies dir die vorgegebenen Antworten mit dem jeweils unterstrichenen Satzteil genau durch, um herauszufinden, nach was oder wem du fragen musst.

a) Who enjoyed the film?
b) What time is it now?
c) What does Lisa have? / What has Lisa got?
d) Which dress does Sarah buy?
e) Where are the Smiths going on holiday?
f) When does the train arrive?

Aufgabe 28

Hinweis: Hier musst du die Zeitangaben und die Satzenden so zusammenfügen, dass der Satz einen Sinn ergibt und die Zeiten (tenses) stimmen.

1	2	3	4
C	A	D	B

Aufgabe 29

Hinweis: Das Present progressive wird u. a. gebraucht, wenn man beschreiben will, was auf Bildern zu sehen ist. Unter „Zeiten – tenses" in der Kurzgrammatik kannst du Bildung und Verwendung des Present progressive wiederholen.

a) What is your sister doing in this photo?
b) My brother is swimming in the sea.
c) Here I am wearing my new dress.
d) The sun is shining in every picture.
e) In this picture we are eating some delicious ice-cream.

Aufgabe 30

Hinweis: Hier musst du die richtigen Formen des Simple past einsetzen. Im Kapitel „Zeiten – tenses" kannst du nachschlagen, wie man die regelmäßigen Formen bildet. Außerdem findest du eine Liste mit häufigen unregelmäßigen Verben.

On Saturday morning Kelly and Sara met in town to do some shopping. They were invited to a birthday party in the evening and wanted to buy a present. At first they couldn't / could not really decide what to buy, but then they saw a cool smartphone case and were sure that that would be the right present for Tim. Now they could take a look around for some trendy clothes for the party. Kelly bought a T-shirt, but Sara didn't / did not find anything. Afterwards they went home to get changed for the party.

most as <u>bad as</u> in France, but it was <u>more exciting</u> to spend the holidays there than with my parents in Scotland. In my opinion, Spanish food is the <u>best</u> in Europe. My holiday in Spain was great, and I met <u>more</u> people <u>than</u> in all my holidays before!

Aufgabe 20

Hinweis: Einen Überblick über verschiedene Konjunktionen bekommst du im Grammatik-Kapitel „Konjunktionen – conjunctions".

a) Danny wants to become a kindergarten teacher <u>since</u>/<u>because</u> he did an internship in a kindergarten last year. He likes the job <u>because</u>/<u>since</u> working with children is never boring.

b) Luisa wants to be a flight attendant. She has always wanted to be up in the air and see the world, <u>although</u> she knows that she will often be away <u>and</u> miss her friends and family.

c) Elise would like to become a doctor. <u>While</u> still at school, she is doing some voluntary work at a hospital near her home. <u>Before</u> she starts to study medicine, however, she is going on a trip through South America.

Aufgabe 21

Hinweis: Wenn du Hilfe bei der folgenden Aufgabe brauchst, sieh in der Kurzgrammatik unter dem Kapitel „Bedingungssätze – if-clauses" nach. Beachte, dass hier nach dem Typ I gefragt ist.

a) "If you <u>help</u> me in the kitchen, I <u>will give</u> you some extra money for your new bike."

b) "If you take the train, you <u>will be</u> in time."

c) "You <u>will get</u> wet if you <u>don't take</u> an umbrella with you!"

d) "If you <u>don't study</u> hard, you <u>will fail</u> your test."

e) "If it <u>gets</u> cold, you <u>should</u>/<u>can put on</u> a jacket."

Aufgabe 22

Hinweis: Achte hier darauf, den Typ II der if-clauses zu verwenden.

a) If we <u>saved</u> enough money, we could fly to Australia.

b) I <u>would go</u> to the USA if I could choose where to go on holiday.

c) If I <u>went</u> to the USA, I would visit Las Vegas.

d) If I <u>had</u> a lot of money, I <u>would</u>/<u>could travel</u> around the world!

e) My parents <u>would pay</u> for my trip to Spain if I <u>learned</u> some Spanish.

Aufgabe 23

Hinweis: Bei manchen Sätzen musst du die Ersatzform des modalen Hilfsverbs einsetzen. Manchmal sind auch beide Formen möglich. Einen Überblick über die modalen Hilfsverben findest du in der Kurzgrammatik unter „Modale Hilfsverben – modal auxiliaries".

a) Before we go on our trip to Washington, your parents <u>must</u>/<u>have to</u> fill in the form I have given you.

b) If you <u>may</u>/<u>are allowed to</u> take part, just give the form back to me.

c) You <u>needn't</u>/<u>don't have to</u> give me the money for the trip now. I'll collect it next week.

d) Perhaps we <u>can</u>/<u>will be able to</u> visit the National Air and Space Museum.

e) You <u>mustn't</u> forget to take something to eat and drink with you!

Aufgabe 24

Hinweis: Hier musst du sowohl persönliche Fürwörter („I, you, he/she/it, we, you, they") als auch Possessivbegleiter (siehe dazu das Grammatik-Kapitel „Fürwörter – pronouns") einsetzen.

Mrs Brown comes into the classroom, looks out of the window and asks her class in surprise, "Whose jacket is that lying outside?" John answers, "<u>It</u> is Lisa's." "Lisa, is that <u>your</u> jacket?" Mrs Brown asks. "Go and get <u>it</u>, please." Then Mrs Brown notices that Lisa is not in the classroom. "Where is <u>she</u> today?" "I think <u>she</u> is ill," says Maggie, who sounds as if she has been crying, "<u>She</u> didn't wait for <u>me</u> this morning like <u>she</u> usually does. <u>I</u> borrowed <u>her</u> jacket yesterday and <u>she</u> told me to look after <u>it</u>. But this morning, Jack and Tim took the jacket and threw <u>it</u> around. <u>I</u> couldn't catch <u>it</u>, and then <u>they</u> threw <u>it</u> out of the window." "Is that true, <u>you</u> two?" asks Mrs Brown, "Did <u>you</u> do that? Go and get the jacket immediately, give <u>it</u> back to Maggie

a) When do you <u>get up</u> in the morning?
b) I don't want to <u>spend</u> a lot of money at the weekend.
c) "What are you <u>looking</u> for?"
d) I am <u>doing</u> my homework at the moment.
e) <u>In my opinion</u>, the film was very interesting.
f) Sarah, please <u>tell</u> me the truth!
g) Wait, it's not your <u>turn</u>!
h) Look, Sarah is <u>taking</u> a photo!

Aufgabe 14

Hinweis: Hier werden dir Wörter zum Einsetzen vorgegeben. Wenn du dir bei einer Lücke sicher bist, streiche die jeweilige Vokabel durch. Dies reduziert die Anzahl der möglichen Antworten für die restlichen Lücken. Beachte, dass ein Wort gar nicht passt.

a) As Jack doesn't speak any Spanish yet, he started a <u>language</u> course in Malaga.
b) The other students are from many <u>different</u> countries.
c) Sarah, for <u>example</u>, is from England.
d) Massimo is from Rome, the <u>capital</u> of Italy.
e) Louise from France speaks German and English, <u>too</u>.
f) Alicia was <u>born</u> in Quebec in Canada. Her native language is French.

Aufgabe 15

a) Lukas had always wanted to go <u>to</u> Australia for a year.
b) However, a holiday at the other end of the world is <u>very</u> expensive and Lukas didn't have enough money.
c) One of Lukas' friends had a fantastic idea: Lukas <u>could</u> go on a "work and travel" holiday.
d) Lukas was happy! Now he would be able to afford the stay in his <u>favourite</u> country.
e) When Lukas finally got to Australia, he <u>worked</u> on a sheep farm.
f) <u>After</u> working for six weeks, Lukas travelled around the country with some friends he had met at the farm.

Aufgabe 16

Hinweis: Wenn du dir nicht mehr sicher bist, wie einzelne Adverbien gebildet werden, sieh in der Kurzgrammatik unter „Adverbien – adverbs" nach.

a) nicely
b) carefully
c) badly
d) well

Aufgabe 17

Hinweis: Beachte bei dieser Aufgabe zu den Adverbien auch die Wortstellung.

a) Sarah <u>always has</u> some cornflakes for breakfast.
b) Joe <u>often plays</u> football with his friends.
c) Tom and Jessica <u>sometimes have</u> dinner in a restaurant.
d) Lisa's parents <u>mostly go</u> to Greece on holiday.
e) Tom <u>never does</u> his homework properly.

Aufgabe 18

Hinweis: Entscheide hier, ob du die 1. oder 2. Steigerungsform einsetzen musst. Wenn du Hilfe brauchst, sieh in der Kurzgrammatik unter „Steigerung und Vergleich – comparisons" nach.

a) At 1.70 m Evan is <u>taller</u> than Jack, who is 1.69 m in height.
b) Sarah is <u>the tallest</u> girl in the class – she is 1.80 m.
c) Sarah, who turns 16 in April, is <u>older</u> than Jack, who was born in June.
d) Jessica's hair is <u>longer</u> than Tina's.
e) Emma is <u>better</u> at maths <u>than</u> Evan.
f) But Jessica is <u>the best</u> pupil in the class!

Aufgabe 19

Hinweis: Entscheide auch hier, ob du die 1. oder die 2. Steigerungsform einsetzen musst. Hinzu kommt der Vergleich mit „as ... as".

The weather in France was much <u>worse</u> than last year. It was raining almost all the time. Our flat, however, was <u>more comfortable than</u> last year. I also like the French food. It's much <u>better</u> than the food in England. In my opinion, France is <u>the most beautiful</u> country in Europe. / I went to Spain with a youth group. The weather in San Sebastian was al-

body" ist der Oberbegriff.
d) ~~knife~~ → vegetables
Hinweis: „knife" ist kein Gemüse, „vegetables" ist der Oberbegriff.
e) ~~meat~~ → dessert
Hinweis: „meat" ist kein Nachtisch, „dessert" ist der Oberbegriff.

Aufgabe 6

a) restaurant
b) theatre/cinema
c) hospital
d) church
e) park

Aufgabe 7

Hinweis: Wenn dir einige englische Begriffe für das Land, die Sprache oder die Nationalität nicht auf Anhieb einfallen, dann schlage sie nach und nimm sie in deine Vokabelkartei auf.

the people	the country	the language
(the) English	England	English
(the) French	France	French
(the) Spanish	Spain	Spanish
(the) Italians	Italy	Italian
(the) Americans	United States (of America) / USA	(American) English
(the) Germans	Germany	German
(the) Dutch	the Netherlands	Dutch
(the) Turkish	Turkey	Turkish
(the) Canadians	Canada	(Canadian) English, French

Aufgabe 8

Hinweis: Hier musst du die Wörter einander so zuordnen, dass sie jeweils ein Paar ergeben, das zwar unterschiedlich geschrieben wird, aber gleich klingt. Am besten sagst du dir die einzelnen Wörter laut vor.

break – brake;   see – sea;   board – bored;
whole – hole;   know – no;   hour – our;
piece – peace

Aufgabe 9

(Kreuzworträtsel mit folgenden Wörtern:)
AWAKE, LIGHT, NIGHT, SLOW, LOUD, WRONG, HIGH, SAFE, CHEAP, BESSER (BEAR?), POOR, DRY, ARROW, SWEET, CROWDED, EXCITING, LOUD, STUPID

Aufgabe 10

Hinweis: Hier sollst du die unterstrichenen Wörter durch ihr Gegenteil ersetzen.

a) I <u>left</u> early this morning.
b) The plane was <u>early</u>.
c) I have just <u>caught</u> the train!
d) Sarah has <u>found</u> her watch.
e) James <u>sold</u> a car yesterday.
f) My water bottle is <u>empty</u>.

Aufgabe 11

Hinweis: Hier musst du ein Wort mit derselben Bedeutung (Synonym) finden.

a) perhaps
b) little
c) <u>Shut</u> the door, please.
d) fast
e) (to) call

Aufgabe 12

a) policewoman
b) princess
c) actress
d) waitress

Aufgabe 13

Hinweis: Hier musst du jeweils das richtige Wort bzw. die im Englischen korrekte Wendung auswählen. Passe dabei auf „false friends" auf.

world …" (Z. 8 f.)
b) E
Hinweis: "She steps into a little room …" (Z. 12)
c) G
Hinweis: "'I want to be part of trying to figure out how to feed ourselves better …'" (Z. 25)
d) H
Hinweis: "'… they're a really, really popular food.'" (Z. 29 f.)
e) I
Hinweis: "Bugs also taste yummy …" (Z. 33)

Kompetenzbereich: Use of Language

Allgemeiner Hinweis: In diesem Kapitel kannst du die Bereiche Wortschatz und Grammatik trainieren. Sie sind die Grundlage für alle anderen Kompetenzbereiche. In der Prüfung werden sie im Teil „Use of Language" aber auch gesondert geprüft.

Aufgabe 1

a) school: chalk, blackboard, teacher, pupil, chair, desk
b) holidays: beach, suntan, sunshade, swimming, tent, hiking
c) animals: bear, bird, horse, monkey, guinea pig

Aufgabe 2

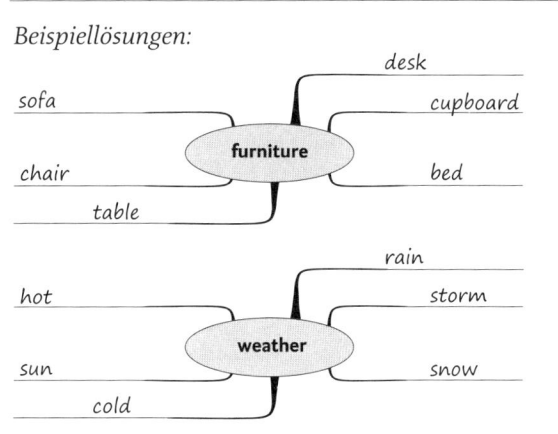

Beispiellösungen:

furniture: desk, sofa, cupboard, chair, bed, table

weather: rain, hot, storm, sun, snow, cold

Aufgabe 3

Hinweis: Hier ist der Oberbegriff nicht vorgegeben. Du musst überlegen, was die aufgelisteten Wörter gemeinsam haben.

a) colours / colors
b) vehicles
c) languages

Aufgabe 4

Hinweis: Zu Beginn jeder Zeile ist der Oberbegriff vorgegeben. Du musst also nur noch überlegen, welches Wort nicht dazugehört.

a) pineapple
   Hinweis: Ananas ist kein Gemüse.
b) CV
   Hinweis: kein Beruf; CV (curriculum vitae) = Lebenslauf
c) vinegar
   Hinweis: Essig ist kein Getränk.
d) fork
   Hinweis: Eine Gabel ist keine Mahlzeit.
e) chips
   Hinweis: keine Süßigkeit (BE: sweets); chips (BE) = Pommes frites

Aufgabe 5

Hinweis: Hier musst du überlegen, welches Wort nicht in die Reihe passt und was die verbliebenen Wörter gemeinsam haben.

a) ~~bag~~ → clothes
   Hinweis: „bag" ist kein Kleidungsstück, „clothes" ist der Oberbegriff.
b) ~~singer~~ → (musical) instruments
   Hinweis: „singer" ist kein Musikinstrument, „(musical) instruments" ist der Oberbegriff.
c) ~~food~~ → parts of the body
   Hinweis: „food" ist kein Körperteil, „parts of the

Hinweis: "... more than three fourths of teachers said technology makes their teaching more successful." (Z. 17 ff.)

c) search for information.
Hinweis: "... it especially helps with activities like research, information searches, reports and presentations." (Z. 19 f.)

d) prepare them for real world experience.
Hinweis: "He says: 'the important thing is to help prepare the students for real world experience'" (Z. 22 f.)

e) students use electronic devices too often.
Hinweis: "Critics of technology in classrooms say that students are spending too much time looking at screens on their computers or electronic devices." (Z. 27 f.)

Aufgabe 3

a) Technology is widely available to students in classrooms across the United States ...
Hinweis: Z. 1 ff.

b) ... classroom technology gets high marks from educators.
Hinweis: Z. 14 f.

c) ... knowledge about technology is something students need.
Hinweis: Z. 23 f.

d) ... technology is just one of many tools available to teachers.
Hinweis: Z. 24 f.

e) So we are making sure that there is a balance with student use of technology.
Hinweis: Z. 30 f.

Reading Test 7: Insects for dinner

Aufgabe 1

a) E
b) C
c) B
d) A
e) D

Aufgabe 2

a) true
Hinweis: "... a great source of protein and minerals known to be important to good health, like calcium and iron. Insect larvae, for example, offer all that, as well as high quality fat, which is good for brain development." (Z. 2 ff.)

b) not in the text

c) false
Hinweis: "The United Nations Food and Agricultural Organization has said that the world's demand for protein from beef and ... chicken is unsustainable. Protein from bugs is one possible solution." (Z. 19 ff.)

d) true
Hinweis: "A carrot supplies their water needs." (Z. 23)

e) false
Hinweis: "... in the Democratic Republic of Congo. In its markets, people sell live wild-caught crickets and African Palm weevil larvae to eat." (Z. 30 ff.)

Aufgabe 3

a) the U.S.A.
Hinweis: "Insects are food in many parts of the world, but not in the United States." (Z. 8 f.)

b) restaurants.
Hinweis: "We raise crickets and mealworms to sell to restaurants and food manufacturers." (Z. 17 f.)

c) grain.
Hinweis: "She feeds them crushed, wet grain." (Z. 22 f.)

d) we will have less land but more people.
Hinweis: "Ms. McGill says: 'I want to be part of trying to figure out how to feed ourselves better as we have less land and water and a hotter planet and more people to feed.'" (Z. 24 ff.)

e) has a bug farm in the Democratic Republic of Congo.
Hinweis: "'And what we do is farm bugs for food ...' Franklin works in the Democratic Republic of Congo." (Z. 28 ff.)

Aufgabe 4

a) C
Hinweis: "Insects are food in many parts of the

c) true
   Hinweis: "The guides ... know how to create a creepy atmosphere and make visitors shudder ... thanks to their special training they know every detail of Edinburgh's history." (Z. 9 ff.)

d) false
   Hinweis: "... historical events. The events usually have to do with executions, murder and other terrible crimes." (Z. 13 f.)

e) true
   Hinweis: "Some of the ghost walks are like theatre performances ..." (Z. 21)

f) not in the text
   Hinweis: Im Text wird zwar erwähnt, dass es auch „normale" Touren gibt, nicht aber, wie viel sie kosten (Z. 27)

Aufgabe 2

a) creepy.
   Hinweis: "... grey buildings, ... the thick fog ... make it a creepy place." (Z. 3 f.)

b) historians.
   Hinweis: "They are often studying history or working as historians ..." (Z. 10 f.)

c) Scottish history.
   Hinweis: "Besides getting the creeps, visitors can also learn a lot about Scottish history ..." (Z. 15 f.)

d) frighten the visitors.
   Hinweis: "... tour guides in monster costumes ... suddenly jumping out of nowhere. In the dark, this can be very frightening ..." (Z. 21 ff.)

e) like to be frightened.
   Hinweis: "Ghost walks are a great experience for those who enjoy the thrill ..." (Z. 25)

Aufgabe 3

a) ... thick fog that sometimes covers the town for days ...
   Hinweis: Z. 3 f.

b) For those ... in the hope of catching a glimpse of a Scottish ghost, a guided ghost walk around town is a must.
   Hinweis: Z. 6 ff.

c) ... they know every detail of Edinburgh's history.
   Hinweis: Z. 11 f.

d) ... visitors can also learn a lot about ... everyday life in medieval Edinburgh ...
   Hinweis: Z. 16 f.

e) In the dark, this can be very frightening ...
   Hinweis: Z. 23

f) ... shrieks are not unusual in Edinburgh at night.
   Hinweis: Z. 23 f.

Reading Test 6: Technology has value

Aufgabe 1

a) false
   Hinweis: "... nearly nine in 10 U.S. public school students say they use digital learning tools ..." (Z. 4 ff.)

b) not in the text

c) true
   Hinweis: "... digital learning tools include websites, application software programs, and online classes, games, videos and programs." (Z. 12 f.)

d) false
   Hinweis: "... 65 percent of U.S. teachers use digital tools to teach every day ..." (Z. 16 f.)

e) true
   Hinweis: "Concerns about technology overuse ... 'So we are making sure that there is a balance with student use of technology,' he says." (Z. 28 ff.)

f) true
   Hinweis: "Nearly all elementary students say digital learning tools are fun." (Z. 32)

g) false
   Hinweis: "... eight percent said they would like to use them less." (Z. 37)

Aufgabe 2

a) at least several days a week.
   Hinweis: "... a study ... It found that nearly nine in 10 U.S. public school students say they use digital learning tools at least a few days a week." (Z. 3 ff.)

b) more successful.

Reading Test 3: India

Aufgabe 1
a) D
b) F
c) C
d) A
e) B
f) E

Aufgabe 2
a) false
   Hinweis: "… *India* … *has a population of about 1.2 billion*. More than <u>twenty million</u> people live in or around the capital city, <u>New Delhi</u>." (Z. 1 ff.)
b) true
   Hinweis: "… the British, who began to colonise India in the 17th century …" (Z. 10 ff.)
c) not in the text
   Hinweis: Es wird zwar erwähnt, dass die beiden offiziellen Sprachen Indiens Englisch und Hindi sind (Z. 14 f.), aber nicht, welche Sprachen die Kinder in der Schule lernen.
d) false
   Hinweis: "In Europe and the USA, people have always been interested in the <u>spiritual side of India</u>. A lot of <u>Westerners travel to India to practise yoga</u> …" (Z. 23 f.)
e) true
   Hinweis: "The <u>textile industry</u>, the car industry and the IT sector … have all been <u>growing fast</u> over the last few decades. (Z. 26 f.)
f) true
   Hinweis: "Millions of people still live in poverty and do not have enough to eat." (Z. 30 f.)

Reading Test 4: Book report

Aufgabe 1
a) E
b) D
c) F
d) B
e) A
f) C

Aufgabe 2
a) children's rights movement.
   Hinweis: "… one of the most famous people in the world and one of the most important children's rights activists." (Z. 3 ff.)
b) both girls and boys get an education.
   Hinweis: "… brave fight for <u>children's right to education</u>." (Z. 11 f.), "… fight for the right to <u>education for every child</u>." (Z. 31 f.)
c) supported his daughter.
   Hinweis: "<u>Both father and daughter</u> also spoke out publicly for girls' right to education." (Z. 21 f.), "Ziauddin Yousafzai <u>suggested his own daughter</u>, and Malala … began writing a blog …" (Z. 24 ff.)
d) wrote a blog.
   Hinweis: "… Malala (then eleven years old) began writing a blog …" (Z. 25 f.)
e) in 2012.
   Hinweis: "… one day in 2012, a Taliban gunman stopped the school bus and shot Malala right in the head." (Z. 28 f.)
f) went on fighting for children's rights.
   Hinweis: "Malala continues to fight for the right to education for every child." (Z. 31 f.)

Reading Test 5: Ghost walks

Aufgabe 1
a) true
   Hinweis: "Edinburgh has always been the perfect setting for ghost stories …" (Z. 1)
b) not in the text
   Hinweis: Im Text steht, dass die Besucher*innen hoffen, einen Geist zu sehen (Z. 6 f.), nicht aber, dass jemals einer gesichtet wurde.

meals, but when I go out for dinner, I sometimes order fish or chicken.

35 **Tessa:** Hi there, I'm Tessa. One of my new year resolutions is to lose some weight. That's why I'm trying to cut down on sugar and carbohydrates. I recently read an article about animal transports, so I decided not to eat any more meat for ethical
40 reasons.

Reporter: Thanks everyone for sharing all this with me and our listeners.

a) Clare – **F**
   Hinweis: "... I've been a vegan for two years." (Z. 6 f.)
b) Finn – **A**
   Hinweis: "There's nothing I enjoy more than a big chunk of steak. All my family love meat, no matter what ..." (Z. 12 ff.)
c) Colin – **C**
   Hinweis: "I'm Colin and I'm a vegetarian." (Z. 20)
d) Hannah – **D**
   Hinweis: "I consider myself a 'part-time vegetarian', because I usually eat vegetarian meals, but when I go out for dinner, I sometimes order fish or chicken." (Z. 31 ff.)
e) Tessa – **H**
   Hinweis: "... trying to cut down on sugar and carbohydrates ... I decided not to eat any more meat for ethical reasons." (Z. 37 ff.)

Kompetenzbereich: Reading

Allgemeiner Hinweis: In diesem Kapitel wird überprüft, wie gut du einen englischen Text verstanden hast. Da du dir hier den Text mehrmals durchlesen kannst, werden genauere Details abgefragt als in den Aufgaben zum Hörverstehen. Lies die Texte also besonders aufmerksam.

Reading Test 1: Signs

a) C
   Hinweis: emergency = hier: Notaufnahme; to pick up = hier: abholen
b) A
   Hinweis: leash = Leine
c) A
   Hinweis: delays = Verspätungen; motorway = Autobahn
d) B
   Hinweis: to report = hier: sich melden; reception = Empfang

Reading Test 2: More signs

a) B
   Hinweis: assembly point = Versammlungspunkt
b) C
   Hinweis: to be allowed to do sth = etwas dürfen
c) B
   Hinweis: speed limit = Geschwindigkeitsbegrenzung
d) A
   Hinweis: to be required = erforderlich sein
e) C
   Hinweis: certain days = bestimmte Tage

d) **B**
  ◆ Hinweis: "Usually I work ... *five days a week. If there's a lot to do, I also work on Saturdays* ..." (Z. 34 ff.)

e) **A**
  ◆ Hinweis: "And it just feels great when a piece of furniture is finished." (Z. 37 f.)

Listening Test 8: Music

1 **Jacob:** Hi, I'm Jacob and I love rock music. When my parents are not at home, I listen to my favourite bands at full volume.
 Amber: I love One Direction, they're so cute! In
5 April, my friends and I are going to their concert in Edinburgh – we're their biggest fans! I hope we get a good place in front of the stage.
 Thomas: Hi, I'm Thomas. Actually, I don't care about music that much – it's just not very important to
10 me. Sometimes, when I'm alone at home, I turn the radio on, but it's more to have some background noise – I don't really pay attention to what is being played.
 Grace: My name's Grace and music is my life! Most
15 of my classmates find this weird but I mainly listen to classical music, like Mozart, Schubert and Chopin. What I like even more than listening to music is playing it myself. I've been taking piano lessons since I was six and I practice at least
20 two hours every day.
 Amelia: Hi, I'm Amelia. A boy from our school took part in "The Voice UK". He didn't win in the end, but for me the show and the songs he performed were really emotional – we all sat there
25 crying! I didn't know music could have that effect on me and really touch my heart.

a) Jacob – **E**
  ◆ Hinweis: "... I listen to my favourite bands *at full volume*." (Z. 2 f.)

b) Amber – **F**
  ◆ Hinweis: "I love One Direction ... we're their *biggest fans*! I hope we get a good place *in front of the stage*." (Z. 4 ff.)

c) Thomas – **C**
  ◆ Hinweis: "Sometimes ... I turn the radio on ..." (Z. 10 f.)

d) Grace – **A**
  ◆ Hinweis: "What I like even more than listening to music is *playing it myself*." (Z. 17 f.)

e) Amelia – **B**
  ◆ Hinweis: "... the *show* and the *songs* he performed were *really emotional* – we all sat there crying!" (Z. 23 ff.)

Listening Test 9: What do they eat?

1 **Reporter:** Hello. My name's Allison Hill of BBC London. I'm reporting live from busy Oxford Street on this rainy Saturday morning, where I'll be interviewing people about what is usually on
5 their plates.
 Clare: My name's Clare and I've been a vegan for two years. My diet is plant-based and I avoid all animal foods, such as meat, dairy products, honey and eggs. I also love Indian food, so I usually
10 have a vegetarian curry for dinner. Vegan food is not as boring as many people think.
 Finn: Vegan food? Not for me, thank you! There's nothing I enjoy more than a big chunk of steak. All my family love meat, no matter what: pork,
15 beef, veal, lamb, chicken – I could go on forever. We also like to try exotic types, such as crocodile. In the summer, we have a barbecue at least once a week. I'm Finn by the way.
 Colin: You should really consider your health, Finn!
20 I'm Colin and I'm a vegetarian. Since I don't have a garden of my own and can't afford to buy organic food all the time, I got involved in a community garden last year. We share a garden and grow all kinds of fruit and vegetables, which is
25 great fun and really rewarding.
 Hannah: My name's Hannah. What a great idea to join a community garden – I moved to London two months ago and I find it very difficult to make friends. I bet being part of a project like this
30 would help me meet nice people who are on the same wavelength. I consider myself a "part-time vegetarian", because I usually eat vegetarian

Tom: That's crazy! You know, I'm really afraid of heights and I wouldn't go to the top of a skyscraper for the world. By the way, did you buy anything in New York?

Jenny: Well, I bought seven pairs of jeans and lots of T-shirts. And make-up, of course.

Tom: I hope you bought me some good jeans too! I'll pay you a good price for them.

Jenny: Oh, I'm sorry, I forgot to get you some. I need them for myself and my family, I'm afraid. By the way, didn't you say you wanted to go to the United States on your next holiday as well?

Tom: Yes, I'd love to. But I haven't got the money for the trip. And I want to take my driving test first.

a) C
Hinweis: "Did you also go to New York?" – "Yes, of course we did." (7 f.)

b) B
Hinweis: "It was also great to take the ferry to the Statue of Liberty and to Ellis Island…" (13 f.)

c) C
Hinweis: "…the Top of the Rock observation desk. From there you have a fantastic view of the city." (18 f.)

d) A
Hinweis: "…I bought seven pairs of jeans…" (Z. 27)

e) C
Hinweis: "I hope you bought me some good jeans too!…" – "Oh, I'm sorry, I forgot to get you some." (Z. 29 ff.)

Listening Test 7: Youth Radio 2FM

Presenter: This is Paula Jones from Youth Radio 2FM with the best shows for young people in town! Our topic this week is "The world of work". A lot of you out there don't know what to do after you graduate, what job or profession to do. You ask yourself "What are my strengths?" or "What would I love to do and what would I absolutely not like to do?". It's a hard decision and we're here to give you some help. Every day this week a young man or woman will be talking about their job. They'll talk about their training and what they like or don't like about their job. Maybe there'll be a job that you find interesting as well and haven't thought about before. Who knows? But now let's start the show. With me in the studio today is Jason Cooper, who's a carpenter from Cleveland, Ohio. Hello, Jason. It's great to have you here on the show today.

Jason: Hi, Paula. It's a pleasure to be here today.

Presenter: So you're a carpenter. Have you always wanted to do that job?

Jason: Yes, I love making things out of wood. I really liked woodwork class at school, and especially building models of houses.

Presenter: So how long was your training?

Jason: That took two years. At the end I took an exam and got my diploma. I was even able to stay with the carpenter's workshop where I did my training.

Presenter: What about your working week – can you give me an idea of what it's like? Is it hard sometimes?

Jason: Yeah, you bet! But I don't mind – I really like my job. Usually I work from 8.00 to 4.00, five days a week. If there's a lot to do, I also work on Saturdays – but that's OK because I get paid for the extra hours. And it just feels great when a piece of furniture is finished.

Presenter: I can imagine! And how much vacation do you get?

Jason: Oh, it's not bad. I get three weeks a year.

Presenter: And what about pay?

Jason: Well, the pay isn't so good, but I don't mind so much because I love the job. But what I really want one day is to own my own carpenter's workshop.

Presenter: Well, I wish you all the best!

Jason: Thank you so much.

a) B
Hinweis: "Our topic this week is 'The world of work'…. Every day this week a young man or woman will be talking about their job." (Z. 3 ff.)

b) A
Hinweis: "So you're a carpenter." (Z. 20)

c) C
Hinweis: "So how long was your training?" – "That took two years." (Z. 25 f.)

Listening Test 5: The meteorite

Presenter: Good morning everyone! This is Tina Smith. Welcome to my show "Strange things happen". With me today are Sam and Lisa McDonald from Phoenix, Arizona. Last month they had an unexpected visitor. At nine o'clock in the morning, just before breakfast, a meteorite weighing 1.3 kg crashed through the roof of their house and landed in their living room! Have you ever heard of such a crazy incident before? Astronomers say what happened to the McDonalds is a very rare event. A meteorite which falls through a roof is absolutely exceptional. Well, now let's listen to Sam and Lisa's story.

Presenter: Good morning, Sam and Lisa. It's great to have you in my show today.

Sam and Lisa: Hi Tina.

Lisa: It's a pleasure for us to be here.

Presenter: Lisa, can you tell me what happened exactly? You were preparing breakfast in the kitchen when a meteorite came down.

Lisa: You're right. I was in the kitchen making breakfast and there was this huge explosion. I thought the ceiling had exploded. You just couldn't see a thing, there was dust everywhere …

Sam: Then I saw a rock lying under the computer, and it was really hot to the touch. The scorched rock must have bounced off the sofa and hit the ceiling before it came to rest underneath the computer.

Lisa: It was sheer luck that nobody was hurt!

Sam: Yes, indeed. Far worse could have happened.

Presenter: What did you do then with the meteorite?

Sam: We dried it in our oven. It's still in our house.

Presenter: And are you planning to sell the rock? Scientists say you could expect to get several thousand dollars for the meteorite from collectors.

Lisa: Well, actually we planned to offer the rock to a museum.

Sam: So that everyone can see it and scientists can examine it.

Presenter: Well, Sam and Lisa, I guess that is a good plan. Thank you so much for sharing your story with us.

a) A
 Hinweis: "At nine o'clock in the morning, just before breakfast …" (5 f.)

b) B
 Hinweis: "… a meteorite … landed in their living room!" (Z. 6 ff.)

c) C
 Hinweis: "You just couldn't see a thing, there was dust everywhere …" (Z. 23 f.)

d) B
 Hinweis: "… before it came to rest underneath the computer." (Z. 28 f.)

e) C
 Hinweis: "Well, actually we planned to offer the rock to a museum." (Z. 37 f.)

Listening Test 6: A trip to the USA

Tom: Hi Jenny. You're back from the US! How was your trip?

Jenny: Oh, it was great. My host family took me to visit a lot of the famous places we heard about in our English lessons such as Niagara Falls and Washington D.C.

Tom: Did you also go to New York?

Jenny: Yes, of course we did.

Tom: What did you see there?

Jenny: We went to all the famous places like the Empire State Building, the Statue of Liberty and Central Park. Central Park is wonderful in spring when the cherry blossoms are in full bloom. It was also great to take the ferry to the Statue of Liberty and to Ellis Island, where millions of people arrived before they could immigrate to the United States. But what I liked best was going on the Top of the Rock observation desk. From there you have a fantastic view of the city. And the people and cars seem so tiny from up there. I'm not afraid of heights, but it was really really weird when I felt the skyscraper swaying a bit.

b) **cloudy** with **sunny** periods
   Hinweis: "The forecast for this morning is not too bad. It will be cloudy with sunny periods" (Z. 4 f.)

c) in the **(late) afternoon**
   Hinweis: "But later in the afternoon we expect some heavy rain." (Z. 6 f.)

d) **25 °C**
   Hinweis: "... much better weather for tomorrow ... temperatures will rise to around 25 degrees" (Z. 10 ff.)

e) **over 30 °C**
   Hinweis: "... temperatures over 30 degrees next weekend." (Z. 15 f.)

Listening Test 4: St Patrick's Day

On March 17, people around the world celebrate the Irish holiday of Saint Patrick's Day. It is a major holiday in Ireland, but the rest of the world has influenced its celebration as much as the Irish themselves.
Most Americans think of Saint Patrick's Day as a big party, but its beginnings in Ireland were religious. Ireland is a mostly Roman Catholic country. Saint Patrick lived on the island more than 1,500 years ago, and he is widely considered to have established Christianity in the country. The Church honoured him with a holy day in the 17th century. March 17 marks the date of his death. Saint Patrick is believed to have served in Ireland as a Catholic bishop. One story says that he drove all the snakes out of Ireland. The average Irish person honoured March 17 quietly. Attending church services was the main activity. In fact, most businesses that served alcohol would close on that day. In the early 1900s, Ireland's government made Saint Patrick's Day an official holiday. By the 1960s, towns across Ireland started celebrating the holiday with parades and music. In Ireland today, Saint Patrick's Day is a four-day public celebration that includes parades, music, food, and games.
For Irish people living outside Ireland, Saint Patrick's Day became a chance to celebrate their Irish identity and culture. Now, countries and cities around the world celebrate March 17 in creative ways. Many countries hold Saint Patrick's Day parades. Famous monuments, including the Great Wall of China, the Colosseum in Rome, the Niagara Falls, and the Gateway of India in Mumbai will all be coloured by green light for the day.
The U.S. is especially famous for its Saint Patrick's Day celebrations. Many cities with large Irish communities, like Boston, New York and Chicago, hold parades and parties. Cities will also colour local rivers green for the day. Ireland is known as the "Emerald Isle" because the country is covered in deep green grass.
However, many modern Saint Patrick's Day traditions were invented by the Irish in America. In the U.S. on Saint Patrick's Day, it is common for Americans to drink green beer or eat corned beef and cabbage, but many of these traditions are not really Irish. Neil O'Flaherty, an Irish citizen now living in the U.S., remembers celebrating Saint Patrick's Day much differently than it is now. Back then, for Catholic families in Ireland, it was the day you had to go to church. It had much more the feeling of a religious holiday than a public holiday. He also remembers everyone wearing small, three-leaf plant pieces, called shamrocks.
No matter how people celebrate March 17, Saint Patrick's Day is a day for everyone to be Irish.

Abridged and adapted from: Phil Dierking and Caty Weaver: Everyone gets to be Irish on St. Patrick's Day, in: Voice of America Learning English

a) **(more than) 1500** years ago
   Hinweis: "Saint Patrick lived on the island more than 1,500 years ago ..." (Z. 8 ff.)

b) **March (the) 17 / 17(th) March**
   Hinweis: "March 17 marks the date of his death." (Z. 12 f.)

c) parades, music, **food** and **games**
   Hinweis: "In Ireland today, Saint Patrick's Day is a four-day public celebration that includes parades, music, food, and games." (Z. 22 ff.)

d) **green**
   Hinweis: "Famous monuments ... will all be coloured by green light for the day." (Z. 30 ff.), "Cities will also colour local rivers green for the day." (Z. 37 f.), "Ireland is known as the 'Emerald Isle' because the country is covered in deep green grass." (Z. 38 ff.), "... drink green beer ..." (Z. 44)

e) people went to **church** on that day
   Hinweis: "Back then ... it was the day you had to go to church" (Z. 48 ff.)

Question 1

B

✏ *Hinweis: "We could invite her to a 3-D film at the new Cineplexx. What do you think?" – "Yeah, that's a great idea." (Z. 10 ff.)*

Question 2

B

✏ *Hinweis: "…I love films about love and heartache even more, so I'd go for 'Mr Right'." (Z. 12 ff.)*

Question 3

C

✏ *Hinweis: "It's called Footie2gether: F-O-O-T-I-E, the number '2' and G-E-T-H-E-R." (Z. 10 f.)*

Question 4

A

✏ *Hinweis: "…we still have vacancies on the weekend before Christmas, or from 2 to 3 January." – "…then I think I'll book the earlier date." (Z. 8 ff.)*

Question 5

C

✏ *Hinweis: "…the purple one over there also looks nice." – "Yes, I think that would suit you really well. Why don't you try it on – the changing rooms are right over there." (Z. 8 ff.)*

Listening Test 2: A flight to London

Good afternoon, ladies and gentlemen. This is your captain speaking. My name is Sandy Brown and I'd like to welcome you aboard on flight 175 from Stuttgart to London Heathrow.
I'm sorry to tell you that our flight will start 20 minutes later than scheduled as the airspace over southern Britain is overcrowded at the moment. Our flight will take about 1 hour and 45 minutes, so we will land at Heathrow Airport at about three thirty. We will be flying at an altitude of 35,000 feet and our average speed will be 600 miles per hour. We should be flying over the Channel at about ten past three. The weather in London is nice and sunny, with temperatures at about 25 degrees Celsius.
I hope you have a pleasant flight and that you enjoy your stay in London. Thank you for flying with British Airwaves. I'm looking forward to seeing you again on board on one of our flights.

a) **20/twenty** minutes
   ✏ *Hinweis: "…our flight will start 20 minutes later than scheduled…" (Z. 5 f.)*

b) **1/one** hour **45** minutes
   ✏ *Hinweis: "Our flight will take about 1 hour and 45 minutes…" (Z. 8)*

c) **35,000** feet
   ✏ *Hinweis: "We will be flying at an altitude of 35,000 feet…" (Z. 10)*

d) **600** miles per hour
   ✏ *Hinweis: "…our average speed will be 600 miles per hour." (Z. 11)*

e) **flying over** the Channel
   ✏ *Hinweis: "We should be flying over the Channel at about ten past three." (Z. 12 f.)*

Listening Test 3: Weather forecast

Good morning, it is now 6.30 and this is Frances McDonald with the weather report for today and tomorrow.
The forecast for this morning is not too bad. It will be cloudy with sunny periods and a temperature of 19 degrees. But later in the afternoon we expect some heavy rain. Tonight the temperature will go back to 10 degrees because of the rain.
Overnight the rain clouds will disappear and we expect much better weather for tomorrow. It will be windy in the morning but with the sun the temperatures will rise to around 25 degrees during the day. There could still be some rain later in the afternoon, but the warm and sunny weather will continue, with temperatures over 30 degrees next weekend.
Now, it's time for the sports news with Harold Jennings.

a) **6.30 in the morning / 6.30 am**
   ✏ *Hinweis: "Good morning, it is now 6.30…" (Z. 1)*

Lösungen

Kompetenzbereich: Listening

Allgemeiner Hinweis: Zum Lösen der Aufgaben zum Kapitel „Listening" musst du dir die Texte genau anhören. Wenn du einen Text nach dem ersten Hören noch nicht verstanden hast, kannst du ihn dir noch einmal anhören. Lies den Hörverstehenstext aber nur durch, wenn du mit den Lösungen gar nicht weiterkommst.

Listening Test 1: Short conversations

Question 1

Buying a birthday present

Sarah: Hi Leo, are you coming to Sue's birthday party on Saturday?
Leo: Yes, I am. But I still don't have a present for her. Do you have any idea what she would like?
Sarah: I haven't bought her anything yet either. But I know that she does all kinds of sports, so maybe a voucher for a sports shop would be good. And she likes going to concerts and to the cinema.
Leo: We could invite her to a 3-D film at the new Cineplexx. What do you think?
Sarah: Yeah, that's a great idea – I'm sure she'll like that.

Question 2

Cinema

Anna: Hi guys. Have you been waiting for long?
Brian: No, Anna, don't worry, we've just arrived.
Anna: Have you decided which movie you wanna see yet?
Brian: No, we can't make up our minds. I'd like to watch the latest James Bond, but Amy doesn't like action films. There's also "Meeting Mr Right", a romantic comedy, and "Squirrels Gone Nuts", an animated film about a gang of crazy squirrels. Which one do you prefer?
Anna: Well, I love squirrels but I love films about love and heartache even more, so I'd go for "Mr Right".

Question 3

New app

Max: Look, David. I've got a new app on my smartphone. It's called Footie2gether. I get a message whenever there's someone in the neighbourhood who wants to play football in the park.
David: Cool.
Max: There're always enough people to make teams. Last time, more than twenty people showed up.
David: Sounds great – what's it called again?
Max: It's called Footie2gether: F-O-O-T-I-E, the number "2" and G-E-T-H-E-R.
David: Great, I'm gonna download it, too.

Question 4

Hotel reservation

Receptionist: Lakeside Hotel and Spa, my name is Anne Forster, how may I help you?
Mr Smith: Hello, John Smith speaking. I'd like to book a weekend for two in December or January.
Receptionist: Let me check this for you. I'm afraid we're fully booked between Christmas and New Year. But we still have vacancies on the weekend before Christmas, or from 2 to 3 January.
Mr Smith: Thanks, then I think I'll book the earlier date.

Question 5

In the shop

Shop assistant: Good afternoon. Can I help you, madam?
Customer: I've been invited to a wedding and I'm looking for a nice evening dress.
Shop assistant: Do you prefer a certain colour?
Customer: Hhm, I don't know. I thought blue maybe, or black? But the purple one over there also looks nice.
Shop assistant: Yes, I think that would suit you really well. Why don't you try it on – the changing rooms are right over there.